DEFORMATIVE FICTIONS

THEORY AND INTERPRETATION OF NARRATIVE
James Phelan, Katra Byram, and Faye Halpern, Series Editors

DEFORMATIVE FICTIONS

CRUELTY AND NARRATIVE ETHICS IN TWENTIETH-CENTURY LATIN AMERICAN LITERATURE

Ashley Hope Pérez

THE OHIO STATE UNIVERSITY PRESS
COLUMBUS

Copyright © 2024 by The Ohio State University.
All rights reserved.

Library of Congress Cataloging-in-Publication Data
Names: Pérez, Ashley Hope, author.
Title: Deformative fictions : cruelty and narrative ethics in twentieth-century Latin American literature / Ashley Hope Pérez.
Other titles: Theory and interpretation of narrative series.
Description: Columbus : The Ohio State University Press, [2024] | Series: Theory and interpretation of narrative | Includes bibliographical references and index. | Summary: "Demonstrates the challenges and opportunities of 'deformative fictions' by examining Latin American literary works that have been misread, underread, or fetishized because they depart from literary norms"—Provided by publisher.
Identifiers: LCCN 2023054205 | ISBN 9780814215654 (hardback) | ISBN 0814215653 (hardback) | ISBN 9780814283431 (ebook) | ISBN 0814283438 (ebook)
Subjects: LCSH: Ocampo, Silvina—Criticism and interpretation. | Vallejo, Fernando—Criticism and interpretation. | Bolaño, Roberto, 1953–2003—Criticism and interpretation. | Narration (Rhetoric)—Moral and ethical aspects. | Latin American fiction—History and criticism—20th century.
Classification: LCC PQ7082.N7 P3798 2024 | DDC 863—dc23/eng/20240208
LC record available at https://lccn.loc.gov/2023054205

Other identifiers: ISBN 9780814259061 (paperback) | ISBN 0814259065 (paperback)

Cover design by Susan Zucker
Text design by Juliet Williams
Type set in Adobe Minion Pro

For Liam Miguel and Ethan Andrés, always

CONTENTS

List of Illustrations		ix
Statement on Land and Responsibility		xi
Acknowledgments		xiii
INTRODUCTION	A First Encounter with Deformative Fiction	1
CHAPTER 1	Narrative Ethics, Deformative Fictions, and Fictional Cruelty	20
CHAPTER 2	Ocampo: Cruelty as Defense and the Contamination of Readers	38
CHAPTER 3	Vallejo: Cruelty as Assault and the Entrapment of Readers	83
CHAPTER 4	Bolaño: Cruelty as Anti-Elegy and the Inadequacy of Readers	127
CHAPTER 5	Strategic Hospitality in World Literature: Bridges from Deformative Fictions to Responsive Readings	178
CONCLUSION	Readers, Deformative Fictions, and Ordinary Life	212
AFTERWORD	Current Attacks on Difficulty in Literature	218
Bibliography		223
Index		235

ILLUSTRATIONS

0.1	Still images from *People Looking at Blood, Moffitt* (1973) by Ana Mendieta	2
1.1	Photograph from *Beyond the Killing Fields* (1992) by Kari René Hall	32
4.1	*Summer* (1573) by Giuseppe Arcimboldo	149
4.2	Illustration of a thaumatrope	152
4.3	Photograph of *Le Readymade Malheureux* (1919–20) by Marcel Duchamp	173
5.1	Sample images of Brás across *Daytripper* (2011)	201
5.2	Scene at Pelourinho in *Daytripper*	203
5.3	*Koinobori* as visual motif in *Daytripper*	206
5.4	Divider image before chapter 10 in *Daytripper*	207
5.5	Iemanjá altar in *Daytripper*	208
5.6	Possessed fisherman as guide in *Daytripper*	209

STATEMENT ON LAND AND RESPONSIBILITY

I wrote this book while living and working in central Ohio, which is the traditional homeland of the Shawnee, Miami, Wyandotte, Delaware/Lenape, and other Indigenous Nations. Despite centuries of genocidal actions and policies by governments and religious organizations, these vibrant and innovative sovereign nations exist. Because of the United States government's disregard for treaties and forced relocation of Indigenous people through the Indian Removal Act of 1830, there are no federally recognized American Indian tribes in the state of Ohio today. But Indigenous people are here, resisting and persisting. I recognize and honor their inherent right to be the principal stewards of this land and its resources. A further responsibility for repair belongs to "land grant" universities like the one where I teach in Ohio. The US government funded these universities through the unjust sale of expropriated Native lands. To acknowledge land and harms is not repair; it only begins to mark the need for justice. US citizens and US institutions have the responsibility to do more than acknowledge. We must act.

Concrete action includes the education we bring to ourselves and others. *Why Indigenous Literatures Matter* by Daniel Heath Justice (Cherokee Nation) demonstrates how Indigenous storytelling and theorizing speak to core concerns of the human experience, and it invites us to rethink literature more broadly in relation to this vital body of work.[1] The public scholarship

---

1. Justice, *Why Indigenous Literatures Matter*.

by Dr. Debbie Reese (tribally enrolled at Nambé Owingeh), collected in the online database American Indians in Children's Literature, provides a critical framework for recognizing and contesting the many harmful stereotypes about Native people in literature and offers resources to support all in teaching, reading, and writing toward redress and fuller recognition of Native sovereignty and dignity.[2] In *An Indigenous Peoples' History of the United States,* Roxanne Dunbar-Ortiz challenges myths of the United States that have been promulgated as fact and provides access to aspects of history that few learn in school.[3]

We can act on what we learn about the lands where we live, work, and travel. The *High Country News* "land-grab" project documents the land seizures and violence-backed treaties that made Native dispossession the foundation of "land grant" universities, and points to remedies: https://www.landgrabu.org/.[4] Voluntary land taxes are one way to recognize our access to stolen Indigenous land. Land tax participants pay an amount that goes directly to Native Nations or organizations in the area. The Native Governance Center (https://nativegov.org/) offers guidance on further actions that follow the leadership of Indigenous Nations and communities.

Even the most robust effort at repair cannot restore what has been destroyed and stolen, but this is no excuse for inaction. Contemporary ownership is the dubious legacy of violent removal and genocide of the land's rightful stewards. The harms of the past persist into the present, and it is our responsibility to address them.

---

2. Reese, "American Indians in Children's Literature."
3. Dunbar-Ortiz, *Indigenous Peoples' History.*
4. See the searchable "Land-Grab" database for information on how specific universities have benefitted from land the government expropriated from Native peoples. Lee, "Morrill Act."

ACKNOWLEDGMENTS

I am deeply grateful for the mentors, colleagues, friends, and loved ones who have walked alongside me on the long way to this book's completion. This book is different, and better, because of you all.

Special thanks to Jim Phelan for pulling me into conversation and helping me to write again during the pandemic. Thank you for seeing the book in the early draft. Philip Armstrong helped me find every resource, opportunity, and support possible over the past five years so that I could keep going with this project. My colleagues in Comparative Studies inspired me with their research and welcomed me to think in new ways about literature, culture, and the world. Students in my world literature courses gave me the chance to make the case (many times!) for reading deformative fictions and for responding to strategic hospitality with care.

I am indebted to many generous readers who accompanied me through drafts of various parts of this book: Anke Birkenmaier, Melissa Curley, Jessica Delgado, Patrick Dove, Pat Enciso, Maggie Flinn, Jared Gardner, Erin Graff Zivin, Harvey Graff, Faye Halpern, Nick Kawa, Patricia Klingenberg, Anna Lieswyn, Herb Marks, Juno Parreñas, Eleanor Paynter, Jerry Reid Miller, Johanna Sellman, Sydney Silverstein, Noah Tamarkin, and John Trimble. More people helped than my memory can hold. Please pardon any omissions.

I value organizations and administrators who have chosen to support humanities scholarship and to consider how work in universities can be more responsive to the communities beyond it. Course releases from the College of Arts and Sciences and funding from the Division of Arts and Humanities made work on this book possible. The TOME@Ohio State initiative, funded by The Ohio State University Libraries, provides free access to the digital version of this book to readers around the world. The OSU Press professionals brought patience, clarity, and rigor to the preparation and production of this book. Thank you to Juliet Williams, Elizabeth Zaleski, and, especially, Ana Maria Jimenez-Moreno for your guidance. Susan Zucker created the striking cover design.

The encouragement, kindness, patience, and practical help of many others sustained my family and me through the writing of this book. My parents, Pat and Terry Ray, have given me courage to pursue my path, even when doing so meant going uphill. I have always felt their steadying hands at my back. Thank you to Charlie Pugsley for steadfast support and for welcoming me back from long writing days with warmth and play. Thank you to Alisa Alering, Shelley Burns, Sarah Derry, David Dubose, Amanda Fox, Mary Harris, Andrew Karre, Judy Parnes, Justin and Starry Ray, Kevin Richards, Carl Schock, and Maurice Stevens. I felt the care of my village, near and far.

And thank you, most of all, to my amazing kids, Liam Miguel and Ethan Andrés. You helped me find more time to write when that seemed impossible. You cheered me on and motivated me to get the day's work done so that we could enjoy our time together. You celebrated each milestone with me. I am proud of this book, but I am much prouder of having written it with your support. We did it!

INTRODUCTION

A First Encounter with Deformative Fiction

To set up her untitled 1973 performance piece (now commonly known as *People Looking at Blood, Moffitt*),[1] Ana Mendieta spread a large quantity of blood and unidentifiable blood-saturated solids in front of an unmarked door. She chose a spot a few blocks from the University of Iowa campus on a busy weekday morning. She then concealed herself in a car nearby and filmed the reactions of people passing by, each of whom became an unwitting participant in a performance piece. Both for these morning walkers and for museumgoers viewing the artifacts of the event, the bloody mess on the sidewalk is what initially attracts attention. Like the passersby, we want to know what we are looking at. The blood hooks us in—what happened here? The subject of most of the images, however, seems to be the walkers' continued movement away from the stained threshold: the blur of moving legs, the determined set of shoulders, the eyes locked ahead or else temporarily detoured by a rubbernecking stare (see figure 0.1).

Over the course of the film, at least twenty-eight people come upon the inscrutable bloody vestiges. Most keep walking, but some stop and stare. One woman probes the blood-soaked solids with the tip of an umbrella. *People Looking at Blood* clearly critiques the failure to respond to what has

---

1. Mendieta, *Untitled (People Looking at Blood, Moffitt)*. This work is also sometimes identified as *Moffitt Building Piece*.

FIGURE 0.1. Two stills from the film documenting *People Looking at Blood, Moffitt* (1973). Performance recorded on Super-8 color, silent film. Running time 3:12 minutes. © The Estate of Ana Mendieta Collection, LLC.

"happened," but those who do stop come off badly as well. They resemble voyeurs and gawkers, bystanders briefly stalled by morbid curiosity or ineffectual sympathy. Art critic Maggie Nelson notes that all of these responses look "from the outside—and likely felt, on the inside—like an uncaring abandonment, even if of an indeterminate or imaginary entity."[2] The scenario turns the defense, "I was just looking!" into an accusation: "*All* you did was look." Yet it is difficult to say what response *would* have been adequate. We might make a phone call, but to whom? The police? City sanitation? Could we stand by the grisly display and insist that others stop and look? Knock on the door and demand that someone answer for the blood that appears to be seeping from beneath it?

Near the end of the film, a man arrives, considers the spill, enters the nearest storefront (its window displays the name "H. F. Moffitt") and returns with a square of plywood. Squatting awkwardly on the sidewalk, he uses the board to scrape the solid bloodied pieces into a cardboard box. Understood from inside the performance's story world, the cleanup job is far from neutral, much less benevolent. We may read it as a demonstration of the prerogatives of private

---

2. Nelson, *Art of Cruelty*, 80.

property ("this mess is near my business; I have a right to address it"), an act of civic duty ("I will take responsibility and spare others the trouble of this nuisance"), or a potential obstruction of justice ("my desire to be rid of this mess matters more than what it might mean as evidence"). Sopping up the blood also seems to fall short of the situation's ethical demands.

Those viewing the video or images from Mendieta's performance must relate not only to the choices of these passersby but also to the artist's intention and motivations. Mendieta created other works during this period that emphasize (or enact) cruelty. The series likely responded, at least in part, to the rape and murder of another young woman studying at the University of Iowa at the same time as Mendieta. These performances also involved depositing "artifacts" of violence onto the canvas of ordinary life in Iowa City. In one, Mendieta placed a blood-splattered mattress in an abandoned farmhouse. In another, she dumped a suitcase with what appeared to be bundles of dismembered body parts in a city park. In *Rape Scene,* Mendieta turned her own body into the artifact of apparent violence, staging her home as if she had been the victim of a gruesome sexual assault. These performances decry several intertwined conditions. First, and most concretely, the structures of society allow, even encourage, the rape and murder of women. Second, people looking at "blood" *only* look; they respond with no meaningful action. Mendieta seems to ask, for example, what signs of "blood" (or distress) did others ignore or walk past the day the University of Iowa student was raped and murdered? Third, society too often treats the intrusion of "blood" on everyday life as the problem, focusing on wiping away the evidence of violence and predation, while failing to address their source. Mendieta inscribes fictional signs of suffering onto the landscape of daily life to protest and counteract the ways the signs of factual suffering get cleaned up, packed away, or otherwise dismissed from public awareness. By forcing blood back into view, these performances challenge the dysfunctional processes that produce and conceal harm in the first place.

The layering of aesthetic and ethical concerns in *People Looking at Blood,* and in Mendieta's body of art more broadly, attracts the attention of art historians and cultural scholars focused on visual media.[3] I open this study of literary narratives with *People Looking at Blood* because it provides a visceral and memorable example of the difficult class of narratives I call "deformative

---

3. Mendieta's art is the focus of extensive cultural analysis. See, for example, Blocker, *Where Is Ana Mendieta?* Conrad James focuses on the literary influence of her art in "Ana Mendieta."

fictions." Experimental or avant-garde works defamiliarize our worlds by stripping away, temporarily at least, our conventional or habitual ways of seeing or reading. Deformative fictions execute a more fundamental disruption. Their authors deliberately undercut understanding and connection in favor of challenge and distress. By unsettling our reading practices and thwarting our expectations, deformative fictions command attention to both. They defamiliarize the act of reading itself and, in so doing, reacquaint us with its ethical weight. Deformative fictions often combine disruptive narrative approaches with thematic intensity in ways that render them haunting and unsettling. Far from compensating for or redeeming challenging content, their aesthetic elements render it even more problematic. The disturbing provocations of deformative fictions persist long after readers' initial encounters with them. They are the narrative equivalent of earworms, those songs that seem designed to loop intrusively in our brains. As "mindworms," deformative fictions chew through the delicate matter of our comfort and security. They infiltrate networks of feeling and thought, taking up residence in ways that disturb and distract. I first encountered *People Looking at Blood* over a decade ago. Whereas hundreds of other aesthetic experiences encountered over those years have settled into the sediment of my memory, this performance remains stubbornly salient. It is exceptionally hard to "finish" deformative fictions, even after we have closed the book, ended the film, or exited the museum.

A second reason for beginning with Mendieta's piece is to underscore a broad view of "fiction." Although I focus on novels and stories in this book, I see fiction as a category that encompasses a wide range of narrative forms that deliberately establish their own internal field of reference.[4] Fiction may be expressed in film, music, video games, dance, visual or performance art, theater, literature, and beyond. That frame of reference may be highly counterfactual as in fantasy, or it may be deeply enmeshed with recognizable external frames of reference as in historical or biographical fiction, or it may be somewhere in between. A work like Mendieta's, for example, might initially seem to be a documentary film in that it records actual reactions to the blood on the sidewalk. But it is intentionally constructed to create its own, counterfactual, frame of reference. The blood was not "just there" when Mendieta began filming. Her placement of it refers to a previous fictional event (whatever would have led to blood being in that particular location). In relating to

---

4. Benjamin Harshav articulates this point clearly: "The issue is not in the amount of demonstrable truthfulness but rather that [fictional works] establish their own IFR [internal field of reference] while [nonfiction works] claim to describe the 'real' world." Harshav, "Fictionality and Fields of Reference," 15.

the blood and its unknown cause, the filmed pedestrians become characters in her fiction.

Lastly, like each of the deformative fictions I examine in the pages ahead, Mendieta's performance makes prominent use of *fictional cruelty* as a narrative resource. Broadly speaking, cruelty describes a relationship to suffering, one characterized by excessive delight or indifference. (I further specify *fictional* to emphasize the distinctiveness of engagements with cruelty in aesthetic works, as opposed to how legal, political, sociological, military, and other discourses have developed the concept.[5]) Cruelty has a layered presence in *People Looking at Blood*. Within the fiction Mendieta created, those who encounter the blood seem to display indifference to the suffering that the blood suggests, whether by ignoring it, gawking at it, or swabbing it up. For viewers of the performance, there is the added question of cruelty on the part of the artist. Mendieta inflicts a disturbing experience on unknown people who have been given no opportunity to consent, or refuse, to participate. The undisclosed recording of their experience, from a remove, also suggests detachment or indifference to the distress of their encounter with the blood.

People Looking at Blood also highlights the etymology of cruelty. The Latin for "cruel," *crūdus*, shares roots with the Latin for "blood" (*cruor*). Whereas *sanguis* refers to the blood that circulates inside the body, *cruor* describes blood from a wound or blood outside of the body. The blood Mendieta spilt across the sidewalk is "out of place" because it no longer maintains life and because the walkers cannot account for it. Their questions of *Who? Why? When? What happened?* have no available answers. They witness *something*, but what? The uncertain status of the blood's origins emphasizes its out-of-place presence. Displaced from any recognizable body, this "blood" stains the sidewalk, the performance, and the viewer. This reflects the Latin etymology for cruelty in a second way: *crūdus* refers to that which is bloody, raw, or indigestible. Like the blood in Mendieta's performance, cruelty evades satisfactory explanation and is, by definition, excessive. The indigestibility of *People Looking at Blood* is, at least in part, why it persists so forcefully in my imagination.

Cruelty is a favored resource of deformative fictions, as I will explore further in chapter 1. For now, I want to make the following observations. First, deformative works are especially likely to confront readers with difficult or troubling instances of fictional cruelty. Second, the experience of relative imperilment in encountering deformative fictions may entice readers to impute cruelty even to texts that do not depict suffering or harm on the level

---

5. For discussions of cruelty as a sociological and psychological problem, see Taylor, *Cruelty*; and Baron-Cohen, *Science of Evil*. For a historical perspective, see Baraz, *Medieval Cruelty*; and Steintrager, *Cruel Delight*.

of the plot. That is, readers may characterize the writing—or the author—as cruel. Third, a focus on fictional cruelty helps illuminate how deformative fictions raise ethical and moral questions about readers and the practice of reading. Fourth, a focus on cruelty offers an important alternative to the prevailing emphasis on violence as a thematic concern in scholarship on Latin American fiction, including on the novels and stories I examine.

WHAT ARE DEFORMATIVE FICTIONS?

The term "deformative fictions" highlights the contrast between the works I examine and other challenging narratives, most notably what critic Joshua Landy describes as "formative fictions."[6] Formative fictions also challenge and frustrate, but as Landy theorizes them, they ultimately support certain readers in developing competency through reading. The formation that interests Landy occurs through a cycle of initiation, challenge, and development. Landy argues that, through repeated encounters, readers' mental faculties and sensitivities shift to respond more fully to the formative fiction they are working with. Gradually, a suitably diligent reader achieves adequacy to the task of reading a particular formative fiction. This virtuous cycle seems to justify the careful attention that literature professors demand (or plead for) from students and that many of us aspire to in our own reading.[7] Above all, what formative fictions ask of readers sounds *fair*. Formative fictions challenge, but they also reward hardworking readers and reinforce reading behaviors that lead to increased understanding and appreciation.

By contrast, deformative fictions subvert the norms that everyday readers (often unconsciously) expect to be upheld. They challenge the idea that stories can be counted on to provide entertainment, enlightenment, humor, emotional connection, broadened perspective, or some other benefit, however deferred it may be. They raise disconcerting questions that persist, unresolved, and that generate uncomfortable feelings of implication, contamination, complicity, and even guilt. They frustrate, disappoint, complicate, and otherwise disrupt prevailing notions of what a text "should" do and how it "should" satisfy us. This is often true even for scholars and professional readers, who tend to hold more sophisticated expectations of literature, and who may derive pleasure from challenging texts in ways that lay readers typically do not.

---

6. Landy, *How to Do Things*, 3–12.

7. Landy asserts a wholesome and positive account of reading as a process of incremental growth, one that fits neatly with the foundational virtues of Protestantism, especially its so-called work ethic. See, for example, *How to Do Things*, 57–59.

The obstructions of deformative fictions differ from more familiar experiences of literary difficulty. We may register the difficulty of Ezra Pound's *Cantos* by counting the footnotes needed to untangle a dense web of allusion, or we might think of the challenge of encountering painful legacies and disavowed histories in literature, as in Octavia Butler's *Kindred* or Palestinian Ghassan Kanafani's *Men in the Sun*. Deformative fictions can and often do create difficulty through unfamiliar syntax, obscure literary allusion, and thematic intensity, among other strategies. They are distinctive, however, in how their authors mobilize narrative resources with the *intent* of disrupting the satisfactions of reading.

Like Heidegger's hammer, which becomes most noticeable when it breaks, the resistant qualities of deformative fictions demand attention by disrupting the "work" of reading and disappointing readers' expectations. Deformative fictions undercut the belief that literature serves as a reliable space in which to develop the self (the old story of *Bildung*/formation through reading). Instead, they thwart familiar positive takeaways and meaning-making tactics and challenge the assumption that careful attention to the author's use of narrative resources will yield a satisfying experience. As mindworms chewing through a reader's consciousness, deformative fictions stimulate unexpected responses in dark recesses and leave behind trails of waste. Or is it fertilizer? If so, what might grow in the soil of our examinations of how deformative fictions function?

NARRATIVE ETHICS AND RHETORICAL READING

My scholarly training and personal investments as a literary critic, professor, novelist, and enthusiastic reader direct my focus to literature. But literature is not just convenient. It provides a valuable reprieve from "fast" platforms such as TikTok and YouTube or the breakneck circulation of memes, GIFs, sound bites, tweets, Instagram posts, and evanescent Snapchat communications. In the digital spaces where we increasingly read and relate, we have become accustomed to sorting, processing, and consuming—if not analyzing—content that appears, and sometimes disappears, at an accelerated rate. By contrast, literature offers the possibility of a slow and sustained encounter with imagined worlds. Proceeding at a less frenetic pace, we may learn (or relearn) to pay attention to complex patternings of relation and expression. The slower, sequential unfurling of meaning in relation to the printed page encourages awareness of our role in generating and interpreting a world from the text. Still, the core dynamics and ethical complexities of deformative fictions retain their force beyond written works, as the opening discussion of Mendieta's performance art suggests. I hope others will extend my efforts to additional narrative modes and media. Even within the realm of literature, the implications of studying deformative fictions extend beyond the Latin American traditions to reading and interpretive practices more broadly.

Deformative fictions invite, or demand, increased attention to often overlooked dimensions and possibilities of narrative texts and reading encounters. In particular, they illuminate the stakes of the stories we tell, how we tell them, and how we receive them. This is the domain of narrative ethics, which Adam Zachary Newton defines as "the ethical consequences of narrating story and fictionalizing person, and the reciprocal claims binding teller, listener, witness, and reader in that process."[8] Whereas it is easy to see the obligations that impinge on those who tell stories, narrative ethics reminds us of the ethical obligations and challenges across the narrative act. Four overlapping domains of narrative ethics orient my discussion of deformative fictions: the ethics of the *told*, the ethics of *telling*, the ethics of *writing*, and the ethics of *reading*. With each analysis, I consider the particulars of each text's story (the *told*); its construction, narrator, and implied author (*telling*); the text as an object created in an existing world under certain circumstances by a flesh-and-blood author (*writing*), and the set of practices we bring to the text (*reading*). A focus on the ethics of the *told* might weigh the ethical implications of characters' choices, actions, and attitudes. The ethics of *telling* centers questions about characteristics of the narration, often as an expression of ethical orientation on the part of character narrators or authors. This focus highlights the ethical significance of narrative and stylistic choices in the evocation of a textual world. The ethics of *writing* addresses the conditions in which writers create and the structures that affect their telling, such as access to publication and literary markets, language of composition, and other external factors. The ethics of *reading* considers the stakes of how readers experience, receive, interpret, or respond to stories.

I reflect especially on the ethics of *reading* deformative fictions. Reading inflects the *told*, the *telling*, and the *writing* with the particularity of a moment and the idiosyncrasies of a specific reader. The ethics of *reading* also includes our retrospective interpretation and the other stories we tell about our experiences of reading. In other words, we interpret the text, but we also interpret our experience of it. Reading is an encounter as immediate as any sensory experience, whether it is characterized by paperboard, fibers, and ink markings; pixels illuminated on a screen or reader; braille read by eager fingertips;

---

8. Newton, *Narrative Ethics*, 10–11.

or soundwaves apprehended by the ears.[9] But most of the "experiences" we speak of when we talk about reading are conjectural and projected. Words penned in another moment bring readers into partial contact with the author that they imagine as the source of textual effects (the implied author). For the reader, the text as artifact implies the existence of an author who can be reconstructed from it imaginatively. The writer anticipates the reader; in response, the reader reconstructs the author. The text expresses the set of resources (e.g., dialogue, description, handling of time and space, intertextuality) mobilized by the author to achieve certain ends and ultimately navigated and coordinated by the reader. Here and throughout the book, I mean "reader" and "author" as position markers, synecdoches for all the responses, intentions, values, beliefs, capacities, and propensities on each side of this communication—the dimensions of author and reader brought to bear on the reading encounter. Even as we acknowledge that there is more to who readers are, and more to who any author is, than what gets expressed in a given act of writing or reading, the narrative encounter invites dynamic and multifaceted expressions of subjectivity and constructions of meaning.[10]

This process is fundamentally relational. Readers at once relate to a unique object (the text) and relate to their ongoing reconstruction or projection of a "somebody" who created it. That "somebody" may be a character narrator within the story world, the implied author whom we imagine writing it, or the actual author at another remove. We may relate to all three at once, seeing them as distinct figures or experiencing them as nested expressions contained within the author. The "real" author possesses flesh and blood, but as far as the reader is concerned, who they are depends just as much on interpretation and imagination as do the identities of a narrator or any character. The bottom line is that these echoes of basic communication imbue narrative with immediacy even when there are large gaps between the time or space of writing and reading.

Some of these observations may seem obvious. But to adopt a rhetorical view of narrative breaks, or at least disrupts, the common sense of two main strains of professional literary interpretation: one that treats narrative as (primarily) an illustration of historical, political, and cultural forces, and the other that focuses on narrative as a structured sign system ("the text is all," "the author is dead"). The former takes literature as an access point to a broader understanding of human experience and sees engaging with *persons* as the

---

9. For a consideration of the embodied experience of reading, see Newton, *To Make the Hands Impure*.

10. An especially clear explanation of the constructivist approach is Hall, "Work of Representation."

source of that understanding. By contrast, the latter emphasizes the structures and modes of play that are particular to literary language and not reducible to ordinary communicative acts. Although proponents of the text's autonomy will often see their approach as a reparative act—restoring language to the primacy it ought to have held already—to those focused on what experiences mean to people, the tropes of text-focused criticism may seem to line up with cruelty to virtual persons: one who cares most about signs comes off as lacking in empathy for the represented or implied human other.

The rhetorical theory of narrative helps coordinate these concerns. It approaches narrative as a complex set of actions, rather than treating narrative as an object. Jim Phelan's definition of narrative as a layered communicative exchange by which *somebody tells somebody else something on some occasion and for some reason(s)* highlights the rhetorical theory of narrative's focus on the interpersonal stakes of communication. When we approach texts as *rhetorical readers,* we direct our attention to the complexity of this communication as a main access point to the particularity of the texts and their deployment of narrative resources.[11] Reading is an encounter, not just with a text, but with the dynamic relationships between stories, tellers, audiences, and worlds.

A basic premise of my understanding of narrative is that authors set terms for these encounters (within the constraints of their position, what we talk about with the ethics of *writing*). The terms they set lead to a range of experiences, from the "thoroughly deformative" at one end of the spectrum to the "thoroughly hospitable" at the other. We can think of "challenging" (or "formative") texts arrayed between the two extremes. Whereas deformative fictions challenge us with narrative experiences designed to be disruptive, hospitable fictions make every effort to accommodate readers. This accommodation has ethical stakes that are just as significant as those of deformative fictions. The strategies and modes of attention we cultivate to read deformative fictions may also benefit our reading of far more hospitable narratives.

For a text to *register* as deformative (or hospitable) depends to some degree on characteristics of readers and situational factors. A critic, seasoned in the interpretation of varied disruptive literary techniques, may not experience a text as deformative even though that was the intention of the author. By contrast, as I've witnessed many times in my world literature courses, students confronting a postcolonial novel for the first time may perceive it as intensely inhospitable even though the author did not set out to write a deformative work. The subjective experience of a text does not override the reality

---

11. Phelan, *Somebody Telling Somebody Else,* 3–29.

of the author's intention, but it does shape the degree to which that intention is received, at least by a particular reader.

This is one reason for inquiring into readers' responses alongside my analysis of the works of literature themselves.[12] Admittedly, much of this is anecdotal and conjectural; I leave studies of readers' brain activity to scholars of cognitive narratology, and I have no empirical surveys of readers' attitudes. But reading experience is so ephemeral, mutable, and intimate, so subject to revision. It is hard to imagine tools sensitive enough to capture it. If I lean into my skill set as a novelist in imagining how various readers respond, I do so with the same intention that animates my fiction writing: to evoke experiences that resonate with reality, even if they do not duplicate them. When my discussion pertains especially to one type of reader, or when the contrast between likely responses by different readers is especially strong, I make a point of noting what kind of reader, specifically, I mean. When I do not specify, I am imagining readers as people who would voluntarily pick up a difficult book. They might be writers or professors, but they might also be readers in a book club or especially engaged undergraduates curious about the diverse possibilities of fiction. I imagine these readers as people who would be relatively unintimidated by "regular" or "formative" literary difficulty, but who would find deformative fictions challenging, especially in terms of the complicated ways that they position us. When I refer to *rhetorical readers,* I mean to highlight these readers' explicit engagement with the rhetorical theory of narrative and the focal points and resources it offers.

CHARACTERIZING DEFORMATIVE FICTIONS

Deformative fictions may chasten presumptions, check expectations, expose the cheap or compromised pleasures for which we sometimes grasp, and halt our sweeping away of difficult-to-account-for details. In other words, they confront us with the problems of how we often improvise meaning to serve ourselves when we read. None of these qualities are absolute, however. A text might be more, or less, deformative depending on what we compare it to. What we are talking about is really a *range* of intentionally difficult fictional narratives, itself one section of a larger gradient of literary difficulty. Many factors impact where we might place a text on the spectrum. These include the other works we compare it to, the relative capacities and experiences of

---

12. This is an approach pursued with sensitivity in Graff Zivin, *Anarchaeologies.*

readers, and the historical moment of authorship and/or of reading. Still, the following characteristics help define the basic range of deformative fictions.

1. *Deformative fictions tamper with the unstated, but presumed, author–reader contract.* They frustrate, disappoint, complicate, subvert or otherwise disrupt expectations of what a text "should" do and how it "should" satisfy readers. Stylistic experimentation generally targets aspects of literary convention (e.g., genre, plot progression, and focalization) or seeks to alter or renew our apprehension of reality (as with tactics of defamiliarization). In contrast, deformative fictions strike closer to the core of narrative exchange. They disrupt what Phelan describes as "the default ethics of telling in literary narrative since modernism,"[13] where "ethics" might be better understood as norms of comportment. As Phelan goes on to describe, the viability of these norms hinges on reciprocity and trust between authors and audiences: "the audience assumes that attending carefully to the author will result in a worthwhile experience, and the author assumes that the audience can be trusted to . . . follow the art of mediated communication."[14] This default implies that the author's primary obligation is to readers, and that effectively coordinating readerly and writerly processes fulfills this obligation. But deformative fictions often establish other priorities, highlighting that the ethical dimensions of literature go beyond whether or how either side of the author–reader contract is fulfilled. Asking, "To what or to whom does this author express a primary ethical obligation, if not the reader?" helps us to assess how they disrupt typical narrative dynamics. For example, Silvina Ocampo prioritizes the integrity of her narratives, their right to exist as they are in the face of some readers' desire for them to be otherwise, as I discuss in chapter 2.

2. *Deformative fictions dislocate us from our usual reading protocols and responses.* Not only do deformative fictions eschew accommodations for readers, but they also obstruct many of our usual ways of reading. They often undermine interpretive objectives, such as defusing or reducing the negative pressure of confusion aroused by a story. Academically trained and practiced readers tend to privilege "certain texts . . . because they work with a normalized strategy or set of strategies."[15] But even professional readers find their interpretive alchemy disrupted—or reformulated to catalyze uncomfortable conclusions. As I demonstrate in chapter 4, Roberto Bolaño's *2666* tantalizes readers with the prospect of a thematic reading that might account for the novel's many parts, bifurcations, and echoes. In the end, however, it makes interpretation feel like an abandonment of ethical engagement. To succeed

---

13. Phelan, *Somebody Telling Somebody Else*, 22.
14. Phelan, *Somebody Telling Somebody Else*, 22.
15. Rabinowitz, *Before Reading*, 212. See also Steig, *Stories of Reading*.

at a satisfactory or comprehensive reading would mean to *stop seeing* or *stop mourning* the murders represented in the novel. Instead, it demands that we continue to see and feel. When we navigate deformative fictions' disruptions of our interpretive protocols, we also cultivate greater curiosity about the often-unconscious grooves of our analysis. This increased awareness benefits our reading of works that are not deformative, but that for other reasons (e.g., subject matter; language of authorship; racial, cultural, sexual, or gender identity of the author) fit poorly with dominant modes of reading. As we learn to read deformative fictions, we cultivate strategies and alternative routes for reading fiction that does not accord with expectations in other ways.

3. *Deformative fictions challenge the belief that literature can (and should) support readers' development—whether of wisdom, discernment, empathy, or some aspect of the self.* Especially in relation to nondominant traditions, like Latin American literatures, we invest a great deal in imaginative engagement with cultural difference. We institutionalize this approach through special editorial imprints and university curricula that feature language like "global citizenship" and "cultural perspectives." Such an approach presents literature as a tool for gaining knowledge of life experiences, circumstances, characters, and settings that differ in substantial ways from what readers are accustomed to. When we frame literature in this way, we enjoy the implicit reassurance that by reading, we discharge some real responsibility to human others.

To be sure, many literary scholars view such claims with caution, even if we espouse them publicly in defense of the humanities or of the courses we teach. But deformative fictions draw particular attention to problems with readers' appetite for empathizing. They tend to expose the ways that this desire to "feel with" is not about the "other," at least not primarily. Fritz Breithaupt enumerates the "dark sides of reader empathy," where the self-focused goal is really the reader's pleasure—even at the cost of the "recipient" of empathy.[16] Although we rarely name this procedure, it might be summed up as something like, "this character must continue to suffer so that I can feel the pleasure of my feelings in response, whether they be compassion, outrage, or something else."[17] Fernando Vallejo's 1994 novel, *La virgen de los sicarios* (*Our Lady of the Assassins*), dramatizes this in the character narrator's agonized response to a suffering dog. What appears to be sympathy for a fellow creature, however, is in fact an occasion for deeper engagement with his own self-pity. Deformative fictions threaten to expose the possibility of similar motivations in our reading practices, at least some of the time.

---

16. Breithaupt, *Dark Sides of Empathy*.

17. See Breithaupt, "Empathic Sadism" for four "flavors" of morally ambivalent, self-focused empathy.

4. *Deformative fictions complicate readers' relationship to the narrative experience, often arousing ambivalent or negative feelings such as stress, disorientation, aggravation, and complicity.*[18] They create webs of implication or otherwise encumber *reading* with an uneasy relationship to the *told*, the *telling*, or the *writing* of the narrative. As I will discuss in greater detail, fictional cruelty serves as a prime resource for generating distressing affective states, but deformative fictions can accomplish this in other ways as well.

5. *Deformative fictions advance an alternative agenda that sets them apart from most other texts. That agenda suggests that, at least some of the time, the education readers need is an "unshaping": a deformation of expectations, presumed entitlements, and patterns of thought and feeling.* This provocative pedagogy leaves readers unprotected and often unrewarded. It may take us significantly beyond our comfort zone or push us right to the edge of what feels like harm. The experience of relative imperilment may seem quite personal. If we persist in our engagement, however, the lack of accommodation we experience with deformative fictions can increase our awareness of the desires and expectations we bring to other reading encounters. This is especially pertinent to changes in our readings of hospitable narratives that seem to make far fewer demands of us, like the one I examine in chapter 5.

Deformative fictions embody these five characteristics to varying degrees, and as readers change—both in their individual development and through generational shifts—the impact of a given textual element may subside or intensify. A deformative fiction received as troublesome or pernicious at one time may be celebrated and read with enthusiasm at another historical moment. We may think, for example, of changing responses to fiction by the Marquis de Sade or Rachilde. This increased legibility may correlate with other shifts, such as gradual acclimation to stylistic innovation (free verse, for example) or acceptance of a genre (the novel as literature, rather than mass entertainment). But a trend toward greater acceptance is not given. Texts that were once celebrated may acquire fraught associations over time and become more, not less, troublesome. Changing understandings of the stakes of representing race complicate the interpretation of racial imagination in works such as Mark Twain's *Adventures of Huckleberry Finn* (1884) and William Styron's *Confessions of Nat Turner* (1967).[19] Because these texts vex contemporary readers in

---

18. For more on aesthetic evocations of unpleasant feelings, see Ngai, *Ugly Feelings*.

19. See Rekdal, *Appropriate* for detailed discussions of American literature and the evolving interpersonal stakes of representing cultural and racial differences. Many of the texts in *Appropriate* function as deformative fictions.

ways that their authors did not intend, though, I would describe them as challenging or provocative, not deformative.

Similar shifts unfold in our encounters with a single work. Some deformations may come to seem less afflictive as we become more familiar with them. Imagine that Mendieta enacted *People Looking at Blood, Moffitt* across several blocks on a likely route to the campus of the University of Iowa, or that she repeated it each morning for a week. The spilled blood continues to disconcert, but we may build our strategies for reading the situation, what significance to attach to it, and to our experience, and other responses that reduce the piece's afflictive potential. Often, although not always, as we spend more time with a text, it is harder to remember the initial shock, sense of disequilibrium, and distress it caused us.

Even as experiences of deformative fictions are variable, I want to stress, again, the importance of authorial intention. Authors shape their works to be deformative and invite readers to recognize and grapple with the deformations they create. Readers may not recognize them for various reasons, whether because of individual reading habits, or because what is deformative in one era might become naturalized, or because what rises to the level of deformativity for one group of readers does not for another. But most authors of deformative fictions ensure that the signature of their projects is deeply emblazoned by deploying a range of deformations.

THE PARADOX OF READING DEFORMATIVE FICTIONS

Ultimately, I argue that our difficult experiences of deformative fictions *do* lead to learning. At first, this might seem like a contradiction. Isn't learning what made Landy's difficult texts "formative"? How does learning relate to deformative fictions' agenda of frustrating readers and withholding the benefits of reading? In some ways, this is simply a reminder that descriptions like "deformative" and "formative" are relative, not absolute. "Deformative fictions" serves as a shorthand for those works in the intentionally (and highly) disruptive range of a spectrum of literary difficulty. Still, they are not *absolutely* deformative. They frustrate and limit readers' drive to meaningfulness, but they do not (or cannot) deny it altogether. Even as deformative fictions gesture toward refusal and negation, insights accrue. We become more reflective about ourselves as readers as we consider the ramifications of our expectations. We gain a more capacious understanding of how and why stories matter even—or especially—when they do not please or satisfy us in normative ways.

The concrete implications of our interactions with deformative fictions emerge most powerfully, not on a first reading, but as that experience resonates through future literary encounters. In the same way that athletes who train at high altitudes do not feel the benefits of their conditioning until they descend to lower elevations, we may not notice the effects of deformative fictions until we discover their influence on our "regular" reading. Like all metaphors, this one has limits. Deformative fictions are not coaches. Their authors are not explicitly interested in teaching us what to do, how to respond, or which actions or approaches might produce ethically adequate readings of their, or any other, works. They do not prescribe solutions or offer resolutions. They confront us with active feelings of stress, inadequacy, disorientation, guilt, and discomfort—all conveyed in writings that are exceptionally effective at implanting themselves and persisting in our consciousness. Although unpleasant, these experiences stimulate shifts in reading and attentional practices as we interpret and negotiate the satisfactions that a text puts before us. This hard-won learning looks quite different from the typical insights of our encounters with literature, but it *is* learning.

It may seem contradictory to speak of a pedagogy or ethics of reading deformative fictions since increasing readability or success runs counter to the deformative projects themselves. Deformative fictions are indeed often counter-pedagogical, invested in projects of unmaking or of disrupting any program of reading. Even as this is a recognizable characteristic of most deformative projects, readers have their own projects and goals. In other words, we are not obligated to remain in the space of unmaking or disruption. Learning to read deformative fictions more effectively is not a contradiction, but it does point to a paradox. On the one hand, careful attention to what makes deformative fictions unique means attending to their particular obstructions, seeing them as they are rather than as it would be convenient for them to be. On the other, all experience produces learning, and I embrace this reality by proposing practices for reading deformative fictions more constructively. Becoming rhetorical readers of deformative fiction offers opportunities to attend to the particularity of the text while also seeing a range of possibilities for navigating the complex resources it mobilizes.

Although our ways of reading may diminish the deformative character of a text to some degree, I advocate for practices that keep us attentive to the implications of our own reading and interpretation. Like most ethically complex situations, reading deformative fictions calls for alertness to our own motives, sensitivity to differences, and curiosity about what we do not understand. I seek to keep in focus the value of recognizing distress and discomfort as part of the experience of deformative fictions, as well as the value of welcoming learning that differs from what we may have expected or become accustomed to in other reading. This is the project I undertake in the chapters ahead.

Chapter 1 examines the hallmarks of deformative fictions, describes how they capitalize on fictional cruelty, and considers the ethical challenges that they present to readers. In chapters 2, 3, and 4, I extend these ideas in case studies of short fiction by Silvina Ocampo and novels by Fernando Vallejo and Roberto Bolaño. I examine the distinct modes of deformative fictions undertaken by each writer and follow their unique engagements with cruelty as a narrative resource. These works of Latin American fiction offer a starting point for exploring what deformative fictions do and how we might read them. I also seek to illuminate core dimensions of these authors' innovative narrative projects. Although my readings may offer a counterweight to sometimes inattentive or imprecise critical treatment of these works, particularly in the English-language press, I do not attempt comprehensiveness or "coverage" of these authors' full body of work, much less of their respective literary traditions. Rather, I seek to orient readers who are less familiar with, but curious about, Latin American literature. I hope to keep the ethical responsibilities of interpretation present, which is especially important when reading works composed in cultural contexts and historical moments at greater removes from our own lived experiences.

I begin in chapter 2 with the *defensive* deformative fiction of Silvina Ocampo's short stories in *La furia y otros cuentos* (The fury and other stories). Ocampo adopts a deformative approach as part of a broader rejection of pressures to conform to notions of feminine literary decorum in the mid-century literary culture of Buenos Aires. Her strategies include flattened affect, persistent ambiguity, unreliability, and narrative framing that multiplies distressing possibilities. Her most effective defense, however, is an offense: she positions readers as co-authors of cruelty by making us the ones to flesh out the disturbing implications of scenarios. Her stories challenge readers' expectation of access to character interiority and reveal how often our impulse toward empathy in reading is self-serving rather than benevolent.

Chapter 3 considers Fernando Vallejo's *assaultive* project in *La virgen de los sicarios* (*Our Lady of the Assassins*). This novel is often discussed as an illustration of drug-related hyperviolence in 1990s Columbia (ethics of the *told*), but I focus on the sites of cruelty in the *telling* and *writing* of the novel. These include the narrator's celebration of death, his evacuation of meaning from the suffering of others, and his parasitic relationship to the teen assassins whom he takes as lovers. The cruelty does not stop with the narrator's afflictive *telling*. The author hijacks the resources of fiction in the service of diatribe.

He also sustains an elaborate project of rhetorical passing, a strategy in which the same narration invites starkly contrasting interpretation by different audiences. The audience of targeted readers presumes that the novel's misogynistic, anti-poor, elitist diatribes belong to an unreliable narrator. By contrast, a second audience of conspiratorial readers understands the continuity between the narrator's views and the author's, recognizes the duping of the targeted audience, and enjoys beholding this extended assault on liberal humanists and professional readers. *La virgen* provides a compelling instance of how assaultive deformative fictions entrap readers and expose them to harm. It also invites consideration of the ethical implications of what rhetorical readers choose to do in response.

Chapter 4 focuses on the *anti-elegiac* approach to deformative fiction in Roberto Bolaño's *2666*. Bolaño places over a hundred accounts of gruesome, unsolved murders at the center of the labyrinthine plot of *2666*, tempting readers to fit the murders into a total reading of the novel even as he ensures that such a reading will fail. Rather than allow literature to function as a site of repair or a source of coherence, Bolaño uses the relational quality of cruelty to create myriad instances of the readers' implication in death, suffering, and global circumstances that render some lives especially precarious. Whereas the experience of guilt sometimes seems to offer consolation ("at least I feel *bad* about it"), Bolaño turns our reading experience into a source of responsibility that we can neither discharge nor dismiss.

In the last chapters, I build on these case studies to consider what encounters with deformative fictions may mean for our reading practices more broadly. Chapter 5 focuses on the narrative and ethical concerns that arise when reading the works of world literature that US readers are most likely to encounter. I focus on the idea of *strategic hospitality* in these works, by which I mean authors' deliberate accommodation of cultural outsiders, whether through minimizing differences, linguistic adjustments, or other choices. I argue that our experiences with deformative fictions can help us increase, rather than relax, our attention to how authors navigate the challenges of their relationship with a world readership. I analyze a popular graphic novel, *Daytripper*, by the Brazilian comics artists Fábio Moon and Gabriel Bá, and demonstrate opportunities for interpreting strategic hospitality with an attentiveness that matches our consideration of difficulty in deformative fictions. In the conclusion, I consider how rhetorical readers' engagements with deformative fictions build greater capacity for contending with uncomfortable narratives, whether fiction or nonfiction, literary or nonliterary.

Each chapter approaches, in a different way, the same core question: How do we understand our work as rhetorical readers, and how might that change if we learn, at least some of the time, to renounce expectations of satisfaction and mastery in our encounters with literature? Deformative fictions ask us, often painfully, to confront discomfort, reckon with privilege, and perhaps become more mobile, responsive, and self-aware in our reading of literature and the world. In the pages ahead, I tell the story of encountering deformative fictions, describe the power of these encounters to change us, and imagine how we may carry traces of these experiences into our reading of other texts.

CHAPTER 1

Narrative Ethics, Deformative Fictions, and Fictional Cruelty

Deformative fictions, especially those that make use of cruelty as a narrative resource, strike at the heart of some of our most dearly held notions about literature. Most book lovers can call to mind satisfying instances of reading that broadened their horizons or transformed their thinking. We remember the times that a book offered much-needed companionship at important junctures in our life journey. Readers pass these books on to their friends. Professors teach them to students. Book jackets and reviews promise, "This book will change you." We often speak of reading as a way of calibrating our intuitions about human experience, which we then redeploy in future reading and living. Reading beyond our cultural comfort zones, this popular story goes, allows us to engage empathetically with differences. Along the way, we develop the kinds of broad awareness that can make us better citizens: more informed, tolerant, sensitive, and culturally aware. This is an appealing notion, and it speaks to important aspects of the reading experience. Its limitations, however, are significant. A joke at my own expense illustrates this. If wide and deep reading improves the reader's moral character, literature professors and English teachers should be the most generous humans in the world. Overwhelming experience to the contrary suggests otherwise. As Rick Gekoski quips, "consider a typical member of a university English department, and despair."[1]

---

1. Gekoski, "Reading Is Overrated."

Of course, books *can* support our growth in clear and recognizable ways. And indeed, this kind of "formative" experience is what we have tended to focus on. But this is only part of the story. By reading deformative fictions, we learn to account more fully for how the diversity of narratives, and our diverse readings of them, matter. Recognizing the value of books that leave us confused, disoriented, uneasy, or upset is often at odds with how we have been encouraged to think about the benefits of reading.[2] Expecting rewards may make us feel entitled to find, or improvise, satisfactions even when they conflict with the character of the texts we are reading. If we fail in those improvisations (as is often the case for deformative fictions), we may be tempted to turn away from a narrative or disparage it as perverse. But doing so makes differences into deficits.

This may not seem like too much of a problem when it is "just" a book that we treat like a resource for our enrichment, or reject as insufficiently hospitable. But imagine what a similar approach would mean if we were relating to other people. In our best interpersonal relating, we respond to a person we encounter with attention and care for their uniqueness and the particularity of their experiences, perspectives, desires, and wisdom. For example, I would do well to set aside the expectations I have of my hearing companions when I interact with a deaf colleague and instead to welcome the particular expressivity of their communication. In so doing, I may attend to, rather than discount, difference. If handled well, the occasion offers the chance to cultivate curiosity about the wisdom that another holds. A veteran affected by PTSD or a neighbor in the late stages of dementia likely will relate to us differently from those with other experiences, and those differences might not feel especially comfortable. But discomfort does not, I hope, make us less responsive or engaged. Nor should it cause us to view other people, or our encounters, as damaged or deficient. Our experiences may draw attention to the *cost* of being responsive and attuning to someone else, or they may make us notice that we are missing out on satisfactions that we had become accustomed to. Nevertheless, we can continue to recognize these interactions as meaningful and "worth our time" even when they do not conform to our expectations or maximize our comfort. In a comparable way, deformative fictions remind us that a meaningful engagement with literature, and narrative ethics, transcends attention to "the good" that a text supposedly does for readers. On the far side of deformative literary experiences, we see the terrain of narrative ethics differently.

---

2. For a discussion and critique of these stories about literacy, see Graff, *Searching for Literacy*.

THE NARRATIVE ENCOUNTER

I want to stay for a moment with the situation I just raised and ask, what does it mean to face a deformative fiction as attentively as if we were facing a human other? To meet the text with a sense of responsibility, not of entitlement? This idea of encounter is rooted in a Levinasian understanding of ethics as infinite vulnerability to the other.[3] I understand the kind of encounter that Emmanuel Levinas describes, and the fullness of responsibility it entails, as an ethical aspiration rather than an outcome achievable (or desirable) in practice.[4] I draw only modest parallels between Levinas's paradigmatic scene of ethics and the actual practice of reading, of a person facing a text. But considering these parallels helps us understand how reckoning with deformative fictions expands the scene of ethics in reading.

According to a Levinasian approach, the call to respond to another—text, human, or otherwise—precedes any knowledge of self or other and unfolds without guaranteeing any experience of worth, goodwill, beauty, lovability, understanding, or other advantage. In the absence of these benefits, what values orient us? I propose neutral curiosity about a text's particularities and attentiveness to the implications of our response to it. Within this framework, we practice recognizing and releasing some of the protective, distancing, and distorting tactics that typically are deployed in readers' attempts to negotiate the difficulty or disruption of these works.

We often resort to self-protective reading practices, shielding ourselves from discomfort at the expense of serious engagement with difficult texts. In one expression of this, we may rush to the release valve of dysfunctional authorial intention to explain our discomfort, perhaps adopting the position of aggrieved victims of the writer. The accusation levied against the writer may be tinged with ethical or aesthetic judgments, or both. The author is cruel, or unskilled in their craft, or otherwise deficient, aggrieved readers may claim. Scapegoating curtails attention to the text. If another is to blame for our discomfort, if the text is the source of unwarranted suffering, we may absolve ourselves of responsibility for engaging with it. To be clear, to make sense of deformative fictions, we do need to think about authorial intention. My point here, though, is that pathologizing the author often functions as a justification for not engaging with the text sincerely, as it is.

---

3. See Newton, *Narrative Ethics*. For essential discussions of literary encounter as ethical experience, see also Graff Zivin, *Ethics of Latin American Literary Criticism*.

4. Levinas, *Totality and Infinity*.

When we divert the resources of reading and interpretation from engaging with the text to reinforcing our innocence, we become rigid rather than reflective, reluctant rather than curious. It diminishes our capacity to inquire into the expectations or desires that we bring to our reading, much less into the degree to which the text's legitimate frustration of these may account for our discomfort. Alternatively, readers may bring scaffolds to the text with the goal of "redeeming" the author or narrative by making sense of its recalcitrance. To force the narrative into a different shape or build a bridge of materials alien to the text, however well-intentioned, demonstrates another expression of failed attention and engagement, an elevation of our ideas about how the text *should* be over what it is.

Readers may be especially likely to force resolution and coherence, or to engage in other modes of misreading, when they approach disturbing books. We seek to protect ourselves against points of view that we find unwelcome or threatening.[5] For example, decades of poorly fitting "explanations" for cruelty encumber Ocampo's short stories. Critics often treat cruelty as a mark of her engagement with the fantastic tradition, as an expression of solidarity with social outsiders, or as the cornerstone of a subversive protofeminist literary project. But in each of these approaches, critics reshape Ocampo's stories to fit their purposes, often working forcefully against the grain of the texts.[6]

To the contrary, I am interested in what happens when we choose to face the text with the openness and receptivity that we aspire to bring to our best human relations while simultaneously reminding ourselves that this stance is heuristic. The text is not a person; it has no responsibility to make readers feel that it is a person. It *matters* in its nonhuman particularity. By attending carefully to this relational model, along with its limitations, we adapt aspects of the Levinasian ethical encounter, shifting from an ideal philosophical space to the lived experience of reading. In contrast to Levinas's emphasis on absolute exposure and vulnerability as a core element of encounter, I believe that responsive reading is possible without self-abandonment or total passivity in the face of a text or its imagined author.

Attention to the particularity of a text is active. It calls for curiosity and imagination as we reconstruct an authorial audience. What kind of readers and what kind of responses does this text invoke? What invitations (or disincentives) does it create for feeling, judgment, and interpretation? Seeking signs of the intended authorial audience for a text allows us to imagine what

---

5. Rabinowitz, *Before Reading*, 201–2.
6. Reading against the grain has its merits, of course, but we should be aware that we are doing it. See Terry Eagleton for discussion of an intentional practice with the goal of "show[ing] the text as it cannot know itself." Eagleton, *Criticism and Ideology*, 43.

kind of reading the author anticipated or sought to stimulate. Difficult or provocative texts call for extra awareness of the difference between indications of authorial expectations of an audience and our relative freedom as actual readers. We can open fully to the challenges of deformative fictions while maintaining a firm grasp on our agency and capacity for consent. More specifically, we may choose not to participate in the authorial audience and instead stand aside from its implied values and perspectives. We may do this for reasons particular to a given text, for example, when the authorial audience seems to be intended to hold views that we find objectionable, or for reasons particular to ourselves, as when our experiences make it too costly to identify, even provisionally, with a perspective, perhaps one that intersects with harm we have suffered. A sexual trauma survivor may exercise special caution when approaching a text that contains representations of indifference to or celebration of sexual abuse.

To emphasize how rhetorical readers may cultivate both agency and receptiveness, I think of engaging with a text through deliberate but provisional *contact*, here understood as a consensually established point of connection. A body may meet a beach with expanses of skin touching warm sand, or with only a single finger resting lightly on the surface. In reading, we have choices about the extent and duration of contact, choices that matter still more when the text we approach feels more like a bed of nails than a stretch of smooth sand.

Choosing to reckon with works that thwart our desires or preferences expands the ethical range of our reading.[7] Responsibility to a recognizable or hospitable text may not tax us much, but deformative fictions demand what Jacques Derrida describes as our "responsibility to the most dissimilar, the entirely other, the monstrously other, the unrecognizable other."[8] Our tendency to characterize the text as "monstrous" may correspond precisely to the intensity of our desire for it to be otherwise. By contrast, if we attend to the text in its difference from what we might wish to find, we adopt a stance of openness, which is itself an expression of ethical aspiration. It sustains the possibility of reckoning more fully with a text as it is, apart from whatever meaning, pleasure, or satisfaction it may offer us. Deformative fictions test that resolve, but they can also help us deepen it.

---

7. Reading only the human—or the humane—in the text amounts, in my view, to what Levinas describes as "the reduction of the other to the same." Levinas, *Totality and Infinity*, 43.

8. Derrida, *Beast and the Sovereign*, 108.

REPRESENTATIVE DEFORMATIONS

Authors of deformative fictions accomplish their effects through a wide range of strategies. Here, without pretending to provide an exhaustive catalog, I describe some of the narrative moves that may accompany a deformative agenda. Or, to put it another way, these features may be part of what causes readers to recognize a deformative fiction as such. Often these deformations cluster in a text in ways that are mutually intensifying.

Disruptions to Psychological Realism. Some deformative fictions manipulate or withhold indications of interiority (e.g., motivation, reaction, and emotion) that typically invite us to treat fiction as an extension of our dealings with others. We may tolerate significant disruptions of realism in general, from the improbable murder rate in the small-town setting of a mystery series to the intricately imagined worlds of science fiction. By contrast, denial of access to the material we need to uncover or interpret characters' motivations can feel like an affront. Blocked access to internal information often heightens the discomfort of encountering morally vexed dynamics in a narrative.

Narrative Impropriety. Our sense of what is acceptable, as much as what is likely, corresponds to a notion of narrative propriety: how ought a story like this—by someone like this, narrated on such and such an occasion—be told? Rabinowitz notes that we read with little concern for how events might play out in reality but draw primarily on our knowledge of what they lead to in the kind of literature we are reading.[9] But what should or could refine our concept of a genre may become *prescriptive* when imposed on a specific text or writer. Cultural elites of 1930s Latin America anticipated that a woman writer would offer considerable emotional access to her characters. This is exactly what Ocampo refused to do.

Activation of Cultural and Narrative Taboos. Vallejo's narrator not only celebrates murder; he delights in the deaths of mothers and pregnant women. Pedro Almodóvar's *Kika* (1993) includes a comically protracted rape scene that proves more upsetting to many viewers than comparably extended scenes of murder.

Highlighting Inconsistencies between Moral Judgments of Narrative and of Lived Experience. Often in tandem with the activation of taboos, deformative fictions foreground differences between the moral judgments elicited by fiction and those elicited by real life. For example, Margrethe Bruun Vaage observes how fictional representations of rape elicit more forceful reactions than murder, but the same does not hold in responses to these harms in real life. Further, for many viewers and readers, representations of rape usually

---

9. Rabinowitz, *Before Reading,* 139.

"cross the line" whereas representations of murder often seem to serve a conventional narrative function.[10] Readers have plenty of experience identifying with male murderers, from King David in the Old Testament to Dostoevsky's Raskolnikov. By contrast, Vaage notes that rape often marks a character as abject and irredeemable in ways that murder does not. Deformative fictions may capitalize on these inconsistencies and foreground the hypocrisy of a moral outrage at *representations* of harm that outpaces the typical reader's response to actual harm.

Exclusion from the Authorial Audience. Some works actively rebuff readers' efforts to join the authorial audience. This textual resistance may be rooted in protectiveness of cultural identity, a gendered perspective, an oppositional stance, or some other particularity. Whatever the cause, the resulting exclusion often generates a deep sense of readerly incompetence.[11] Ocampo deliberately disappoints readers' expectations that they will be brought into the fictional world or the hearts and minds of characters. She confronts them instead with impenetrability and resistance, withholding and withdrawal. Her defensive approach denies access to interiority, and readers who cannot adjust their expectations accordingly find themselves at odds with the authorial audience.

Problematic Inclusion in the Narratorial or Authorial Audience. Deformative fictions discomfit through inclusion as well as exclusion. In Vallejo's *La virgen*, the narrator presents himself as our guide to a Columbian underworld of killers for hire and addresses readers as voyeurs of violence. We may dislike this positioning, but an intellectual interest in what Vallejo intends for his authorial audience brings us close—too close for comfort—to the complicity his narrator's address implies, and to the disturbing views that the author shares with his narrator.

Forestalling Interpretation. The resistant characteristics of deformative fiction may also prevent readers from absorbing distressing content into an interpretation to ease the discomfort the narrative causes. We rarely want to rush through our reading encounters with love or tenderness, but we almost always want to get past the cruelty as quickly as possible. A deformative fiction like Bolaño's *2666* works against that desire by extending the reader's exposure to unredressed suffering. Unable to position these deaths in a satisfying interpretation or to judge the cruelty that causes them, we are denied the consolation of "witnessing" and release.

---

10. Vaage, "On the Repulsive Rapist."

11. See Sommer, "Resistant Texts and Incompetent Readers." See also Rabinowitz, "Betraying the Sender."

Activating, Then Blocking, Readers' Expectations. Deformative fictions make use of the process by which we come to have expectations. Kenneth Burke describes form as a twofold element. First, "the creation of an appetite in the mind" and second, the eventual "satisfying of that appetite."[12] Deformation, by extension, entails activating appetites and then refusing to satisfy them. The classic expectations of a detective story include the notion of just one culprit, the triumph of the detective, and success through logic rather than force.[13] A deformative fiction whets the appetite for genre satisfactions but then withholds them. *2666* activates the codes of detective fiction only to discard them. First, there are more sources of crime than can be accounted for in the narrative, much less by the bumbling detectives within it. Second, all potential avatars of justice fail. Third, although force cannot redress the hundreds of murders of women, neither can reason.

These are just a few of the strategies and approaches that authors of deformative fictions may mobilize. Each of these could be the focus of a longer study of deformative fictions, and I return to many of them in my close readings. In this book, however, I have chosen to focus on fictional cruelty, a narrative resource that proves especially powerful in deformative fictions. This is true for the Latin American stories and novels I examine, but it also holds for many deformative fictions from other traditions. The rest of this chapter delves into the particularities of cruelty as a narrative resource. I highlight the rhetorical moves that cluster around it, outline its affordances as a critical concept, and propose it as an alternative to a focus on violence in Latin American literature.

DELINEATING FICTIONAL CRUELTY

Twentieth-century Latin American fiction constitutes a formidable chapter in cruelty's long and grueling career in fiction. In the *Iliad*, Achilles drags Hector's body; in *King Lear*, Regan and Cornwall gouge out Gloucester's eyes; in *Don Quixote*, the barber and the priest cage the would-be knight. These and other scenes of cruelty trigger contradictory responses. Visceral horror mixes with fascination; the impulse to turn away competes with the desire to see and the hope that some understanding may follow. Whatever its challenges to readers, cruelty offers potent dramatic possibilities to writers. It plays

---

12. Burke, "Psychology and Form," 31.
13. Rabinowitz, *Before Reading*, 196.

to literature's strengths in bringing human psychology and emotion together with the high stakes of suffering. Cruelty is not always expressed physically, which means that literature can confront us with less spectacular, more indirect, but equally chilling scenarios.

Cruelty differs significantly from the concept of violence, which is far more widely invoked in discussions of Latin American literatures. Popular culture critics writing about Latin American literature in translation often treat portrayals of violence as marks of authenticity. When used to describe human behavior, violence implies inflicting harm. Identifying instances of violence does not require a judgment about the agent(s) causing harm, their intentions, or their attitude toward harm. This offers researchers and readers the advantage of apparent objectivity. We can locate violence in the world or in a text by identifying the application of force and the harm it causes. When readers focus on violence, it remains "out there." That is, it is possible to detect violence while maintaining separation from the causes of harm or responsibility for the resulting pain.[14]

By contrast, one of the most striking qualities of cruelty is its ability to creep outward from a location in a text. Texts or reading practices may recruit us into various positions—from agents to victims, bystanders, and potential beneficiaries—by virtue of the observations, judgments, and feelings that accompany encounters with represented or implied pain. By beholding or reflecting on cruelty, we may also feel that we enact it at another remove. In this way, cruelty can spill outward from the text, drawing us into complex and disconcerting experiences of narrative worlds, and of our own minds. In my readings, I will highlight three main expressions of fictional cruelty: *cruelty in the told* (cruelty as a dimension of plot), *cruelty in telling* (cruelty as a dimension of style), and *cruelty in reading* (cruelty as a dimension of reader response or interpretation).[15]

---

14. An interesting semantic difference distinguishes cruelty from related concepts. For violence and evil, nouns are the primary word form. What violence *is* anchors the concepts of what it means to be violent or act violently. This is also true for evil. The frequency of use of "evil" as a noun outstrips its use as an adjective. In contrast, cruelty gains specificity from what it means *to be* cruel. In most dictionaries, at least one meaning of cruelty refers readers to the definition of the adjective "cruel." This difference may seem trivial, but it suggests the centrality of affect and intention to cruelty. See the Oxford English Dictionary for documentation of the dominance of the use of "evil" as a noun. *Oxford English Dictionary,* s.v. "evil." Representative instances of these patterns in definitions of cruelty appear in the Oxford, Random House, and Merriam-Webster dictionaries. *Merriam-Webster,* s.v. "cruelty (n.)," https://www.merriam-webster.com/dictionary/cruelty.

15. For two important treatments of cruelty in literature, see James Martel and José Ovejero. Martel's reading of *Thus Spoke Zarathustra* highlights how a text can strategically activate and disappoint the reader's expectations. What Ovejero calls "ethical cruelty" resonates espe-

1. *Cruelty in the Told.* This is the cruelty we recognize most readily: cruelty *in* the story, as part of its "content." This cruelty unfolds between characters within the story world, as a dimension of plot. Readers typically have a high level of tolerance for this expression of cruelty, if it is framed in ways that assist us in judging or making sense of it. The cruel villainy of the witch in the story of Rapunzel or the stepmother in Hansel and Gretel, for example, patterns familiarly into our reading of fairy tales. Formal elements, especially genre markers, offer a frame that tells us how to read cruelty. In horror novels, we savor our safety from narrated suffering; even terror becomes a form of pleasure in the carefully controlled environment of the genre.

Similarly, when authors choose, they can provide us with full access to the mental states of characters. Even gestures that would be too ephemeral to sustain judgment in lived experience are, in fiction, suspended in amber, becoming usable material for our assessments of mental states. They may offer us less information than we receive through nonverbal communication in real life, but we gain more opportunity to keep processing and reinterpreting with further context or greater scrutiny. These conditions may lend a certainty to judgments that we rarely experience in daily life. In the works of Stendhal, Balzac, Henry James, George Eliot, and authors who follow their example of psychological realism, access to the inner worlds of characters allows us to make sense of behaviors and attitudes that otherwise might evade understanding. By offering insight into characters, many works of literature contain cruelty in the *told* as something that we can recognize, judge, and reject.

2. *Cruelty in the Telling.* This is cruelty as a dimension of *how* a story is related, expressed in genre, style, form, voice, and other elements of texts. Readers may impute this cruelty to the narrator, the implied author, or both. Cruelty in the *telling* may be directed at characters. For example, in the final pages of Émile Zola's *Nana* (1880), the narrator abandons any notion of Nana as a dying woman and presents her instead as a disintegrating body. The scene completes the dissolution of her humanity, an outcome Zola aggressively prefigures in the novel. We may register cruelty in the *telling* in how Zola turns someone we had related to as a person into a mere device. In Ana Castillo's experimental epistolary novel, *The Mixquiahuala Letters*, the narrator recounts the story of a forced sterilization endured by the woman she writes to—a story her recipient already knows because she experienced it. This simultaneously

---

cially with the subtractive and obstructive pedagogy I identify in deformative fictions: it subverts expectations and specifically targets readers' intellectual habits. I value Ovejero's analysis, but I find his terminology less helpful; to label one type of cruelty "ethical" confuses the issue because it implies that only certain texts or certain uses of cruelty have ethical weight. Martel, "Nietzsche's Cruel Messiah." Ovejero, *La ética de la crueldad* (The ethics of cruelty).

reopens a deep wound and imposes the narrator's reading of the experience's significance, overwriting whatever it may mean for her correspondent.

Although it may appear on its own, most often cruelty of *telling* intensifies cruelty of the *told*. In the Old Testament story of the Levite's concubine (Judges 19), the Levite turns his concubine out of his host's home to be raped by the men of the town. The next morning, he divides her body into twelve parts, which he sends to the tribes of Israel. The narrator's measured, distant telling of the horror repeats the Levite's indifference to the suffering he allows and perhaps also perpetrates. The chronicler's distance intensifies the narrated cruelty and enables him to withhold critical information, specifically whether the concubine is alive or dead when the Levite dismembers her. Here, cruelty in the *told* and in *telling* may focus on characters, yet we may feel that we, too, are victims of the writer or narrator's cruelty. We may attribute cruelty to the writer and/or narrator when (in our judgment) their telling encumbers our reading excessively, and they appear indifferent to or delighted by the distress these challenges cause.

3. *Cruelty in Reading.* This is readers' experience of indifference to or pleasure in suffering, where "read" might also mean "watch" or "hear" or whatever mode of processing is relevant to a specific narrative form. It may be present in our response (or nonresponse) to characters, texts, and textual situations (the *told*) and/or to dimensions of the *telling*. Whereas encountering cruelty in the *telling* often leads to experiencing a text as deformative, there are many experiences of cruelty in reading that do not trouble us. For example, we experience delight in a presumed evildoer's painful comeuppance in a revenge narrative (cruelty of the *told*). We may move quickly, even lightly, through the bleak scene of the crime in a mystery novel with little attention to the suffering it caused, while we focus on how the scene or details of the crime provide the framework needed to understand the rest of the novel. Within the genre frame, the crime itself may be a source of reassurance in that it holds the clues that facilitate the discovery of the wrongdoers and the reimposition of social order.[16]

An experience of cruelty as part of our *reading* may result from some feature of the *telling*. Formal elements such as framing and focalization limit our ability to respond to the pain of characters. Dispassionate descriptions of suffering offer little purchase for emotional response, depriving readers of empathy's relief, as in Ocampo's short fiction. Or we may struggle with a narrator who insistently seeks to recruit us into their delight in the distress of

---

16. My thanks to Faye Halpern for reminding me of readers' orientation toward the restoration of order.

other characters, as in Vallejo's *La virgen*. Even if we resist, our long exposure to this stance over the course of the novel may prompt worries about complicity with the narrator's cruelty. With respect to cruelty in reading, the issue is not adjudicating whether a reader's response "qualifies" as cruel. Our reading responses are personal, varied, transient, and subject to revision. Still, describing these responses is important to clarifying the effects of deformative fictions. Certain qualities in texts can cause readers to experience pleasure or indifference to portrayed suffering. Because cruelty encompasses responses that can exist without direct perpetration, these responses may make readers feel complicit with cruelty of the *told* or *telling*.

FICTIONAL CRUELTY'S ASSETS: CONTEXT, RELATIONALITY, AND CONTAMINATION

I want to consider a bit more closely the assets fictional cruelty brings to a deformative project, which stem from the fact that it defines a *relationship* between one person's mental or emotional state and another person's suffering.[17] To name cruelty, we make several judgments, although they may seem to happen simultaneously. We recognize suffering, we assess the perpetrator's mental state as including indifference or pleasure, and we determine a causal relationship between the suffering and the response. The nature of this relationship is usually more difficult to ascertain than the presence of suffering or force. Context is key. The face of a field surgeon performing an amputation without anesthesia might possess the same impassivity as a psychopathic killer butchering a victim. Yet we attribute dramatically different mental states to them: necessary professional objectivity in the former case versus extreme cruelty in the latter. A more moderate example is laughter from an employee of a funeral home during a eulogy that may be taken as a sign of indifference or delight in the suffering of the mourners. Laughter by an attendee is likely be understood more generously as a case of nerves or some fond recollection of the deceased. The ambiguity of context paves the way to reconfiguration and reframing in accusations or justifications of cruelty. The speculative and

---

17. Some treatments of cruelty focus on the degree and type of pain required for an experience to "qualify" for consideration under the rubric of cruelty. John Kekes asserts that cruelty is only relevant to those cases where pain "harms the victim in a way that endangers the victim's functioning as a full-fledged agent." Kekes, "Cruelty and Liberalism," 837. By contrast, Philip Paul Hallie argues that cruelty can still be relevant in the absence of "dramatic pain." Hallie, *Paradox of Cruelty*, 24. For a discussion of varying perceptions of "legitimate" pain depending on historical period and cultural context, see Baraz, *Medieval Cruelty*, 2–9.

FIGURE 1.1. Untitled photograph of a boy kicking a dog. © Kari René Hall, *Beyond the Killing Fields* (New York: Aperture Books, 1992).

flexible character of cruelty opens possibilities for reconfigurations that widen the scope of implication. For a visual analogy, consider the photograph in figure 1.1.

This photograph, taken in a Cambodian refugee camp, presents one act of violence that produces multiple refractions of cruelty. The child's foot striking the dog is the act of force that causes harm, but the cruelty does not stop there. The photograph also captures an older child witnessing this act with what appears to be smirking amusement or delight. The photograph's existence implies a photographer who did not intervene, at least not immediately, to stop the abuse. Even accounting for this layering of cruelty, we might expect the response demanded by the image to be straightforward. Shouldn't we feel horror at this delight in and indifference to suffering, then sympathy for the injured animal? The ripples of cruelty continue outward. Without dismissing the gravity of the boy's abuse of the dog, we could consider how, and by whom, he has been brutalized. Another instance of potential cruelty emerges in awareness of our relative detachment from suffering that takes place in geographically or culturally distant spaces.[18] Multiple configurations of cruelty

---

18. These children count among over 190,000 Cambodian refugees living inside Site 2 on the Thai-Cambodian border after Vietnam's invasion of Cambodia. Established in January of 1985, the camp was not closed until 1993, when refugees were repatriated to Cambodia.

may exist simultaneously in a text, increasing the potential for outward spillage toward readers.

How do we understand the dance between deformative fictions and fictional cruelty? Deformativity, as I have stressed, is rooted in authorial intention, whereas fictional cruelty is a *resource* often mobilized in these works. Neither requires the other. Fictional cruelty may be, and frequently is, present in texts that conform to reader expectations rather than challenging them. By the same token, the presence of cruelty is not essential to deformative fiction. But how might each appear in the absence of the other? I disentangle these threads here, by way of demonstration, even as they will remain tightly interwoven across the case studies from Latin American fiction.

Fictional Cruelty Apart from Deformative Fictions. Works with a high index of fictional cruelty abound, and most fall outside the deformative range because they ultimately reassure rather than distress their readers. In general, readers tend to have a high level of tolerance for cruelty of the *told,* provided that the other forms of fictional cruelty are not present or are present at lower levels. For example, in many horror and mystery novels, genre-specific schema help to contain cruelty in familiar formulas, often allowing readers to relate to suffering primarily in terms of how it catalyzes events in the plot. Bloodshed and suffering in a Stephen King novel or a police procedural are part of how these works function in their respective genres. Like the detectives or determined survivors who are protagonists in these novels, we make our way through the carnage to get on to the next thing; we understand this cruelty as a necessary catalyst for subsequent events in the plot. In many instances of *fictional cruelty apart from deformative fiction,* cruelty is one mark of genre accommodation. As such, it does not disrupt the author–reader contract. In fact, it upholds it.

Deformative Fictions Apart from Cruelty of the Told. Texts may frustrate or vex readers in ways that threaten the reading experience, and the reader, without explicitly engaging with cruelty. For example, authors may challenge and deform reading experiences through unexpected uses of satire, the dilation or contraction of narrative time, aesthetic distortions, alarming allegorical parallels, and disruptions of ontological assumptions, to name a few strategies.[19]

The Vulnerability of Deformative Fictions to Charges of Cruelty of the Telling. Although it is relatively easy to assert the widespread presence of fictional cruelty *without* deformative qualities, the possibility of imputing cruelty of *telling* always remains open. This is because cruelty is relational and subjective,

---

19. For related discussions of techniques of disruption, see Hume, *Aggressive Fictions,* 10–11.

and its possible relationships include the "someone" whom we imaginatively construct as the source of a text. We may attribute cruelty in *telling* to the narrator or author, especially if we perceive aspects of the narration to be marked by callousness or indifference. For example, readers of *Madame Bovary* (1857) might impute cruelty to the narrator, or to Flaubert himself, in response to the framing of Emma's suicide.[20] Flaubert does not construct it as a dramatic high point (as Emma likely would have wished), but rather as an occasion for a drowsy dialogue between a priest and a pharmacist. Readers may see the scene as a crowning demonstration of the narrator's refusal to take Emma, or her suffering, seriously. In this case, the character Emma seems to be the target of the cruelty of *telling*. In other examples, readers frustrated or distressed by the deformative qualities of a text may feel that they are the victims of cruelty, that the author or narrator has done something cruel to them through the text.

SHIFTING PARADIGMS IN READINGS OF LATIN AMERICAN LITERATURES

A fuller examination of fictional cruelty offers one way to shift problematic patterns evident when works of Latin American literature are presented as "world literature." Especially in US-based media, cultural critics may fetishize violence as a grisly signifier of authenticity. At times, Latin American literary criticism mirrors this popular obsession, albeit with more subtlety.[21] When critics do address cruelty, they often approach it as another name for violence and focus on its thematic, symbolic, or allegorical possibilities. For example, the cruelty in Ocampo's stories becomes less troublesome when presented as expressing the rage of marginalized members of society.[22] Some critical readings contain the distressing resonances of rape, torture, and mutilation in Osvaldo Lamborghini's novella *El fiord* (*The Fjord*, 1969) by treating them as elements of political allegory.[23] An even more common tactic presents cruelty

---

20. I address Flaubert's aggressive stance toward women who write in Pérez, "Against *Écriture Féminine*." Flaubert presents Emma as an incompetent woman writer to highlight, by contrast, the accomplishments of his own narrative technique.

21. A sample of scholarly titles highlights the frequency with which violence offers the frame for reading Latin American literature: Biron, *Murder and Masculinity*; González, *Killer Books*; Avelar, *Letter of Violence*; Manzoni, *Violencia y silencio* (Violence and silence); Kaplan, *Género y violencia* (Genre/Gender and violence); Close, *Contemporary Hispanic Crime Fiction*; Herlinghaus, *Violence without Guilt*; Nemrava, *Disturbios en la tierra sin mal* (Troubles on earth without evil).

22. Chapter 3 provides an expanded discussion of this tendency.

23. For one such reading, see Kraniauskas, "Porno-Revolution."

as a direct reflection of historical or contemporary lived experience. A notable example is *Cruel Modernity* (2013) by renowned pioneer of Latin American literary studies Jean Franco. In it, Franco offers nuanced reflections on a constellation of twentieth-century historical atrocities in Latin America. Ultimately, however, she employs literature primarily to illustrate historical realities and attends far less to how fictional treatments of cruelty are distinctive.[24] Prematurely or superficially assigning a testimonial or documentary function to a literary text distracts from the full range of its narrative effects and their ethical implications.

Critics have reasons for the priorities they set, and I value a diversity of approaches. What is concerning, though, is the pervasive avoidance of the texts' specificity—and the deformative challenges they may hold for readers.[25] Extractive colonial logics persist in what Idelbar Avelar diagnoses as "exotic expectations" on the part of privileged critics outside of Latin America. In his telling, these critics are interested in Latin American literature as a source of raw materials, especially novelty and manageable difference. He imagines them shouting, "'Give us more García Márquez, more magical realism, give us what we don't have, after all there are plenty of people doing this theoretical stuff in English departments!'"[26] Those of us reading and writing about Latin American literatures from geographic and cultural removes, in particular, would do well to cultivate openness, vulnerability, and curiosity. The goal, in Avelar's words, is to experience the text as something that "places in crisis

---

24. Other scholars follow this pattern, such as Leonard, *Cruel Fictions, Cruel Realities*. The title frames fiction as offering access points to "realities."

25. Because this book is not a comprehensive survey of deformative fictions across Latin American literatures, I want to be cautious about making claims regarding their relative prevalence and reasons why deformative strategies may appeal. Still, although they are beyond the scope of this book, I hope that naming a few of the questions that others have asked about deformative fictions in Latin American traditions may be useful in directing further attention. For example: Are deformative strategies more prominent in Latin American literatures than in other traditions? If so, why? How do Latin American authors of deformative fictions situate themselves in relation to trends, movements, and other networks of literary influence? What particularities of Latin American readerships may shape authors' choices to work with deformative strategies? In terms of Latin American literature as world literature, how does traveling beyond its context of composition influence whether a text is perceived as deformative? Do deformative qualities function as disqualifying factors when texts are considered for translation, and what is the role of the author's nationality and positionality, and readers' expectations of each, in shaping this outcome?

To go beyond speculation in answering these questions would require knowledge of a diversity of traditions and contexts that likely exceeds the expertise and capacity of a single scholar. It certainly exceeds mine. I hope that future work (including my own) will contribute to this effort, but for now I want to stress the goals of this book, which focuses on case studies to build a vocabulary and a set of practices for critical engagement with deformative fictions.

26. Avelar, "Ethics of Interpretation," 97.

the epistemic stance of the one who studies it."[27] With its webs of potential relationships and capacity for implicating readers, fictional cruelty offers a focal point for explorations of this crisis and what it may signify for readers, stories, and the narrative acts that bind them together.

Deformative fictions provide an exceptional arena for this challenging work. Conversations deepen with the recognition that it is normal—even desirable—to reckon with experiences, and texts, that challenge us in ways we did not expect and whose value we may not recognize immediately. We can expand the frame of our reading to include the benefits of navigating deformative fictions. At the same time, we should avoid approaches that might harden into a protocol for processing texts into something we can recognize and handle, and from which we merely extract more subtle satisfactions. The difference is that what we learn from deformative fictions derives from the experience of engaging with them. Rather than expecting a ready resource, we find value in grappling with their absence of generosity. Deformative fictions influence us in ways analogous to fasting, silent retreats, and other rituals of subtraction. Elective deprivation can expand awareness and offer us the opportunity to apportion our attention differently. If we know we are not going to eat or hear words spoken aloud, we may begin to pay attention to other sensations and stimuli in the world around us. The same is true for the attentuation of literary satisfactions. We may notice aspects of the reading encounter that we had no occasion, before, to register as significant.

Deformative fictions demand readers' reckoning. As we attempt to understand and interpret a text, we find ourselves called to account for our reading and its ethical consequences. Experiencing the instability of common assumptions about reading turns them into questions. *Does* empathy promote good behavior? Does persistence deserve a reward? Is the desire for connection and resolution benign? Is reading "safe" for the reader? Does literature lead to enlightenment or deepened understanding of ourselves or humanity?[28] The response to each of these questions, if we attend closely to deformative fictions, is *no,* or at least, *not always.* Authors of deformative fictions anticipate and reject simple notions about how cruelty or other difficult material "should" be presented and understood. They tactically leave expectations unfulfilled, and sometimes shatter them.

Deformative fictions have much to teach us, although not necessarily about the world, nor about how to be more moral or empathetic persons, nor

---

27. Avelar, "Ethics of Interpretation," 98.

28. For a thorough accounting of many of these notions, several of which are central to Landy's theorization of formative fictions, see the introduction of *How to Do Things with Fictions,* especially 32–38.

about how to become better readers. We may make gains in any or all of these areas; indeed, I argue that we can. But we can't skip past the difficulty to the rewards, and trying to do so will cheapen and spoil them. Reading deformative fictions productively begins with an acknowledgment of the degree to which our readerly moves and desires are self-focused and self-serving. Deformative fictions assert their independence from the modes of engagement we prefer. They withhold the lessons we might hope for. Instead, they institute a pedagogy of refusal, diversion, and abrasion. Deformative fictions ask: Do we have enough courage and curiosity to engage inhospitable approaches as a valid mode of literary expression worth our time and care? I urge this aspiration, but it is not easy. As we see in the next chapters, deformative fictions present some of literature's most distressing facets, especially when they intertwine with fictional cruelty.

CHAPTER 2

Ocampo

Cruelty as Defense and the Contamination of Readers

A family gives a child a loaded gun to play with in hopes—perfectly fulfilled—that he will "accidentally" shoot a tyrannical grandfather. An adult narrates, without remorse, the events of his fourth birthday party during which he instigated the other children to set fire to the house with all their mothers still inside. A woman poisons a neighbor on the suspicion that he has written an offensive note about her relationship with her deceased lapdog. A prostitute placidly awaits her death while trapped in the basement of a building being demolished.

Welcome to Silvina Ocampo's fiction. In her stories, narrators and characters—whether adults or children, wealthy or dispossessed, apparent wrongdoers or victims—seem to accept acts of harm as unremarkable. A sinister atmosphere hovers over even those stories that lack explicitly destructive or deadly outcomes. The result is a complex, often uncomfortable, experience for readers. This chapter expands upon the theories of deformative fiction and fictional cruelty offered in chapter 1 by providing the first of three case studies on twentieth-century Latin American writers. I argue that Ocampo pursues a deformative approach as a *defensive* measure. Fictional cruelty functions as a key narrative resource in that project, and I consider the effects of this approach on rhetorical readers' responses.[1]

---

1. See also Pérez, "Reading Cruelty."

Engagements with cruelty raise the stakes of interpretive and ethical judgments, and deformative effects inhibit our ability to judge with confidence in the first place. A story that operates in this way can seem frustrating, unsatisfying, or downright perverse. Some readers may even feel that the story, or its author, subjects them to cruelty. This is especially likely when cruelty already has a thematic presence in the literature in question, as it does in Ocampo's short fiction. The daughter of Buenos Aires social elites and a regular collaborator with the far-better-known Jorge Luis Borges, Ocampo was most active from the 1930s to the 1960s. This was a time when critics valued literature by Latin American women primarily for emotional expressivity and intimate portrayals of domestic experiences. By contrast, Ocampo shaped a deformative agenda in her fiction to defend against gendered expectations of access to character interiority or emotional depth. Her defensive aesthetic deliberately disappoints readers' expectations of admission to the theater of characters' hearts and minds. Ocampo's stories offer a steady diet of flatness, opacity, affective estrangement, obfuscation of causality, and narrative ambiguity. By refusing to accommodate presumptions of access and connection, Ocampo exposes and disarms "ordinary" reading practices that, assessed skeptically, might be characterized as *intrusive* rather than merely engaged. These rebuffs are further intensified by a strategic activation of fictional cruelty's potential to creep outward from a story or its narrator.

What might seem perverse to a frustrated reader may also be purposeful. One clear goal in Ocampo's project is to prevent readers from treating characters and texts as screens upon which to project their assumptions and desires. In addition to this protective function, Ocampo's approach has two other dimensions. First, as in military rhetoric, *defense* in Ocampo's work entails a show of force. Her deterrence of unwelcome readerly behavior is rooted in narrative firepower. And second, like an excellent defense attorney who shields her client from suspicion by building a case for someone else's guilt, Ocampo protects the integrity of her short fiction by positioning readers as complicit in the very effects they may wish to criticize.

Ocampo's defensiveness stems at least in part from a reaction to the literary culture of mid-century Buenos Aires, but its effects are still felt by readers coming to the stories today. Faced with impenetrability and deflection, withholding and withdrawal, readers may wonder: what does Ocampo's fiction offer beyond refusals and rebuffs? Are we to remain chastened but unsure of what, if anything, we can do about our readerly presumptuousness? Ocampo's harsh pedagogy disrupts readers' expectations (of the stories, of the characters, of the narrator, of the author) in part to shift how we engage with fictional worlds more broadly. The stories force awareness of and reflection on what are often nearly reflexive reading behaviors. In other words, despite the initial helpless or hapless response many readers feel in the face of Ocampo's unaccommodating narrative, hers is ultimately a *calling in* rather than a calling out. She calls us into a different relationship with narrative inventions (especially those that don't accommodate our desires or assumptions), a greater level of scrutiny of our own motives, and a skepticism toward any sense of "innocence" we may cling to in reading.

In this chapter, I bring Ocampo's distinctive project into focus and show how it exemplifies qualities of deformative fiction and a tactical engagement with fictional cruelty. I begin by offering literary and critical context for her body of work, then offer a thought experiment to assist in foregrounding the essential qualities of Ocampo's approach to the short story. The greater part of the chapter unravels the effects of Ocampo's disruptive narrative strategies through close readings of five short stories from the height of her career. These stories demonstrate both the consistency and range of her literary project, and they showcase her distinctive use of narrative resources. Approaching the stories as deformative fiction brings greater definition to key ideas in narrative theory, including narratorial unreliability, estrangement, the implied author, and rhetorical ambiguity. Across these considerations, I examine how rhetorical readers may navigate encounters with Ocampo's stories—including the temptations, traps, frustrations, and other challenges that her deformative project poses.

LOCATING OCAMPO'S FICTION

In 1999, Argentine publisher Emcé gathered Ocampo's complete short fiction in a two-volume collection that preserved the original arrangement of the published stories.[2] Until recently, however, Ocampo's fiction has been mostly inaccessible to those who are unable to read in Spanish. Before 2019, only one collection of Ocampo's stories was available in English-language markets: *Leopoldina's Dream*, a selection of stories from across Ocampo's career, translated by Daniel Balderston (1988). In 2015, the Balderston collection was revised, expanded, and reissued in the New York Review of Books Classics series along with an edition of Ocampo's selected poems.[3] Then in 2019, City

---

2. Silvina Ocampo: *Cuentos Completos* (Collected Stories).

3. I leave Ocampo's poetry aside in this chapter, but it is worth noting that, during her lifetime, she was more acclaimed for her poetry than her stories. Although her poetry received a number of prizes, including Argentina's Premio Nacional de Poesía for both *Los nombres* (The names) (1953) and *Lo amargo por dulce* (Bitter for sweet) (1962), her fiction was never recognized with a major award. In the years since, however, the ratio of critical attention paid to Ocampo's short fiction as compared to her poetry suggests that her stories may have the most enduring appeal.

Lights published *Forgotten Journey,* a translation of Ocampo's first book of stories (*Viaje olvidado,* 1937), as well as *The Promise* (*La promesa*), a novel begun in 1960 and published posthumously in Spanish in 2011. Recent reviews and features in the English-language press, including NPR and *The Guardian,* suggest a broadening visibility of and receptiveness to her work.

There is reason to hope, then, that more of her stories will become available in their original arrangement as collections, including the one I focus on here, *La furia y otros cuentos* (The fury and other stories).[4] Published in 1959, *La furia* offers a mature expression of Ocampo's style and thematic array. The individual stories stand alone as compelling fiction, but Ocampo also plays with the expectations that accumulate as readers proceed through the collection. I will return to this point. Attention to the collective impact of Ocampo's stories is particularly important for taking proper stock of her defensive aesthetic.

At first glance, Ocampo's stories resemble those of other Latin American women writers of her era. They unfold in a petit-bourgeois Buenos Aires milieu and often center women and children in home spaces and community celebrations.[5] Hers is a world of dinners, birthday parties, baptisms, weddings, hairdressing, and home decorating. Beyond the familiar furniture of domesticity, though, Ocampo's stories present a distressing fictional world: children frequently witness, commit, or suffer harm and acts of violence; self-mutilation and rivalry abound; and vengeance outstrips offense.

Perhaps unsurprisingly, then, references to cruelty have become de rigueur in discussions of Ocampo's fiction.[6] These tend to fall into two main categories. First, especially early in her career, there are the scandalized reactions to the fiction, often expressing some variation of the claim that only a cruel writer would persist in inventing story after story in which abuse and suffering are so prevalent. "Dijeron que era muy cruel" ("They said I was very cruel"), Ocampo noted in an interview by way of explanation for why she

---

4. Unless otherwise noted, translations are my own.

5. Buenos Aires is featured in so many of her stories that it becomes a kind of default setting for any story that does not clearly indicate a specific location.

6. Mario A. Lancelotti's 1962 review of *Las invitadas* (The guests) is one of the first explicit references to cruelty as a feature of Ocampo's fiction. In a 1974 introduction to a collection of stories by Ocampo, Jorge Luis Borges declares his perplexity at her "strange taste for a certain kind of innocent and oblique cruelty," which he explained as "the astonished interest that evil inspires in a noble soul." Borges, "Preface," vii–viii. This remark possesses the ring of authority characteristic of Borges's pronouncements, but subsequent critics have demurred. Fiona Mackintosh notes that Borges "recuperates and domesticates" Ocampo's treatment of cruelty, and Gisle Selnes argues that he mistakenly assumes that a woman's engagement with cruelty must be a mere "flirtation." Mackintosh, *Childhood,* 114. Selnes, "The Feminine (Ob)Scene of Cruelty," 520.

never received Argentina's Premio Nacional for fiction.[7] Second, there are Ocampo's defenders, many of whom have focused on explaining or justifying the presence of cruelty in her fiction. Both tendencies—the scandalized accusations of cruelty and the parade of justifications for it—fail to take seriously the inventiveness and distinctiveness of the narrative strategies evident in Ocampo's body of short fiction.

Whereas more recent scholarship sometimes downplays or ignores the deformative qualities in Ocampo's oeuvre,[8] critics of her day applied conventional standards to her stories and thus often found them lacking. As we will see, though, the narrative choices they objected to—distortion, vernacular language, strange syntax, "flat" descriptions that refuse any serious mimetic obligation, an obsessive focus on objects—are not flaws but features of Ocampo's aesthetic. They reflect her systematic disregard for the prevailing tenets of "well-made" fiction at the time of her writing. To do justice to the complexity, subtlety, and efficacy of Ocampo's fiction, we need first to take her narrative project seriously, to treat it with the same appreciation of innovation afforded to other masters of the short story.

PIGLIA'S THOUGHT EXPERIMENT

To trace the broad outlines of Ocampo's aesthetic and consider what expectations we bring to short fiction, I expand a thought experiment proposed in Argentine fiction writer and critic Ricardo Piglia's "Tesis sobre el cuento" ("Thesis on the Short Story"). Piglia's premise is that every work of short fiction tells two stories that unfold through the narration (and its silences). He further argues that the unique genius or strategy of a writer lies in the relationship they establish between the two stories.

---

7. Ulla, *Encuentros* (Interviews), 92.

8. A genuine interest in situating Ocampo within an emerging canon of Latin American women writers leads some critics to smooth away the deliberate coarseness of her aesthetic. Readings that fixate on the feminine tend toward declarations of triumph that have more to do with notions of how a properly protofeminist Latin American woman *ought* to write than with the accomplishments specific to Ocampo's work. For example, Marcia Espinoza-Vera concludes that Ocampo's depiction of female rogues "obviously challenges the romantic masculine ideal of femininity" and that these women escape "the obligations a patriarchal society attempts to impose upon them." Espinoza-Vera, "Unsubordinated Women," 226. In expecting a female author to denounce patriarchy and offer positive, empowering images of women, these critics often appear to determine their conclusions before they even engage with the stories themselves. On this point, see Carlos Gamerro's discussion of tropes in Ocampo criticism. Gamerro, *Ficciones barrocas* (Baroque fictions), 150–52.

Before we engage with Piglia's thought experiment, we need a few terminological distinctions. Spanish has three words that may be rendered in English as "story." The first is *cuento,* which is a text that belongs to the short fiction genre. The second is *historia,* which maps onto the broader idea of "story" across literary and nonliterary contexts. (*Historia* also is used where English speakers would say "history.") The third is *relato,* or "recounting," which aligns with the most basic notion of narrative, including its everyday sense of "somebody telling somebody else on some occasion and for some purpose(s) that something happened."[9] Piglia's claim, then, is that every story (*cuento*) contains the telling (*relato*) of two stories (*historias*). That is, two stories—each with its own system of causality—can be discerned from the same discourse contained in a single work of short fiction.

Masters of the short story, in Piglia's estimation, find a unique way to confront the challenge of "telling a story at the same time as another story is being told."[10] The passive voice of "another story is being told" ("se está contando otra") is important because, even as the author is the orchestrator of the short story and all its narrative machinery, the magic of short fiction lies in the illusion that the second story is "happening" on its own or by virtue of the existence of the first. A central source of readers' satisfaction comes from the opportunities that a story (*cuento*) creates for them to discern, in the telling (*relato*), the connection between the two stories (*historias*) in a flash of illumination. The delight of altered vision that emerges by the end of our reading offers an experience of secular revelation.[11] Retrospective coherence is one of the most significant expectations that everyday readers bring to stories, but Piglia's thought experiment demonstrates that what satisfies is less the coherence itself than the particularity of its arrival, which functions as an authorial calling card or signature.

Piglia develops his argument by hypothesizing how various masters of short fiction would develop the same story seed sketched in one of Chekhov's notebooks: "A man in Monte Carlo goes to the casino, wins a million, returns home, commits suicide."[12] Although the "two story" idea might seem, in this example, to refer to two events in a single narration (the gambling and the suicide), Piglia's discussion makes plain that he sees two stories (*historias*) here that make use of the same events: one story appears in the constellation of details that readers connect to the gambling, and the second appears in those details patterned as relating to the suicide.

---

9. Phelan, *Somebody Telling Somebody Else,* 5.
10. Piglia, "Tesis sobre el cuento," 95.
11. Piglia, "Tesis sobre el cuento," 100.
12. Piglia, "Tesis sobre el cuento," 92.

According to Piglia, Poe's "classic" approach to the short story would place the tale of gambling in the foreground and elaborate the suicide as a secret story that runs beneath it. Only at the end of the narrative would the secret second story (the suicide) come to the surface of the previously visible story of the happenings at Monte Carlo.[13] Kafka would focus on the gambling alone but would imbue it with the menacing character of the suicide.[14] Whereas the story of the suicide arrives as a "surprise" or a "reveal" in Poe, in reading Kafka we would have a sense, at least retrospectively, of the suicide story having been hauntingly present all along, throughout the telling (*relato*). Hemingway would tell the story of the gambling as if the suicide were imminent, marking the significance of this second story not by intimation but by total elision.[15] In "Big, Two-Hearted River," for example, the surface story is of a fishing trip, but the devastating effect of war on the protagonist's psyche is the unnamed second story. This hidden story is the invisible bottom of Hemingway's proverbial iceberg, with only the details of fishing visible above the ocean waves.[16]

Shifting to an Argentine context, Piglia argues that Borges (Ocampo's friend and frequent creative collaborator), would present the story about the casino according to a specific genre, with its elements lightly parodied.[17] (Borges is famous, for example, for stories that draw on tropes from detective fiction and *gaucho* frontier adventure tales.) Embedded in this typified story would be a second, the telling of which provides the theme of the first. The act of suicide would crystallize the meaning of the man's entire life, culminating in the night of gambling.[18] In contrast to Hemingway, who would keep the secret story (the bottom of the iceberg) out of view, Borges would dramatize the perverse construction of a secret plot with the elements of a visible story. That is, the genre-determined depiction of events at the casino would establish the ineluctability of the man's suicide.

Now let's consider what Piglia's experiment reveals about Ocampo's fiction, starting with a hypothesis about how she might handle the events of Chekhov's scenario. I propose that she would narrate the gambling and the suicide consecutively, without clarifying the relationship between the two or elevating either in significance. Characters would respond with the same

---

13. Piglia, "Tesis sobre el cuento," 92.
14. Piglia, "Tesis sobre el cuento," 97.
15. Piglia, "Tesis sobre el cuento," 96.
16. Hemingway first mentions this "theory of omission" (often now called the "iceberg theory" in fiction writing circles) in *Death in the Afternoon*: "If a writer of prose knows enough about what he is writing about he may omit things . . . The dignity of movement of an iceberg is due to only one-eighth of it being above water" (132).
17. Piglia, "Tesis sobre el cuento," 98.
18. Piglia, "Tesis sobre el cuento," 98–99.

equanimity to the big win and to the protagonist's loss of life. The journey to Monte Carlo, the winning of the money, the subsequent suicide, and any other events would be treated with equal narratorial detachment. There would be little, if any, description of character interiority—even of the protagonist. References to emotion, if they appear at all, would be eerily at odds with the situation. Ocampo would introduce narrative opacity and ambiguity at precisely those junctures where Poe would plant the clues to the interweaving of his two stories. Whereas Hemingway's tactic of using the tip of the iceberg to intimate submerged depth encourages a kind of satisfying knowingness in the reader, Ocampo would suggest that the ice exists only above the water's surface—nothing but murky ocean beneath that tip, no discoveries to uncover in imagined depths. Instead of the sense of ineluctable fate chaining one event to the next in Borges, Ocampo would create a free-floating sense of fatality that could not be located in any one narrative element or fully accounted for otherwise.

In many ways, Ocampo is most interesting because of what her approach *subtracts* from the experience readers expect to have; what is taken away or deformed must be read in relation to what we might think "should" be there. In her fiction, the expected second story simply might not emerge at all. Or it might be glimpsed as a partial possibility in tension with other possibilities, none of which pattern strongly enough onto the textual details to prevail in providing clear motivations or thematic resonance. We could even say that the second story in Ocampo's fiction is often the story of readers' disappointment or confusion when they await the flash of revelation or the slow luminescence of intuited connection.

The frequent flatness of Ocampo's story worlds may seem to suggest character-to-character relations that lack the possibility for empathy, compassion, or meaningful connection (ethics of the *told*). But this amoral or premoral ethos doesn't mean that Ocampo imagines her audience as having no judgments of characters or actions. In fact, the distinctiveness of deformative fictions is dialogic, emerging in part through each text's way of contesting, distorting, or otherwise relating to readers' expectations of typical narratives, especially in relation to portrayals of cruelty. Ocampo anticipates readers who will *expect* to have material and guidance for judgments of characters and situations—and then she deliberately does not provide it. Varying degrees of ambiguity, obfuscation of causality, and flattening or obscuring of character affect and motivation forestall many of the interpretive resolutions that might make sense of cruelty in the stories. Ocampo activates expectations only to defend against them with an aesthetic that undercuts the desire for mimetic illusion or empathetic attachment. The absence of insight into character interiority or opportunities for empathy heightens readers' discomfort, and their attention may shift to the implied author's refusal of this access. Frustrated readers may experience narratorial reticence in Ocampo's fiction as a withholding of information that "ought" to be made available to them because it often is in other stories (the ethics of *writing* and *reading*).

Before our closer look at Ocampo's stories, I offer a final observation about Piglia's thought experiment. Piglia sketches the central narrative strategies of his authorial dream team by describing what they *would* do in a short story that none of them ever wrote because this allows him to create a clear basis for comparison. The persuasiveness of his claims ultimately depends on the degree to which it resonates with our sense of the narrative projects these writers seem to undertake across their short stories. And the approach's utility lies in demonstrating how we come to have a sense of a short story writer's "project" as at once distinctly manifest in a given short story *and* discernible across significant portions of a body of work. Rather than imagining this project as an author's signature on the title page of a collection, repeated indistinguishably with each signing, we might think of it in culinary terms as a collection of favored ingredients and techniques that will be employed to varying degrees in each signature dish. Piglia's approach is good at signaling the likely ingredients or the kinds of experiences often set up for readers, but we need close readings to get a fuller sense of the specific articulation of them. Thus, I attend to ambiguity and flatness in Ocampo's fiction, for example, but I examine these and other narrative features as they are expressed along a continuum, like key ingredients that often appear in a chef's dishes, but in varying proportions that lead to distinctive flavor profiles.

DEADLY DRESSES, CHILD NARRATORS, AND AFFECTIVE ESTRANGEMENT

Frequently taught and anthologized, "El vestido de terciopelo" (The velvet dress) showcases many of the thematic concerns and stylistic strategies that predominate in Ocampo's work. Here, as in many of her stories, an unnamed child narrator relates events that precede or precipitate another character's death. In this case, the narrator is a working-class girl of indeterminate age who accompanies a seamstress named Casilda to the house of a wealthy socialite to complete the final fitting of a black velvet dress sequined with a dragon. In a chatty but slightly off-kilter narration, the narrator relates the events that set up the story's dramatic conclusion. She begins by describing their journey from a poorer neighborhood outside Buenos Aires, and from the start her account is colored by vexation (she does not want to go along with Casilda in the stifling heat). She then proceeds to recount their arrival at the client's fancy home in an upscale neighborhood, the difficulty of getting the woman into the dress, and the woman's vacuous small talk throughout the visit.

The situation deteriorates rapidly once Casilda and the narrator finally get the garment onto the client. By the story's end, the woman lies on the floor, immobile and pronounced dead by the seamstress:

> La señora cayó al suelo y el dragón se retorció. Casilda se inclinó sobre su cuerpo hasta que el dragón quedó inmóvil. Acaricié de nuevo el terciopelo que parecía un animal. Casilda dijo melancólicamente:
> —Ha muerto. ¡Me costó tanto hacer este vestido! ¡Me costó tanto, tanto! ¡Qué risa!

> The lady fell on the floor and the dragon writhed. Casilda leaned over the body until the dragon lay still. Again I stroked the velvet that resembled an animal. Casilda said sadly,
> "She's died. It cost me such work to make this dress! It cost me so much, so very much!"
> What a laugh![19]

The simple sentences of the story's final lines seem straightforward, concealing nothing, but they offer no commentary or contextualizing information that would indicate motives, no causal connections to help us knit events together. Instead of some coherent emotional response that we could graft our own feeling onto, the story ends with the return of "What a laugh!"—a canned phrase the narrator repeats throughout the story in response to a wide variety of events. Attempts to navigate back from the ending to an explanation of what has "really" happened in this story do not lead to a convincing or conclusive reading, but rather to a proliferation of possibilities that persist in uneasy tension. First, I examine how Ocampo leverages reader expectations to enable these possibilities. Then I explain how she negates the satisfaction of embracing any of them. The activation and then disappointment of reader expectations is one of deformative fiction's signature subtractive moves. To show how Ocampo defends against any satisfying conclusion about the story's

---

19. Ocampo, *La furia*, 147. Subsequent citations from *La furia* appear parenthetically in the body of the text.

central event, I examine the textual evidence for six possible explanations for the woman's death and consider their limitations.

1. *Supernatural Causes.* A fantasy-focused reading treats the velvet dress as the agent of death in the story, an animated object squeezing the life out of the woman and literalizing what initially seem to be figurative references to the "sickening" and "suffocating" qualities of velvet. Turns of phrase such as "arrugas de género sobrenatural" ("otherworldly wrinkles" or "wrinkles of supernatural fabric") reinforce the implication that the dress and the dragon embroidered on it are not mere matter, and the narrator notes that "la señora respiraba con dificultad. El dragón también" ("the woman was breathing with difficulty. The dragon was, too," 146). By the end, the dragon "writhes" and "lies still," and the velvet seems alive, like an animal. These details appear to attribute a kind of animacy to the dress itself, activating expectations associated with fantasy tales in which objects with mysterious powers act upon the characters. Further, although the narrator describes the woman's encounter with the dress from the outside, she seems in several moments to fall under its power. For example, when she agrees that she also would like a velvet dress, the speaker feels that "el terciopelo de ese vestido me estrangulaba el cuello con manos enguantadas" ("the velvet of that dress was strangling me with gloved hands," 146). This shift from animacy to personification in the narrator's descriptions deepens the possibility of the dress's murderous intent.

Throughout the story, the dress exercises a mesmeric pull on the narrator. In contrast to her usual practice, during this visit the girl doesn't run to the window to see what is happening on the street below because "no me cansaba de contemplar las pruebas de este vestido con un dragón de lentejuelas" ("I didn't tire of watching the fitting of this dress with a sequined dragon," 146). The involuntary nature of the narrator's curious attraction to the dress is underscored in her description of how touching the velvet's plush sets her teeth on edge ("hacía rechinar mis dientes," 145). This turn of phrase resurfaces just a few paragraphs later in the woman's monologue about fabrics and flowers: "El terciopelo hace rechinar mis dientes, me eriza . . . y, sin embargo, para mí no hay en el mundo otro género comparable . . . me atrae aunque a veces me repugne" ("Velvet sets my teeth on edge, it makes my skin crawl . . ., but still, for me no other fabric in the world is its equal . . . I'm drawn to it even though at times it makes me sick," 145). The woman seems resigned to her fate as the dress's captive. When the dress cannot be removed, she concludes, "Tendré que dormir con él" ("I'll have to sleep with it on," 146). The multiple connotations of "sleep," including as a euphemism for death, add a subtle irony to her comment given the story's end. The dress's association with death is reinforced by the woman's comparison between velvet and her favorite flower, the tuberose, which has historically been used in funerary floral arrangements because of its extremely strong aroma. Ocampo is often read in relation to the fantasy genre. For readers focused on intimations of the supernatural, this constellation of details makes a murder-by-velvet finale plausible.

2. *Natural Causes.* Perhaps the woman simply suffocates in the heavy, too-tight dress. Ocampo emphasizes the dangerous heat on the day of the fitting from the story's first words: "Sudando, secándonos la frente con pañuelos, que humedecimos en la fuente de la Recoleta, llegamos a esa casa, con jardín, de la calle Ayacucho. ¡Qué risa!" ("Sweating, wiping our foreheads with handkerchiefs we wet in the Recoleta fountain, we arrived at that house, with a garden, on Ayacucho Street. What a laugh!" 143). More references to the stifling temperature occur throughout the story, and the narrator's mention that Casilda is often sickened and weakened by the long transit to the city lends plausibility, in this story world, to the deleterious effects of the heat and its potential to compound health issues.

The socialite's physical distress begins early in the story. She exclaims, "me asfixio" ("I'm suffocating") during Casilda's first attempt to get the dress onto her, and our young narrator describes her as on the verge of fainting once it is removed (144). In the moments before she falls to the floor, her face has become pale and her chest is visibly moving with her heartbeats (this, according to the child narrator, although the latter is hard to imagine!). A "natural causes" reading finds support in the story's particularized setting (recognizable streets and neighborhoods) and its naturalistic dialogue, as in the client's vapid, tone-deaf small talk. This reading is also bolstered by instances of rich sensory detail focused on everyday sights, sounds, smells, and sensations—the whiff of mothballs as they come up the carpeted staircase; the texture of the velvet; the shouts, whistles, and dings from vendors on the street below; and the *señora's* strong perfume. These narrative investments in verisimilitude activate the expectation that events—including the woman's death—follow the same laws of causality that govern our world.

3. *Seamstress Turned Murderer.* Or does Casilda strangle her vain client in a brief departure from her unassuming and subdued demeanor? This explanation hinges on the most ambiguous line of the story (just before the woman's death): "Casilda se inclinó sobre su cuerpo hasta que el dragón quedó inmóvil" ("Casilda leaned over the body until the dragon lay still," 147). The opacity of this moment in the scene has an immediate source: the positioning of Casilda's back obscures the narrator's line of vision, so neither she nor we can see what happens in this moment. But given the gravity of the situation, it is striking that she does not run to Casilda's side, ask what is happening, or

react in any way oriented toward a better understanding of the situation. This might imply that the narrator is reporting what she "sees" without grasping its significance, her narration rendered unreliable because of her youth and immaturity.

In a charged narrative instance like this, readers are unlikely to simply stop at what an unreliable narrator describes. Instead, we often assemble details that supplement or correct the narrator's (mis)understanding. The story does offer possible indications of murderous activity. For example, the narrator describes feeling gloved hands at her neck when she says that she would like to wear a velvet dress. Does this mark her displaced knowledge of a murder by strangulation that she cannot consciously recognize? Is mild-mannered Casilda's increasing vexation enough to suggest a further escalation in these final moments? If so, what would account for it? From the speaker's perspective, one offense may be the socialite's uninformed idealization of childhood ("¡Qué edad feliz!" ["What a happy age!"]), which comes with the classic uninvited caress associated with elderly aunts and strangers: "me tomó del mentón" ("she grabbed me by the chin," 144).

This is one instance of the woman's air of entitlement, privilege, and petulance. Ocampo also foregrounds her refusal to accept guidance. (The narrator informs us that Casilda had recommended silk, a more seasonally appropriate fabric, but the woman insisted on velvet.) This set of details patterns with a murder hypothesis based on a logic of escalation: the extreme heat brings Casilda's irritation to a boiling point. Vexation might be insufficient to motivate murder in most narrative worlds. But it fits comfortably among the extreme actions of the rebellious children, negligent governesses, resentful relatives, and spiteful spouses who hold center stage in Ocampo's stories.

4. *Casilda's Negligence.* This point is less an independent "explanation" and more a complication or supplement to other explanations of the woman's death. Even if we cannot come to any conclusions about what happens in the opaque moment when Casilda leans over the woman, it's clear enough that the seamstress doesn't render any aid or call for help—help she knows is nearby. (At the beginning of the scene, a servant ushers Casilda and that narrator in, and voices can be heard from the next room.) Combined with the fantasy explanation (1), Casilda may also be under the dress's sway, turned accomplice to its murderous mission. If the woman is suffering from a natural medical emergency (2), the exhausted seamstress may lack the physical strength, mental clarity, or initiative to aid her. Elsewhere in the story, Casilda is frail and trembling—she spills her glass of water when taking an aspirin and requires the narrator's assistance to retrieve the pins that fall from her hands. But the best explanation for the seamstress's silence and inaction is that the woman's

death is her goal (3). Some further motivation seems needed, though, since Casilda reacts with distress soon after her client becomes immobile, and the situation creates a real problem for her as she despairs of ever getting her dress *off* the woman's body.

5. *"Trick" Ending and Other Variations.* Although Casilda announces that the woman is dead, perhaps she has only fainted. There is no conclusive evidence of her death: Casilda doesn't take her pulse, and her work as a seamstress gives her little expertise in medical matters. Although it can't be ruled out based on any textual details, this explanation seems deeply unsatisfying because it would unmake the rest of the story, hollowing out the reader's evaluations of preceding events and motivations in a move akin to the "it was all just a dream" conclusions that plague amateur short fiction. Still, I include this reading since Ocampo frequently flouts the tenets of well-made fiction.

In addition to this "trick" ending, each explanation above may be modified to reflect existing thematic and metaphorical approaches to Ocampo's body of work, such as the role of fantasy as a "subversive" tool and Ocampo's presumed identification with the marginalized in society.[20] Variations focused on the supernatural enact what Sylvia Molloy describes as a prophylactic strategy of relocating cruelty and/or disturbing events to an "innocuous zone" of fantasy.[21] Readings focused on the marginalized reflect a tendency to treat cruelty in Ocampo's stories as a universal strategy for the powerless to react against subjugation, as Erika Martínez Cabrera and others have argued.[22] Critics following this logic often assume that literary representation of the marginalized is necessarily accompanied by solidarity. Ocampo encouraged this assumption

---

20. For example, critics who reframe disturbing events in Ocampo's stories as marks of fantasy and/or expressions of repressed class resentment might offer the following variations:

> *Class-focused variation on "supernatural causes"*: The magical dress has absorbed Casilda's suppressed disgust and frustration with her wealthy clients, and it silences the woman on behalf of working-class people everywhere.
> *Class-focused variation on "natural causes"*: The client dies naturally, but her indulgent lifestyle is implicated, as symbolized by the fancy dress she wears at the moment of her death.
> *Class-focused variation on "seamstress turned murderer"*: Casilda acts as a representative of those made to serve the upper class quietly to the detriment of their own health, avenging this harm unrecognized by the wealthy.
> *Fantasy-focused variation on "Casilda's negligence"*: Casilda's passivity in the face of the woman's distress as a mark of the degree to which she, too, is affected by the dress's mesmeric force.

21. Molloy, "Silvina Ocampo," 23.
22. Martínez Cabrera, "Silvina Ocampo," 132. See also discussions of the victimization and revenge of women, children, and "deviants" as a key element of Ocampo's critique of marginalization and hegemony in Klingenberg, "Mad Double" and *Fantasies of the Feminine*.

in interviews; for example, she often mentioned feeling closer to governesses and household servants than to her family members. But Ocampo's portraits of monstrous mothers, child criminals, animal accomplices, and other misfits are almost universally unflattering and tend to block rather than facilitate identification. As I show in the next section, what appears to be primarily a problem of the ethics of the *told*—what causes the woman's demise, and who is responsible?—is more fully explained by attention to the ethics of *telling* and the ethics of *reading*.

NARRATOR UNRELIABILITY AND AFFECTIVE ESTRANGEMENT

Disentangling the varied potential explanations for the story's ending highlights Ocampo's defense against interpretive resolution. This pushes rhetorical readers to shift their attention from the ethics of the *told* to the ethics of *telling*, but there we encounter new barriers. When it comes to *telling*, how should readers make sense of the narrator's unreliability? From a narratological perspective, the unreliability of child narrators is most often linked to their innocence and naïveté; paradigmatic instances are Scout in *To Kill a Mockingbird* or young Jack in Emma Donaghue's *Room*. In these novels, children faithfully report what they see, but their inexperience prevents them from accurately assessing events and the causal relationships between them.

The limitations of unreliable narrators do not typically keep us from deducing what we think the implied author wants us to know, even when that differs significantly from the narrator's conclusions. We come to unreliable narration with the expectation that we will be able to overcome the narrator's limitations. Rather than functioning as an insurmountable barrier, distortion in a narrator's reporting is usually just one more feature of the narrative for readers to interpret as they imagine the implied author's intentions. Phelan illustrates this with an example from *Huckleberry Finn*. Twain's bewildered Huck describes waiting for "the widow to tuck down her head and grumble a little over the victuals, though there warn't really anything the matter with them," an account that leads most readers to recognize that Huck mistakes the widow's dinner prayer for inexplicable "grumbling."[23] Huck's naïve description defamiliarizes the blessing for a beat in the narration, but readers quickly catch up. In addition to understanding what is happening, rhetorical readers

---

23. Phelan, "Estranging Unreliability, Bonding Unreliability," 229.

enjoy the pleasure of knowing something the narrator doesn't and, perhaps, the amusement of Huck's irreverently fresh perspective on prayer.

But whereas the naïve defamiliarization at work in Huck's account may bond readers to him, unreliability in "El vestido" estranges readers from the narrator. The description of the woman's suffocation does jolt us out of normal seeing, but several factors compromise any novelty or delight in her perspective. We recognize the direness of the defamiliarized situation; this is no confusion of prayer for grumbling. We experience dismay at how the narrator's misrecognition of events leads her to gravely underestimate their seriousness. What will future reflection on this experience mean for her? At the same time, our distress has no resonance in the narration, which withholds access to character interiority. Estranged as we are from our narrator, it is mostly beside the point whether she apprehends events correctly (we strongly suspect that she does not). We seek indications of what the implied author intends for our *assessment* of the narrator's unreliability. But these are largely absent.

To navigate textual ambiguity and establish a coherent interpretation, readers often turn to tonal markers of emotion for guidance. These are rare in "El vestido" and offer little help. The speaker aptly describes the scent of the *señora*'s perfume and the tactile quality of the velvet dress, among other sensations, but her attentiveness to sensory detail finds no parallel in relation to affective experience (her own or anyone else's). Casilda's melancholy—expressed in dialogue after the woman's death—initially appears appropriate. However, what she says—"¡Me costó tanto hacer este vestido! ¡Me costó tanto, tanto!" ("It cost me such work to make this dress! It cost me so much, so very much!" 147)—trivializes her initial "sadness" and reverses the apparent coherence of her response. There are only two other clear mentions of emotion in the story. The first takes place at the opening when the narrator announces that she was "in a bad mood" because of having to accompany Casilda to the city. The second is the refrain, "¡Qué risa!" ("What a laugh!"), which is the concluding line of seven paragraphs across the story's five pages. This marker of mirth (or derision) appears first after an odd street name. We see it also on the heels of apparent mistakes: Casilda fumbles with an aspirin and a glass of water, the client incorrectly concludes that the narrator is Casilda's daughter, and Casilda drops a handful of pins to the floor. The last instances of "¡Qué risa!" center on the woman and her dress, after their failed attempt to get the dress onto the woman, and then, most disturbingly, after the woman's apparent death at the story's end.

Does the girl's laughter center on the squandered labor that the dress represents to Casilda? Or does she celebrate the death of a vain, wealthy woman? The narrator's showy assertion of laughter seems to perform the delight in the face of another's pain. If the narrator were to react with canned laughter only at the moment of the woman's death, we might conclude that it does reflect a cruel celebration of suffering. But the apparently indiscriminate invocation of "¡Qué risa!" for events both trivial and tragic troubles the relationship between narrative performance and the ostensible emotions of the speaker.

A similar disjunction between situation and emotion appears in many of Ocampo's stories. In "La casa de azúcar" (The house made of sugar), the speaker explains his tears not in relation to his current state of crisis but rather as the consequence of a speck in his eye (57). Speaking of her close relationship with her employer, the cook who narrates "La propiedad" (The property) brags, "¡Yo era su paño de lágrimas!" ("I was the handkerchief for her tears!" 57), and another narrator describes a woman who "lloraba cuando reía" ("laughed when she cried," 70). Such commonplaces and contradictions may make Ocampo's narratives persuasive as dramatic monologues, but they possess an artificiality and impenetrability that makes it difficult for readers to imagine them mapping onto an interior affective world. References to emotion draw attention to their own awkwardness and unhelpfulness, like labels haphazardly affixed to canned goods at random. Are these references to emotion offered ironically? Do we see clichés as a reflection of the expressive resources of a working-class narrator? What do we do when we wish to be oriented by feeling but find no such compass in Ocampo's stories? How do rhetorical readers navigate purported markers of emotion that create a point of estrangement from characters rather than a catalyst for imaginative identification with them?

Of course, "estrangement" and "identification" are relative terms. When reading Ocampo, though, most of our experiences fall closer to estrangement, diverging significantly from the feeling-focused and highly interior narratives that predominated in the writing by Latin American women during the first half of the twentieth century. Ocampo's characters often resemble placeholders more than persons, and their flatness makes it difficult to either absolve or condemn them. In the case of "El vestido," it is certainly a problem for readers that the narrator is fascinated and apparently unbothered by the events she recounts, but the proliferation of possible explanations for the death obstructs the emergence of any "most plausible" reading. The absence of emotional content makes it difficult to determine where to locate cruelty in the narrative—with Casilda, with the speaker, with the narrator, with the implied author—or with all of them.

The difficult point is not so much the possibility of the characters' indifference to the *señora*'s suffering, nor is it what the child narrator thinks or feels in response to events. Rather, it seems to me that readers often recoil out of a peculiar sense of propriety: the conviction that the narrator (or Ocampo) should not *narrate* in this fashion. Whereas fiction often serves as an occasion for imaginative access to other minds, Ocampo regularly capitalizes on our foraging for affective satisfactions only to send us away hungry. Yes, we experience a sense of disappointment when we do not get to the bottom of a character's mind or motives. But we also gain an opportunity to consider the degree to which our desire to know how to feel about (or with) characters may stem from a wish to resolve—however provisionally—the disorienting hermeneutic challenges of the text. That is, Ocampo's stories enact a pedagogy of deprivation that can make even the most determinedly empathetic reader pause to consider who, in the end, that empathy serves. This forced reckoning cultivates an uneasy sense of culpability where we usually experience (the illusion of) our innocence.

OCAMPO'S RESISTANCE TO MIMETIC NORMS

So far, I've focused on the dynamics within Ocampo's fiction (the ethics of the *told* and the ethics of *telling*) and on what challenges or opportunities they present to readers (the ethics of *reading*). I want also to consider how her narrative project illuminates the ethics of *writing*: the ethical weight of authors' choices as they navigate external realities, such as their access to literary markets, how critics receive their work, and what expectations readers bring based on their perceived identities. Understanding the fundamental refusal at the core of Ocampo's writing—the "why" behind her defensive deployment of deformative fiction—calls for attention to her privileges of wealth and ready access to publication through her eldest sister's highly regarded literary magazine *Sur* (South). The challenges she faced are also pertinent, including being positioned as a "woman writer" often in the shadow of her more acclaimed husband, fiction writer Adolfo Bioy Casares, and their close friend and frequent collaborator, Borges. During her literary prime, Ocampo weathered the disapproval of critics, who focused their praise of women writers on the intimacy and depth of feeling in their stories.

The writer María Luisa Bombal offers a prime example of this model of success. A young Chilean living abroad in Buenos Aires in the 1930s, Bombal also published fiction in *Sur* and was briefly a member of the same literary circle as Ocampo and Borges. An early review of her novella *La última niebla* (The final mist) by Amado Alonso celebrated the author's lyricism and what he called her "typically female" evocation of the character's emotional life, and her attention to the speaker's "temperamento íntegramente femenino" ("wholly feminine temperament").²⁴ To Alonso and many of his contemporaries, the virtues of Bombal's writing—especially her emphasis on the interior world of her characters—were intimately linked to her fulfillment of their notion of appropriate comportment as a woman writer.²⁵ Like entitled guests who take for granted that their female host will lubricate any awkward interaction (the nervous laugh to ease tension, the sad story to elicit sympathy), these critics expected women writers to make them feel at home through compelling and relatable portraits of their inner lives, but they left stylistic innovations unremarked.

Mimetic skill and lyricism garnered praise for many women writers, a pattern that also encouraged Ocampo's readers to expect emotional access in her stories. Catering to these expectations did not interest Ocampo, but neither could she ignore them. Her financial security and social status, however, gave her the option to challenge them. Ocampo's refusal of representational propriety prompted sharp critiques, including from her own sister, Victoria Ocampo. *Viaje olvidado* (Forgotten journey), Ocampo's first collection of short stories, was published in 1937 by the editorial arm of *Sur*, which Victoria herself controlled. But this did not stop Victoria from telegraphing her disapproval in a tepid review of the book. Mixing muted praise with cutting remarks, Victoria's published review demonstrates the degree to which Ocampo's approach ran afoul of prevailing norms for women writers. She began by comparing Ocampo's representations of things and people to stories in cartoons. By the end of the essay, her assessment turns especially harsh:

> Todo eso está escrito en un lenguaje hablado, lleno de hallazgos que encantan y de desaciertos que molestan, lleno de imágenes felices—que parecen entonces naturales—y lleno de imágenes no logradas—que parecen entonces atacadas de tortícolis. ¿No serán posibles las unas sino gracias a las otras? ¿Es necesaria esa desigualdad? Corrigiéndose de unas, ¿se corregiría Silvina Ocampo de las otras? Es ése un riesgo que a mi juicio debe afrontar. Antes de renunciar a la destreza, es preciso que se haya tomado el trabajo de investigar qué porcentaje de negligencia entra en la composición de sus defectos y qué pereza la lleva a no ser más exigente consigo misma cuando todo nos demuestra que puede serlo.

---

24. Alonso, "Aparición de una novelista" (Appearance of a novelist), 25 and 27. First published in 1936 in *Nosotros* (Us), the essay later served as a preface to the second edition of *La última niebla*.

25. I discuss how these assumptions about Bombal's fiction hamper attention to other aspects of her narrative that are not as strongly identified with femininity in "Translating *La última niebla*."

All of this is written in the language of speech, full of charming finds and of errors that irritate, full of apt images—that come off as natural—and full of failed images—that seem to suffer from torticollis. Is it that one is not possible without the other? Is this unevenness necessary? Correcting the one type, would Silvina Ocampo inevitably be forced to change the other? This is a risk that, in my judgment, she ought to take head on. Before giving up on craft, she ought to have taken the trouble to find out to what degree negligence may be counted among her defects and what sort of laziness prevents her from being more demanding of herself when everything shows us that she is capable of it.[26]

In Silvina Ocampo's deliberate rejection of formal perfection, Victoria saw only evidence of laziness, negligence, and limited artistic aspiration.[27]

This severe critique may reflect Victoria's (perceived) authority over Ocampo. Given her powerful position at *Sur*, Victoria likely voiced her objections during the editorial process but was unable to persuade Ocampo to "correct" her style and bring it in line with prevailing canons of taste. The rhetorical questions in Victoria's review—"¿No serán posibles las unas sino gracias a las otras? ¿Es necesaria esa desigualdad?" ("Is it that one is not possible without the other? Is this unevenness necessary?")—seem to challenge, publicly, what may have been Ocampo's privately stated justifications for her stylistic choices. The *Sur* review suggests Victoria's concerted effort to publicly distance herself from the "flaws" in *Viaje olvidado*. But distortion, vernacular language, "stiff-necked" images, imperfect form, the interplay between rhetorical agility and deliberate awkwardness, and an obsessive focus on objects all emerge as important elements of Ocampo's mature aesthetic—and as strategies for defending her characters, narrative worlds, and stories from the impositions of readers.

FUNCTIONS OF FLATNESS IN "EL CUADERNO" AND BEYOND

Although Ocampo came from an elite family and enjoyed the privileges of wealth, her stories are crowded with servants, hairdressers, laborers, shopkeepers, seamstresses, children, immigrants, and people with disabilities. Her

---

26. Ocampo, review of *Viaje olvidado* (Forgotten journey), 119–20.
27. In José Amícola's estimation, Ocampo resists the structural perfection that became an article of faith in the growing cult of Borges. Amícola, "Silvina Ocampo," 136. For Hiram Aldarondo, Ocampo's thematic preoccupation with cruelty is part of her strategic renunciation of refined, "tranquilizing" beauty. Aldarondo, *El humor* (Humor), 13–14.

reputation for centering what others might view as undesirables is so complete that one critic describes her characters as "una galería de pequeños *freaks*" ("a gallery of little *freaks*").[28] These characters are often positioned in ghastly scenarios that impart a sinister air to domesticity, propriety, celebration, material accumulation, and maternity. For example, a home-cooked meal turns fatal in "Mimoso" when the main character serves her neighbor the taxidermied flesh of her former pet. Hairdressing turns deadly in "La boda" (The wedding) when a young girl plants a poisonous spider in a bridal headpiece in hopes of winning the approval of the bride's rival. In both "La furia" (The fury) and "La oración" (The prayer), children cause the deaths of their playmates. Some critics have taken Ocampo's focus on the marginalized as an expression of a certain cross-class solidarity. But solidarity depends largely on empathy, which Ocampo's stories limit rather than invite.

"El cuaderno" (The notebook) is free from fatalities, but its characters are as two-dimensional as the figures in the notebook that gives the story its name. Left alone in her apartment at the end of her pregnancy while her husband is out watching a holiday parade, the central character Ermelina contemplates her unborn child. The narrator relates that she has been able to envision the child (whom she assumes will be male) fully, except for his face. As if in response to this gap in Ermelina's imagining, a neighbor arrives for a visit with her two sons and brings along a notebook full of images cut from magazines. Ermelina thumbs through the pages and pauses before "la cara de un chico muy rosado, pegada entre un ramo de lilas" ("the face of a very pink boy, glued under a branch of lilies"), which she announces is the face she wishes for her child to have (73). At this moment in the narrative, it appears to be a throwaway line, but its significance emerges at the story's end, when her wish is fulfilled: in a haze of obstetric sedation following the delivery of her child, she recognizes her son's "pink face" from the notebook (76).

The story invites a tension between the attribution of fantasy—a modern exploration of maternal impression, the folk notion that images presented to pregnant women can alter the appearance of their unborn children—and the notion that it is her perception that has been affected, whether by the sedatives used during delivery or, perhaps, by maternity itself. What is most interesting is how rigidly readers are held at bay, unable to connect to Ermelina's internal experience as a source of clarification or orientation to aid our interpretation. Instead, we watch a kind of progressive deformation of Ermelina's perception in the hours before her labor begins:

---

28. Díaz, "Como el agua" (Like water), 92.

De repente Ermelina vio que el menor de los hijos de la vecina se parecía extrañamente a la sota de espadas; era una suerte de hombrecito pequeño aplastado contra el suelo, vestido de verde y rojo. El otro parecía un rey muy cabezón con una copa en la mano, donde bebía una cantidad incalculable de agua. (74)

Suddenly Ermelina saw that the younger of her neighbor's sons strangely resembled the jack of spades; he was a sort of little man-child flattened against the floor and dressed in green and red. The other looked like a king with a very big head and a cup in his hand, from which he was drinking an incalculable quantity of water.

The narration underscores flatness even in the moments when readers are likely to expect affective access, culturally primed as we are to imagine pregnancy as a receptive state that invites "feeling *onto*" as in strangers' unsolicited comments—"You must be so delighted!"—or presumption to touch a pregnant belly.

Ocampo disrupts the romanticization of maternity or childhood.[29] Despite formal marks of the diminutive—"el menor" ("the younger one") and "hombrecito pequeño" ("little man-child")—the stress on deformity in this passage blocks any possibility of finding the children endearing. Words such as "extrañamente," "aplastado," and "incalculable" ("strangely," "flattened," and "incalculable") highlight Ermelina's sense that the children are alienating, unknowable creatures. The comparison to playing cards in the description frames the children as two-dimensional, stylized figures, and the narrator describes the images on the cards in far more detail than the boys themselves. Even Ermelina's newborn child is all hard surface, and his face has "el mismo color chillón que tienen los juguetes nuevos" ("the same garish color found on new toys," 76). Although Ermelina's solitary birth experience may be a cause for concern for modern readers, she does not react to it, and nothing comes of the story's dark intimations. The deadpan narration serves as an ironic indication of the degree to which the "disaster" signaled by the story's menacing

---

29. Ocampo's portrayal of children draws frequent comment. Richard Browning notes the distancing effect of seeing "grotesque, violent or sexual acts" performed by people we expect to be innocent; see Browning, *Childhood and the Nation*, 103. Graciela Tomassini describes the cruelty of children as one element in Ocampo's demystification of childhood in *El espejo de Cornelia*, 38. Thomas Meehan discusses the "widening abyss between children and adults" in Ocampo's stories in "Los niños perversos," 35. Fiona Mackintosh highlights Ocampo's stress on the inaccessibility of childhood from the perspective of adulthood (*Childhood*, 98). See also Klingenberg, *Fantasies of the Feminine*, which deals at length with childhood and holds up transgressive little girls in the stories as sites of intense readerly distress.

mood is not an outside event but rather resides, perhaps, in Ermelina's own passivity and complacency.[30]

In "El cuaderno" and other stories by Ocampo, flat portrayals of unsympathetic characters function as preventative measures against readers' intrusions, however well-meaning (empathy, curiosity, class solidarity) or self-serving (escape, projection, penetration). They are part of Ocampo's refusal to play the "woman writer" game of serving as a midwife to readers' feelings. In other words, Ocampo's fiction defends against the notion that her stories (or characters) ought to provide access to the hearts and minds of imagined persons. Flatness emerges as a hallmark of textuality. The impenetrable surfaces and hard edges of characters serve as a protection against readers' projections of sentiment.

Ocampo's stories offer little occasion for sentimentality or sweetness, and often instantiate what Daniel Harris calls the "anti-cute": a rejection of cuteness as a pathological aesthetic that is *inflicted* on persons and objects (as opposed to inhering in them).[31] In Harris's formulation, cuteness prioritizes the affective needs of beholders and creates "a class of outcasts and mutations, a ready-made race of loveable inferiors whom both children and adults collect, patronize, and enslave in the protective concubinage of their vast harems of homely dolls and snugglesome misfits."[32] Were they written into existence by a different sort of writer, it's not hard to imagine Ocampo's characters—that "gallery of little *freaks*"—recruited into a literary corollary of this kind of collection. But Ocampo defends against that outcome with deliberately unflattering, deliberately flat portraits of monstrous mothers, child criminals, and animal accomplices.

Deviations from what readers expect can be a refreshing change or a stimulus to redouble interpretive efforts. In Ocampo's case, though, it is felt more often as a rebuff. Like Shakespeare's Cordelia, Ocampo undermines authority by refusing to pander to it.[33] Instead, the stories pit superficiality, opacity, and incomprehensibility against the expectation of emotional and interpretive access. Ocampo's eschewal of mimetic illusions of interiority becomes

---

30. A possibly feminist or protofeminist inclination can be detected here, but only with caution. Evelyn Fishburn points out that even the most persuasive feminist interpretations of Ocampo "serve only to open up certain possibilities of meaning . . . but can never be offered as more than a tentative and partial reading" of the stories, which always exceed the "attempted 'explanation.'" See Fishburn, *Short Fiction*, 108.

31. Harris, "Cuteness."

32. Harris, "Cuteness," 179.

33. For a discussion of the "Cordelia effect," see Sommer, "Resistant Texts and Incompetent Readers." Sommer argues that this tactic is especially evident in "marginal" or "minority" fiction.

even more discomfiting in those stories that pair impenetrability with situations of varying degrees and types of cruelty. Beauty may be in the eye of the beholder, but cruelty is often in the eye of the victim. The repeated rejections in Ocampo's fiction may feel like cruelty, a refusal to alleviate the discomfort we experience in reading. The readings that follow highlight the artistry of her defenses and the distinctly deformative nature of her narrative project to demonstrate how efforts at interpretation become increasingly fraught.

DECORUM AS DYSFUNCTION IN "LA CASA DE LOS RELOJES"

Earlier, I advanced the hypothesis that readers of "El vestido" are more troubled by the story's narrative impropriety than by thematic darkness. Here, I focus on "La casa de los relojes" (The clock house), and I examine how narrative decisions expose readers to ethical instability, uncertainty, and a proliferation of potential sites of cruelty. Like "El vestido," this story features a child narrator who describes harm without offering any sign that he comprehends the significance or causes of the suffering. In this case, Ocampo anchors the narrator's unreliability and limited capacity to judge events to a distinct distortion of priorities, an obsessive preoccupation with propriety. The narrator repeatedly stresses his efforts to behave well. Yet this emphasis on avoiding social gaffes apparently causes him to misrecognize or disregard the cruelty he witnesses, even when it targets someone whom he claims to love. My goal here is to develop a deeper understanding of how this story generates rhetorical and ethical complexity but withholds any satisfying resolution. In other words, how might rhetorical readers recognize the signature of Ocampo's deformative fiction in this story?

"La casa" takes the form of a letter from a nine-year-old boy to his teacher. His pretext for writing is to fulfill a promise to practice his composition skills. He opens with a brief account of a summer visit to a lake but quickly shifts the focus to a party that has taken place the night before he writes his letter. The story of the party—a celebration of a neighbor child's baptism—begins casually, without any hint of menace. This only adds to the shock of its culmination in what readers recognize as an act of violence against a local man, Estanislao Romagán. Estanislao runs the neighborhood clock shop next to the narrator's home (the title's "clock house") and proves to be a ready target for the malicious urges unleashed in the drunken revelry of the party. His vulnerability has multiple sources, including his vaguely foreign-sounding name (Is he Slavic? Roma?), his timidity, and his most noticeable physical difference: the pronounced curve in his back. Kyphosis, the condition that prompts the narrator to use the derogatory label *jorobado* (hunchback) to describe him, relegates Estanislao to a childlike, subservient position in the community. He does not protest when children chase him and ask to touch his back for good luck. He apologizes profusely for his wrinkled suit upon arriving at the party, and he promises free watch repairs to the other guests. Then he obediently follows the sinister instructions of the neighborhood men when they decide to transport him to the local dry cleaner's shop to redress the wrinkles in his clothing. Once there, the men express their intention to "iron out" not only Estanislao's suit, but the hump beneath it as well.

The child narrator—who has ignored his mother's pleas to stay home—goes along with the men and witnesses a chaotic scene in the cleaner's workshop. Tripping over one another, the men rush around with "trapos húmedos, frascos, planchas" ("damp rags, bottles, irons") and perform what appears to the narrator to be "una operación quirúrgica" ("a surgical operation," 63). The boy becomes suddenly and violently ill, and he is sent home before the "operation" is completed. This means he can offer us no direct access to the outcome of the men's actions. However, he does note that "no volví a ver a Estanislao Romagán" ("I never saw Estanislao Romagán again") and describes his neighbors helping themselves to watches and clocks from Estanislao's shop the next day (64). When the narrator asks his mother about Estanislao, she tearfully refuses to answer his questions except to say, "Se fue a otra parte" ("He went somewhere else") and to shush any mention of the incident (64). These events are chilling, no question. But their afflictive potential—how they unsettle and linger with readers—is rooted most of all in their telling. Ocampo shapes this experience in three main ways. First, her brand of narrator unreliability contributes to the distressing ethical implications of events in this story. Second, she makes decorum appear dysfunctional, even pathological. Third, through the story's framing, she highlights the possibility of transferring responsibility for cruelty. Because these effects are largely intertwined, I address them jointly. Their combined impact makes the story unsettling—and an excellent example of Ocampo's defensive deformative fiction.

The story begins this way:

Estimada señorita:
   Ya que me he distinguido en su clase con mis composiciones, cumplo con mi promesa; me ejercitaré escribiéndole cartas. ¿Me pregunta qué hice en los últimos días de mis vacaciones? . . . Me divertí mucho en la laguna Salada, hicimos fortalezas de barro; pero más me divertí anoche en la fiesta . . . para el bautismo de Rusito. (59)

Dear Miss:

    Now that I have distinguished myself in your class with my compositions, I am keeping my promise; I will stay in practice by writing you letters. You ask what I did during the last days of my vacation? . . . I had a great time at Lake Salada, we made mud forts; but I had even more fun last night at the party . . . for Rusito's baptism.

The boy presents his account as if it were a solicited response to the unimaginative question perennially posed to schoolchildren, "What did you do on your vacation?" Further, he frames it as a fulfilment of a promise to practice writing, one rooted in his previous accomplishment in the teacher's class. His childlike language—and self-presentation as a pupil addressing an adult— primes readers to recognize that the letter comes to them in an envelope of unreliability. From the start, we expect to compensate for the child's perspective: reinterpreting the details that he provides, filling in where he fails to direct attention, and more generally correcting what we take to be his misunderstandings. The story's opening hints at what will quickly become an overt preoccupation with comportment; by the end of the story, etiquette will have displaced ethics entirely as the boy's framework for judging behavior. Although there is no hint of the dark turn the story will take, seasoned readers of Ocampo know not to conflate unreliability with innocence.

Of particular note is how the narrator recruits his teacher into corroborating his assessments of breaches in decorum. Throughout the letter, he provides commentary on the adult behavior he sees, often reprising the teacher's past instruction and invoking, as if given, what he imagines would be her assessments. In the dry cleaner's shop, when the various chemical smells make the speaker sneeze, he assures his teacher, "me tapé la boca, siguiendo sus enseñanzas, señorita" ("I covered my mouth, following your teachings, miss," 63). And when he describes one of the men exclaiming, *cochino* ("filthy pig"), he parrots adult disapproval, perhaps the sort of phrase he has heard his teacher say: "¡Qué ejemplo para un chico!" ("What an example for a child!" 63). Several of his judgments are followed by the rhetorical question, "¿no le parece, señorita?" ("Don't you agree, miss?"), as if to stress his expectation of her agreement (60, 62). In another story, these prim pronouncements might be charming in their mimicry of adult middle-class values. But the narrator's narrow focus on social propriety displaces any moral evaluation of the actions that lead to Estanislao's unhappy end.

This is made more distressing because the boy presents himself as having a close connection to Estanislao, upon whom two rare references to emotion are focused. The narrator notes, "yo lo quería mucho a Estanislao Romagán" ("I really loved Estanislao Romagán"), and he describes his excitement to see Estanislao treated like "el rey de la fiesta" ("the king of the party") in a scene that echoes Quasimodo's short-lived glory as the "king" of the Feast of Fools in Victor Hugo's *Notre-Dame de Paris* (60, 62). The narrator's announcement at the letter's opening that "más me divertí anoche en la fiesta . . . para el bautismo de Rusito" ("I had even more fun last night at the party . . . for Rusito's baptism") undermines these mentions of care and concern (59). Since this assertion comes after the speaker's full experience of the party's events, it suggests that the violent character of the evening's end does not register with the boy (or does not deprive him of enjoyment).

Further, the narrative becomes opaque precisely where readers likely wish for clarity:

> Me detuve para mirar el lugar donde iban a planchar el traje de Estanislao.
> —¿Me desnudo?—interrogó Estanislao.
> —No—respondió Gervasio—, no se moleste. Se lo plancharemos puesto.
> —¿Y la giba?—interrogó Estanislao, tímidamente.
> Era la primera vez que yo oía esa palabra, pero por la conversación me enteré de lo que significaba (ya ve que progreso en mi vocabulario).
> —También te la plancharemos—respondió Gervasio, dándole una palmada sobre el hombro.
> Estanislao se acomodó sobre una mesa larga, como le ordenó Nakoto que estaba preparando las planchas . . . Todos los hombres tropezaban con algo, con los muebles, con las puertas, con los útiles de trabajo, con ellos mismos. Traían trapos húmedos, frascos, planchas. Aquello parecía, aunque usted no lo crea, una operación quirúrgica. Un hombre cayó al suelo y me hizo una zancadilla que por poco me romp[ió] el alma. Entonces, para mí al menos, se terminó la alegría. Comencé a vomitar. Usted sabe que tengo un estomago muy sano y que los compañeros de colegio me llamaban avestruz, porque tragaba cualquier cosa. No sé lo que me pasó. Alguien me sacó de allí a los tirones y me llevó a casa.
> No volví a ver a Estanislao Romagán. Mucha gente vino a buscar los relojes y un camioncito de la relojería LA PARCA retiró los últimos. (63–64)

> I held back to look at where they were going to iron out Estanislao's suit.
> "Should I take my clothes off?" asked Estanislao.
> "No," answered Gervasio, "Don't bother. We'll iron it while it's on."
> "And my hump?" Estanislao asked timidly.

It was the first time that I had heard that word, but I figured out what it meant by listening to the conversation (you can see how I'm making progress with my vocabulary).

"We'll iron it for you, too," answered Gervasio, patting him on the shoulder.

Estanislao lay down on a long table as Nakoto ordered him to. Meanwhile, Nakoto was getting the irons ready . . . All of the men were bumping into things—the furniture, the doors, the tools—they even bumped into each other. They brought damp rags, jars, and irons. You might not believe me, but it looked like a surgical operation. One man fell on the floor, knocking into me so hard that it nearly broke my heart. That's when, for me at least, the fun was over. I started to vomit. You know that I have a very strong stomach and that my classmates call me ostrich because I can eat anything. I don't know what came over me. Someone dragged me out of there and took me home.

I never saw Estanislao Romagán again. A lot of people came to get the watches and then a truck from LA PARCA watch repair shop took away what was left.

Whereas in "El vestido" the narrator's view of a wealthy stranger's misfortune was literally blocked by Casilda's back, here the boy makes plain that he can *see* what is happening. He describes the drunken confusion of the scene. But beyond providing us with the ominous vision of Estanislao stretched out on a table like a patient, he does not address the specific events that follow. A certain callousness shadows his narration, as when he interrupts the grizzly exchange about "ironing" the watchmaker's hump to inform his teacher about his increased ability to draw on context clues to understand new words. He describes being trampled by one of the men, an experience that "por poco me rompió el alma" ("nearly broke my heart") and that marks the point when "para mí . . . se terminó la alegría" ("for me . . . the fun was over"). Despite marking this turn in his own experience, he does not express any distress in response to what is happening to Estanislao. By underscoring the strength of his constitution, the speaker insists that his vomiting must be attributed to something other than having had too much to drink. To read this as a bodily expression of unarticulated horror is an interpretive choice compatible with his naïve misunderstanding. But the fact remains that the narrator himself does not acknowledge this physical response as information about the troubling character of the incident he witnesses. Except for his reproachful comments on poor etiquette, the narrator offers almost no judgment of the events he narrates. Even as readers can—and likely do—attribute cruelty to the men who make Estanislao the victim of their ridicule and brutal acts, this judgment doesn't feel like *enough*.

If we knew the narrator to be innocent and uncomprehending, we would have the consolation of locating cruelty in what is done to Estanislao and, by extension, in the child's exposure to that act of harm. Alternatively, if we knew the narrator to be aware and complicit in the perpetration of harm, we could judge him a guilty party to the men's cruelty. We cannot be certain of either, and the ambiguity of the narrator's response to events lends a fundamentally incomplete character to any judgments we might make of cruelty in the story's content. I think this is because we expect (consciously or not) that the narrator will share our assessment or at least that the implied author will provide sufficient clues to facilitate solid judgments apart from or "working around" the narrator's faulty conclusions. As with "El vestido," the issue is not discerning unreliability, but rather determining how to *interpret* that unreliability. It floats freely between multiple explanations, including the narrator's misunderstanding, inexperience, lack of moral or ethical sensibility, and willful abuse of his narratee. The ambiguity of the unreliability, rather than the unreliability itself, creates problems for the ethics of *reading*, which centers on the judgments we make of the *told, telling,* and *writing*.

Ocampo resolutely disappoints the expectation that the implied author will offer clarity or provide confirmation of our judgments. We remain uncertain of the child's emotions in relation to the central events—or of those of any characters directly involved. The closest we come is the mother's tears, first when she tries to keep the narrator from going with the men and when he asks about Estanislao after the party. These instances do serve as signals of unreliability, opportunities for readers to be reminded of the limits of the child narrator's perspective. Like Huck taking a prayer as unwarranted grumbling, the narrator mistakes his mother's sadness about Estanislao for dismay at damage done to her furnishings during the party. By contrast, readers likely infer that her tears derive from her worries about what will happen, and later, her distress at what *has* happened to Estanislao. Although minimal, this emotional response reinforces the sense that the narrator, too, should respond. But his outraged and offended asides respond only to the mild curses and other improprieties that he reports.

"La casa" leads readers to navigate a narrative landscape where breaches of etiquette are treated like mountains and acts of mutilation or murder shrink into inconsequential molehills. Far from setting us at ease, the unperturbed quality of the narration is one of its most disturbing aspects. The opening invocation of normalcy is particularly perplexing given that the letter offers a *retrospective* account of events that, as the narrator will reveal, eventually lead to Estanislao's "disappearance." Ostensibly, if we focus on naïve unreliability, the narrator neglects to begin with the most important event because he hasn't fully grasped its potentially deadly significance. Still, by the time that he begins his letter, the boy already knows that the events he relates lead to the "disappearance" of Estanislao. If the goal were to mimic an actual letter, we might expect the whole narration to be influenced by a state of bewilderment and concern. In fact, this story is *framed* as a child's letter, but its actual exposition more closely resembles short fiction than a grade-school-aged boy's correspondence.

Before concluding that this is a flaw, a mark of a less-than-effective mimetic spell, we should recall that realism—psychological or otherwise—is not Ocampo's goal. Instead, the letter frame adds another layer of uncertainty in the narrative, multiplying the distressing implications of our encounter with cruelty in the story. It also introduces the possibility of a double location for fiction, first as the genre home for the story "La casa de los relojes," and secondly in the (potentially) invented story of the party that is told in the letter. Readers recognize the text as fiction (it appears in a collection of short stories) but assume that we are invited to accept the mimetic illusion that the letter is "actually" written by a young boy. Within this ostensibly epistolary frame, however, we can imagine an additional layer of fictionality, where the narrator, within the world of the clock house and the teacher, has completely invented this tale of the baptism and operation. Consider what changes for the ethics of *reading* the story if the tale of Estanislao is not only fictional to us as readers of a short story but also fabricated *within* the narrative world (more on this below).

If you find yourself confused by these complications, you are not alone. You may even wonder why it matters if the story is inside the boy's letter if the letter is ultimately inside Ocampo's story (and so on). How rhetorical readers parse Ocampo's narrative choices has consequences for their judgments about the story (the *telling* and the *told*). Who is harmed, and who knows about it? Who tells about it, to whom, and why? One expression of the ethics of *reading*, I think, is to have the patience to untangle the possibilities for reading the ethics of the *told* and of its *telling*. Here, I begin with the most straightforward reading and proceed to those options that seem most an expression of the deformative in Ocampo's fiction.

1. *Accidental Transmission of Horror.* Within the narrative world, Estanislao is harmed, but the narrator doesn't understand what he sees. Thus, the narrator unknowingly transmits the horror of the event to his teacher, who can discern the cruelty that has been perpetrated.

2. *Intentional Transmission of Horror.* Within the narrative world, Estanislao really is harmed, and the narrator recognizes that cruel actions cause the suffering he sees. We understand his narration as intended to "inflict" the story on the teacher as a further act of cruelty. With its stubborn silences and elisions, the letter incites her to imagine the dark recreations that ensue between "someone . . . took me home" and "I never saw Estanislao Romagán again" (64). The "operation" on Estanislao seems to be the narrator's focus, yet his actual goal is the narrative transmission of opaque disaster to the teacher.

3. *Intentional Transmission of Counterfactual Horror.* Within the narrative world, Estanislao is unharmed. The story about the baptism party is a sophisticated prank by a precocious student. His apparent goal is exposing his teacher to the disturbing visions evoked by his letter *and* invoking in her the distress of being a bystander after the fact. The student's insistence on having been faithful to her "teachings" insinuates a link between what happens to Estanislao and the teacher, as if the letter's purpose were to transfer *responsibility* for the cruel events, or for the story of the events.

4. *Fiction to "Instruct" the Teacher.* Within the narrative world, nothing has happened to Estanislao. The narrator has made up a disturbing tale, the telling of which exaggerates his teacher's concern with propriety, extending it in alarming ways. Understood from this angle, the boy's letter inflicts suffering on its recipient, but it is about more than mischief. It institutes a correction, reversing the roles of student and teacher and transforming the banal, "What did you do on your vacation?" into the more ethically substantive, "What happens to a story if it is told as if nothing matters more than manners?" Rather than demonstrating the degree to which he has internalized the teacher's lessons as he purports, the narrator subtly challenges her mistaken priorities by demonstrating their consequences. Defenders of cruelty, most notably Nietzsche and Artaud, often justify it as a form of necessary instruction or intervention.[34] However, the pedagogical function of the story is buried in this innermost narrative layer, where its moral implications are most complicated by the possibility of irony on the part of the implied author.

---

34. Nietzsche's *Beyond Good and Evil* (1886) explicitly valorizes cruelty as a response to society's deceptions. In Nietzsche's telling, the strong philosophers of the future perform a public service by "tak[ing] the vivisector's knife to the breast of the very virtues of their age" (137). By exposing fictions masquerading as virtues and lies peddled as wisdom, Nietzsche imagines cruelty as an essential precursor to healthy exposure to life's "truths." In theorizing his Theater of Cruelty in *Le Théâtre et son double* (*The Theater and Its Double*) (1938), Artaud similarly celebrates cruelty as the opposite of falsehood, affectation, and illness. He imagines it as a tool for expelling authored language (such as plays) and other contaminants associated with traditional theater. Artaud's Theater of Cruelty produces an unrepeatable event (92). This event, best thought of as a confrontation or an ordeal, corresponds approximately with the "cut" of Nietzsche's philosopher-surgeon.

5. *Fiction to Involve the Reader.* We cannot discern the status of the events within the fictional world in which the letter is written, and the story of oblique harm to Estanislao is fundamentally ironic. The narrator's insistence on decorum is to be decoded as a critique of how propriety can shelter pathological dysfunction. Within the world of the narrative, the recipient of the boy's letter is his teacher, but it is also (and perhaps primarily) directed *past* her, to the reader located one remove beyond. "Doesn't it seem to you?" and other asides from the narrator can be taken as verbal winks at the reader standing behind the teacher. We, not she, are intended to grasp the irony of his relentless focus on comportment. It is as if he were saying to us, "You and I both know that covering your mouth when sneezing is far less important than breaking out of one's bystander stupor and intervening when someone is being harmed." The problem, for readers, with this kind of tactical inclusion is that it reflects an attempt, on the part of the narrator, to establish a sense of conspiratorial connection. That connection between narrator and reader may bleed into feelings of complicity with the narrator's placid acceptance of the harm done to Estanislao. In other words, in this interpretation, inclusion in the narratorial audience creates an uneasy bond between reader and narrator, one that implies an alignment of perspective that can be disconcerting, to say the least.

Close examination of "La casa de los relojes" underscores how significantly the *telling* of a story can intensify the ethical weight of the *told*—and intensify the discomfort of reading. Here, flattened affect and antimimetic effects are less prominent, but the story's relatively high index of ambiguity undermines many of the usual ways we might account for or absorb thematic cruelty into a reading. The rhetorical complexity of narratives like Ocampo's creates multiple possible sites for distressing content, and we experience them differently depending on how we parse the *telling*. We may argue about the merits of each reading, but it is not possible to fully dismiss any of them or elevate one definitively above the others. The story insists instead that readers grapple with their simultaneous existence. Navigating ambiguity in Ocampo's fiction entails contending with the *fact* of multiple possibilities—and of an (implied) author who stubbornly holds them open.

ETHICS, RHETORICAL COMPLEXITY, AND IMPLIED AUTHORS

Readers are left in an uneasy position as they encounter possible sites of cruelty in "La casa." This heightened challenge also shapes how readers imagine the person(s) responsible for the story. The narratological concept of the implied author helps us navigate more effectively the question of whom to hold responsible for the cruelty that *feels* pervasive in a text. An implied author is essentially a figure deduced by readers based on the kinds of effects that occur in the narrative. This conjectured entity should not be confused with the flesh-and-blood person of the author. Rather, the implied author is what readers construct as *the kind of person or creative presence who would tell the story this way, make these narrative choices.* Among scholars interested in narrative theory, debate continues about the utility of imagining an "implied author" in literary analysis, as opposed to dispensing with this intermediary and referring only to the narrator and "real," biographical author. When it comes to deformative fictions, however, the concept of an implied author demonstrates its value through the definition it brings to dimensions of the texts that otherwise would remain indistinct.

Since implied authors function as hypothesized *telling* agents who manage what is *told* according to the *reading* that they anticipate, they sit at the center of overlapping ethical domains of narrative. The ethics of the *told* underscores the stakes of what happens in the narrative world, including our judgments of what we *believe* happens even though it is unconfirmed by our narrator. For example, we may consider our view of Estanislao's fate, our feelings about this letter being delivered to the teacher, and our assessments of other acts described in the narrative. The ethics of *telling* includes the stakes of our judgments of various forms of communication in the story, such as the narrator's address to his teacher in his letter (what he includes, what he leaves out, how he [mis]interprets events). It also includes the implied author's presentation of this letter *as* a story. Because readers construct an implied author from the signals they discern in the text, the ethics of *reading* are equally relevant to a thorough assessment of what is at stake in navigating "La casa" (or any other story). This calls for considering the expectations, frustrations, past experiences, and assumptions we carry as readers as well as how these may condition our imagining of the implied author.

In reading, our assessments of the *telling* and the *told* shape how we imagine the intentions of an implied author. Ocampo was keenly aware of the tendency of her readers to attribute cruelty, not just to her stories or speakers, but to her as author, a tendency she resisted by pointing to the narrator as intermediary. Explaining her frequent use of first-person narrators in an interview, she noted, "Muchas cosas tienen menor responsabilidad: si está mal dicho, la culpa es de esa persona, y si hay cosas horribles que piensa, bueno, es otra persona" ("Many things come with less responsibility: if it's poorly said, the fault belongs to that person, and if that person thinks terrible things, well, that's someone else [other than the author]").[35] The question of responsibility

---

35. Ulla, *Encuentros*, 49.

for elements of the narrative becomes still more complicated when narrators write rather than speak, as is the case with "La casa." For example, a tension emerges between interpreting lapses or apparent errors as unintentional "tells" by the narrator on the one hand or deliberate rhetorical moves, whether on the part of the narrator (functioning as the writer within the story) or on the part of the implied author. (In Vallejo's *La virgen de los sicarios*, which I examine in the next chapter, we will see the overlapping of narrator-as-writer and implied author deployed to even more distressing effect.)

There is a great deal of irony in Ocampo's implication that the use of a first-person narrator offers "cover" against bad reviews or reader complaints. First-person narration in her fiction often accomplishes the opposite of providing any "cover." Many of her stories activate expectations of bonding through the immediacy of the speaker's address, but then undercut these expectations with highly particular, and often concerning, perspectives. Rather than provide emotional access, these narrators multiply the possible sites of cruelty in the story's events, their own narration, and in readers themselves. In such cases, reader dissatisfaction with the vantage point offered by the narrator may prompt a *less* generous imagining of the implied author. The complexity of Ocampo's fiction, however, makes it difficult to simply peg perversity on the implied author and leave it at that. As the next section illustrates, Ocampo's deformative strategies incite intense feelings of contamination, an experience that rhetorical readers contemplate rather than resist.

PERVERSE PEDAGOGY IN "LA FURIA"

The title short story of Ocampo's 1959 collection, "La furia" (The fury), invites further exploration of the link between pedagogy and cruelty, between narrative and contamination. In "La furia" the narrator recounts his attempts to initiate an affair with a Filipina governess named Winifred, beginning with their meetings in public and culminating with the deadly conclusion of their first and only assignation. The initial encounters center on a shared interest in poetry and language study, but in frequent asides the narrator makes plain his focus on sexual conquest. His amorous intentions are doubly thwarted, however. First, the young boy who accompanies Winifred wherever she goes is a source of constant distraction (ostensibly, she is paid to care for the young boy, but the story leaves open the possibility that he is her son). Second, Winifred repeatedly diverts the conversation to grim reflections on a childhood relationship she had with a schoolgirl named Lavinia. These embedded stories center on Winifred's abusive treatment of the girl, both casting doubt on her fitness as a caregiver and foreshadowing her capacity to facilitate the harm implied at the story's end after Winifred disappears, leaving the boy behind with the enraged narrator.

The events leading up to the story's last lines alternate between the speaker's awkward advances, the boy's obnoxious behavior (he incessantly plays a drum), and Winifred's stories of her efforts to "educate" Lavinia through a series of escalating cruelties:

> Yo vivía dedicada como una verdadera madre a cuidarla, a educarla, a corregir sus defectos . . . Para corregir su orgullo, un día le corté un mechón que guardé secretamente en un relicario; tuvieron que cortarle el resto del pelo, para emparejarlo. Otro día, le volqué un frasco de agua de Colonia sobre el cuello y la mejilla; su cutis quedó todo manchado . . . Para combatir sus inexplicables terrores, metí arañas vivas adentro de su cama. Una vez metí un ratón muerto que encontré en el jardín, otra vez metí un sapo. A pesar de todo no conseguí corregirla. (116–18)

> I lived dedicated like a true mother to caring for her, educating her, correcting her faults . . . To correct her pride, one day I snipped off a chunk of her hair that I kept hidden in a reliquary; they had to cut off the rest of her hair to even it out. Another day, I splashed a bottle of perfume on her neck and her cheek; her skin got completely stained . . . To combat her inexplicable terrors, I put live spiders in her bed. One time I put in a dead rat that I found in the garden, another time a toad. But in spite of it all I didn't manage to improve her.

Winifred's presentation of cruelty as a means of instruction echoes Nietzsche in *Beyond Good and Evil*; the philosopher, in Nietzsche's telling, must possess "a certain levelheaded cruelty that knows how to handle a knife surely and subtly, even when the heart bleeds."[36] Winifred asserts that Lavinia's failure to respond appropriately to instruction necessitated more drastic measures, the last of which unfolds during a Christmas pageant. Winifred frames the event in ambiguous terms: "una de las alas de Lavinia se encendió en la llama del cirio que yo llevaba en mi mano" ("one of Lavinia's wings caught fire on the flame of the candle that I held in my hand," 115). Relegating the introduction of *yo*—the first-person subject pronoun—to an adjective clause at the end of the sentence, Winifred distances herself from this final "lesson" despite the credit she takes for the other "instruction" she focuses on Lavinia. Perhaps her reluctance to claim this act resides in the fact that it cannot be recuperated as benevolent.

---

36. Nietzsche, *Beyond Good and Evil*, 134.

Until Lavinia's death by burning, Winifred can disregard her victim's pain by imagining herself as "operating" on a patient for her own good. As with the drunken men's supposed surgery on Estanislao, the boundary between misguided intention and pretext for perversity remains determinedly blurred. Winifred describes the day of Lavinia's death as the "más feliz y más triste de mi vida" ("the happiest and saddest of my life," 115) leaving us to reckon with the idea that the sadness of the day may reside not in the girl's death but in the loss of a patient who otherwise could be made subject to her corrections.

The embedded story of Winifred's ministrations appears to offer an obvious instance of cruelty. That judgment becomes disconcerting, however, when we learn that this view is shared by the speaker, whose actions and motives appear even more suspect than Winifred's. In a direct reference to cruelty (rare in Ocampo's stories), the speaker exclaims, "Qué cruel fuiste con Lavinia" ("How cruel you were to Lavinia"), to which Winifred responds, "Cruel soy con el resto del mundo. Cruel seré contigo" ("I'm cruel to the rest of the world. I will be cruel to you," 119). This exchange occurs when the two are finally alone in the hotel room. Before the speaker can make any advances, however, Winifred abruptly requests that he find the boy. (She has smuggled him into the hotel under her raincoat—the narrator had told her that children are not allowed—and then left him to wander the halls unsupervised.)

When the narrator finds the child urinating against a tree in the courtyard and returns him to the room, he finds that Winifred has disappeared. The speaker fails to extract from him any of the information needed to reunite him with his family. The boy cannot or will not give his name, his address, or even his governess's full name. Meanwhile, the boy continues to play his drum, prompting the narrator to threaten, "Si tocas el tambor, te mato" ("If you play the drum, I'll kill you," 121). The story concludes:

> Comenzó a gritar. Lo tomé del cuello. Le pedí que se callara. No quiso escucharme. Le tapé la boca con la almohada. Durante unos minutos se debatió; luego quedó inmóvil, con los ojos cerrados . . . Siempre fui así: por no provocar un escándalo fui capaz de cometer un crimen. (121)

> He started to yell. I took him by the neck. I asked him to be quiet. He didn't want to listen to me. I covered his mouth with a pillow. For a few minutes he struggled; then he was still, with his eyes closed . . . I was always like that: to avoid causing a scandal, I was capable of committing a crime.

Like the narrator of "La casa de los relojes," the speaker in "La furia" brings propriety and violence into uneasy proximity.

But even as cruelty is named and judged in relation to Winifred's past, its precise location in the rest of the story remains unclear. Should we conclude that the circumstances at the hotel merely activate the speaker's capacity for cruelty, which he himself seems to recognize with his final observation, "siempre fui así" ("I was always like that")? What responsibility lies with Winifred? Perhaps she is tired of her exchanges with a presumptuous and overeager suitor, but this does not account for the apparent abandonment of the boy. Might it be that, having refined her methods over years, she prepares the speaker with narratives of cruelty and then maneuvers him into a situation in which his obsession with avoiding embarrassment can be neatly translated into murderous violence? What is the status of the embedded tales of Winifred's childhood? Did Lavinia ever exist, or were these accounts simply an elaborate enticement to cruelty? Answers to these questions do not come easily. Where cruelty seems to animate the narrative, possible configurations of details seem to multiply, and their significance shifts depending on how we parse the various layers of the narrative.

Although the narrator of "La furia" is an adult, like the narrator of "La casa," he addresses a narratee outside of the immediate action but still inside the textual world. In this case, however, the relationship between narrator and addressee is less clear; his audience is identified in the narrator's asides only as "Octavio." For example, when he claims to have fallen in love with Winifred upon her recitation of an Alexandrine verse, he notes, "Octavio, me enseñaste métrica" ("Octavio, you taught me meter," 114). Elsewhere he notes parenthetically, and still more disturbingly, "Recordé tus consejos, Octavio, no hay que ser tímido para conquistar a una mujer" ("I remembered your advice, Octavio, that you can't be timid if you want to conquer a woman," 115). The remark recalls the child narrator's references to his teacher's instruction and advice in "La casa de los relojes." Were it not for Octavio's lessons, the speaker suggests, he would not have become involved with Winifred. Once again, the narrative finds its ostensible motivation in the illustration of a student's faithful attention to his teacher's lessons and, by extension, an implicit attribution (by the reader, at least) of some responsibility to the teacher.

Ascertaining the place of Octavio as narratee is further complicated by the fact that the story is preceded by a dedication, "Para mi amigo Octavio" ("For my friend Octavio," 113). Should this be taken to establish the narrator as not merely speaking to Octavio but instead directing a written story to him, placing the narrator and the implied author much closer together than we typically would imagine? Or is the dedication Ocampo's, to *her* friend? Octavio Paz dedicated his 1947 poem "Arcos" to Silvina Ocampo; perhaps here—a decade later—she returns the favor. Whereas Ocampo makes no appearance in "Arcos," Octavio emerges as a discreet but important presence in "La furia," with the speaker addressing him repeatedly during the course of the narration. The typographical similarity between the dedication and the asides, all of which appear in parentheses, suggests that the function of "dedication" might also be doubled in the remarks within the story. By dedicating his actions to Octavio and marking them as consequences of his instructions, the speaker appears to transfer, or attempt to transfer, responsibility to his purported mentor. Like the teacher in "La casa de los relojes," this speaker's addressee becomes vulnerable to contamination via narrative.

The story's title seems to link Winifred to the Furies, the relentless, cronelike avengers of mythology. Responsibility seeps outward from the *told* to the *telling*, from the *telling* to our *reading*, diffusing steadily away from the author and proliferating potential contamination. Ocampo's stories highlight the capacity of narrative to implicate us. The resolutely flat surface of her fiction provides a stage for the dramatization of a reality of reading usually tucked discreetly out of view. As readers, we are not merely beholders of a narrative performance; we direct and *perform* our reading. Although a story precedes our reading of it, only our apprehension can activate its capacity to pursue, distress, and bedevil, or delight, entertain, and move.

REFUSING THE READER'S INNOCENCE

Ocampo's stories often seem to neutrally accept any action, any scene, any plot, any character, no matter how grotesque or potentially disturbing, treating all equally, as the ordinary furniture of fiction. The notion that her fiction plays out the "final consequences" of a given scenario has become commonplace among scholars studying her work, who repeat the phrase in myriad contexts to equally varied ends.[37] What motivates these invocations of extremity is an attempt to account for the intense discomfort Ocampo's stories sometimes

---

37. Although what critics see Ocampo carrying to extremes varies, references to "final consequences" abound in readings of her fiction. Martínez Cabrera writes that Ocampo's aesthetic carries Quiroga's narrative strategy of using commonplaces in bad faith "hasta sus últimas consecuencias" ("to its final consequences"), a judgment that echoes Molloy's earlier assessment. See Martínez Cabrera, "Silvina Ocampo," 136; and Molloy, "Simplicidad inquietante," 248. Balderston writes that Ocampo questions "el énfasis en lo fantástico" by "llevándolo a sus últimas consecuencias" ("the emphasis on the fantastic" by "carrying it to its final consequences"). Mónica Zapata asserts that "on détecte dans certains récits une application rigoureuse de la loi jusqu'à ses conséquences ultimes" ("one detects in certain stories a rigorous application of the law all the way to its final consequences"). See Balderston, "Los cuentos crueles," 743; and Zapata, "Rire," 16. For Díaz, the quest for experience in Ocampo is "llevado a sus límites" ("carried to its limits"). See Díaz, "Como el agua," 95.

arouse. But they aren't accurate. As the stories discussed in this chapter illustrate, most often it is not Ocampo, not the implied author, and not the narrator who takes things to "extremes" or to the "final consequences." It is we the readers who are enticed to elaborate imaginatively the horrors that lead to an extreme outcome.

In "El goce y la penitencia" (Pleasure and penitence), the narrator makes a now-familiar move, directing our attention to the possibility of tragedy. After locking her son in the attic of an artist's studio to facilitate her affair with the artist, she ruminates on alarming scenarios: "No se habrá suicidado . . . Podría tirarse por la ventana . . . puede comer pintura. Es un niño violento" ("He won't have killed himself . . . He could throw himself out the window . . . he might eat paint. He's a violent child," 213). Although nothing tragic occurs on this first occasion, as the trysts and the attic detentions recur, these possibly ruinous ends accumulate. The scenarios have the potential energy of a boulder poised at the edge of a precipice, but no definite harm occurs on the page of the story. Instead of pushing the boulder off the ledge and determining its disastrous path, Ocampo often guides us to the surface of the rock and directs our gaze to all that it might destroy as it falls. At other times, as in "El vestido de terciopelo," she seems to position her readers at the base of the cliff, where we apprehend destruction but cannot discern, with certainty, the cause of the disaster we see around us.

It is the bread and butter of fiction writers to spark imaginative amplification in readers, but Ocampo's stories render that participation problematic. Ocampo herself insisted on describing the reader as a "collaborator," with all the dubious implications of that term. Once we begin to elaborate the sinister possibilities between the lines of a story, we may find ourselves in the position of co-authors of cruelty. As Rosario Castellanos diagnoses, the effect creates an unexpected abyss within the quotidian habit of reading, a reckoning with the fact that reading is not an innocent act.[38] Instead, it renders us vulnerable to contamination.

Denying the reader's innocence is a key aspect of the *defensive* method that characterizes Ocampo's deformative fiction. She does not merely deflect intrusive practices but actively *works* on readers. The stories generate uncomfortable feelings of responsibility, which are made all the more vexing by the uncertainty of for whom or for what we are responsible. The texture of this experience becomes more palpable with increased exposure to the stories. As we progress through *La furia y otros cuentos,* we learn to expect a disrupted and disturbing narrative reality, despite titles that suggest the innocuous simplicity of items in a household inventory: "El cuaderno" (The notebook), "Los

---

38. Castellanos, *Mujer que sabe latín*, 150.

objetos" (The objects), "La propiedad" (The property), "Carta perdida en un cajón" (Letter lost in a drawer), "Voz en el teléfono" (Voice on the telephone), and "El vestido de terciopelo" (The velvet dress). Dresses, notebooks, telephones, photographs, portraits, toys, magazines, and other objects appear repeatedly across the stories in *La furia,* as if Ocampo were a theater stage manager showily reusing all the same props across productions rather than particularizing them for each new set.[39] There is a feeling of recognition as a familiar object reappears, reminding us of our earlier experience with it in another story. Connections and associations seem to accumulate meaning. By the end of our reading, we feel we *ought* to understand what objects signify throughout the collection, but we still do not.

Similarly, the expectation of cruelty—and cruelty enacted in ways that spill out across various narrative levels—becomes more salient with every exposure to Ocampo's fiction. So does our awareness of her uses of ambiguity, affective flattening, and disruptions of mimetic illusions. As we attune our palate to Ocampo's signature ingredients, we notice them even when they are less prominent than in other stories. We anticipate (or generate) cruelty as we read, even in instances where it is only faintly suggested.

AN INTERTEXTUAL FINALE

The last story I discuss, "Informe del Cielo y del Infierno" (Report on Heaven and Hell) comes near the end of *La furia*. It thematizes the reader's experience and revives associations from across the collection. Part accusation, part report, part instruction manual, part cautionary tale, "Informe" presents Heaven and Hell as twin warehouses and describes the objects they contain. These items function as part of a strange test that determines one's final destination after death. The unidentified first-person narrator addresses this "report" to an undefined *tú* (you), ostensibly with the purpose of providing advice on how to handle the scenario that will unfold at life's end: "los demonios y los ángeles, parejamente ávidos . . . llegarán disfrazados a tu lecho y, acariciando tu cabeza, te darán a elegir las cosas que preferiste a lo largo de la vida" ("demons and angels, equally eager . . . will arrive in disguise at your bedside and, stroking your head, will give you the choice of the things you preferred throughout your life," 225). The narrator repeatedly warns the addressee to take care in selecting objects in these final moments, since these choices will decide their fate in the afterlife. Initially, the narrator lists

---

39. On the idea that objects and details form a kind of language by way of repetition through Ocampo's works, see Klingenberg, *Fantasies of the Feminine,* 184–206.

household items. Gradually, though, *cosa* ("thing") expands beyond objects to include cities, gardens, mountains, reflections, temperatures, tastes, perfumes, sounds—"toda suerte de sensaciones y de espectáculos [que] nos depara la eternidad" ("every sort of sensation and spectacle [that] eternity offers us," 225).

There is no discernable pattern governing which objects correspond to heaven and which correspond to hell: "Ten cuidado. Conozco personas que por una llave rota o una jaula de mimbre fueron al Infierno y otras que por un papel de diario o una taza de leche, al Cielo" ("Be careful. I know people who, because of a broken key or a wicker cage went to Hell and others who, for a page of the newspaper or a cup of milk, went to Heaven," 226). Even if the hapless person targeted in this situation could crack the code and learn to identify specific objects as "belonging" to heaven or hell, the relationship between objects and destination is also unclear. The report explains, "si eliges más cosas del Infierno que del Cielo, irás tal vez al Cielo; de lo contrario, si eliges más cosas del Cielo que del Infierno, corres el riesgo de ir al Infierno, pues tu amor a las cosas celestiales denotará mera concupiscencia" ("if you choose more things from Hell than from Heaven, perhaps you will go to Heaven; on the other hand, if you choose more things from Heaven than from Hell, you run the risk of going to Hell since your love for heavenly things may signify mere acquisitiveness," 226). An arbitrary, potentially changeable law is in force: choosing more hellish objects *may* lead to a heavenly destination (and vice versa), but there is no guarantee. The report also presents the two destinations in the afterlife as functionally indistinguishable from the outside. The demons and angels move through this world in disguise, and with the same ease; they are described as "equally eager" as they arrive to harvest souls. The narrator urges the narratee to exercise caution, but how is this possible? The report's addressee lacks knowledge of which objects correspond to Heaven or Hell, how choices will be weighed, or what the relative merits of either destination are in this world of reversals.

The narrator further intensifies this dilemma by identifying the addressed "you" as the source of any deformation or ugliness found in exploring the contents of the warehouses:

> Si el viento ruge, *para ti,* como un tigre y la paloma angelical tiene, al mirar, ojos de hiena, si el hombre acicalado que cruza por la calle, está vestido de andrajos lascivos; si la rosa con títulos honoríficos, que te regalan, es un trapo desteñido y menos interesante que un gorrión; si la cara de tu mujer es un leño descascarado y furioso: [la vista de] *tus ojos,* y no Dios, *los creó así.* (225, my emphasis)

If the wind roars, *for you,* like a tiger and if the angelic dove has, when you look, a hyena's eyes, if the man who crosses the street on his bicycle is wearing indecent rags; if the rose with honorific titles, which they gave to you, is a faded cloth less interesting than a sparrow; if your wife's face is an angry stick stripped bare: (the vision of) *your eyes,* and not God, *made them this way.* (my emphasis)

Although deformation often appears in elements internal to the narrative world—grotesque scenarios, unsavory characters, moral reversals—here the speaker names us (or the narratee) as the *source* of the very deformity we perceive. We presume that the characteristics we observe inhere in the objects before us, but "Informe" suggests that our *ways of seeing* (and sensing more broadly) determine what we discern. As readers, we are constitutionally incapable of apprehending objects with any neutrality, but the speaker will not accept that as an excuse. Our perceptions and affective impositions are *our* business; any hostility or cruelty we attribute to objects is our own projection of something within us. I think of John Ruskin's famous illustration of the pathetic fallacy in a line of poetry that refers to "The cruel, crawling foam" of an ocean.[40] As Ruskin curtly observes, "The foam is not cruel, neither does it crawl."[41] One can similarly imagine the narrator of the "Informe" insisting, "the wind does not roar," or the implied author adding, "the *word* is not cruel, nor does it threaten." We can extend the speaker's assertion in light of Ocampo's deliberate emphasis on superficiality and her view of words as objects.[42] In doing so, we arrive at the signature defense found in her deformative fiction: her ability to create a sense of distressing responsibility in us as readers. Ocampo guides us back repeatedly to the uncomfortable impression that our readings reveal more about us than they do about the stories or their author. Once we stop reading, we may protest that Ocampo wrote the stories, not us, but the fact remains that Ocampo effectively contaminates us with *feelings* of responsibility.

CONCLUSION: DEFORMATION AS DEFENSE AND CATALYST TO DIALOGIC ENGAGEMENT

Silvina Ocampo's short fiction awakens a desire for a plausible narrative world but often instead confronts us with the hard edges of her characters, and her

---

40. Ruskin, "Of the Pathetic Fallacy," 205.
41. Ruskin, "Of the Pathetic Fallacy," 205.
42. Ulla, *Encuentros,* 78–79.

stories. She flouts expectations of psychological depth, choosing flatness as a defense against affective intrusions. Readers of Ocampo may feel like the narrator in "Voz en el teléfono" (Voice on the telephone), disappointed to discover cardboard horses and little plastic automobiles instead of "real" things. One could argue that this is always the case, that the mimetic claims of literature are always only ever approximate. Yet the great majority of authors respond to this fact by using their talent to inflate the value of their currency. Their words conjure up visions and feelings, histories and possible worlds that engage our minds as if they were as real as our own. Ocampo resists the notion that readers are somehow entitled to these illusions. Her stories withhold the imaginative access that makes us feel like we are in a familiar world populated by characters with hearts and minds we recognize. For readers accustomed to using narratives as prostheses for feeling, these deformations may feel like a cruel deprivation, a refusal to provide the experiences and feelings that "belong" to fiction. Ocampo refuses to bring the mimetic component of her fiction in line with readers' expectations and calls us back, instead, to the synthetic character of the text.

The foregrounding of textuality may delight when we encounter it in a modernist experimental text, but it vexes and distresses in Ocampo's fiction. The challenge of her deformative project resides in what it implies for the experience of reading, most evident in the problematic scenarios or possibilities of the stories. A desire to *know* intensifies the expectation that engagements with cruelty will open some crucial insight or make the way for desired forms of feeling. Instead, the disconcerting effects of Ocampo's stylistic and narrative choices accumulate and compound one another across the body of her work. Going beyond the uncomfortable feelings of responsibility for the outcomes of specific stories, Ocampo pushes rhetorical readers to recognize the more global responsibility that legitimately accompanies reading: we are not mere observers of literature but rather are participants in creating a textual experience. Like the addressees of "Informe," "La furia," and "La casa de los relojes," we are exposed to the fury of narrative, a presence that contaminates by making us the authors of our own unease. Ocampo's stories haunt readers in part because they make us accountable for a textual world that differs fundamentally from what we might choose for ourselves. The consistent signature of her deformative fiction is to insist on our responsibility even as she curtails the interpretive possibilities available to us. Ocampo's most powerful defensive move is to ensure that any visions of cruelty we think are the author's turn out, instead, to be our own.

•

My hope has been to articulate, across these readings, a case for the distinctiveness of Ocampo's deformative project without downplaying the vexations of reading her stories. Ocampo's fiction merits attention, not in spite of how it disappoints readers' expectations, but precisely because of these defensive measures. Although often unsatisfying if read according to expectations of a "good" woman writer, Ocampo's deformative fiction functions as a check against our impositions. It is a defense that demands recognition of the autonomy of both author and text, their mattering beyond what their contemporaries (or we) wish to make of them.

My examination of Ocampo's deformative project does not settle the "why" of her engagement with cruelty. There *are* reasons for cruelty in her work. She uses cruelty in part to resist expectations of women writers, making a point about the society in which she lived and the literary culture in which she wrote. Relatedly, cruelty in her stories is foundational to a defensive project, one that seeks to protect her writing from readerly impositions and intrusions. These reasons feel insufficient to the cruelty in the stories. They do not allow us to feel satisfied or provide any resolution. When assessing the significance of this experience, we should remember that cruelty is, by definition, excessive. The absence of a satisfying "why" is part of what makes cruelty what it is. This is not a shortcoming of Ocampo's writing but rather an element of how fictional cruelty often works, especially in the deformative projects I examine.

What makes these deformative fictions worth our attention? A decade ago, I felt this was the wrong question to ask—it seemed to me that such a question bespoke impatience with difference if it inconveniences us. With each passing year, though, I have become more inclined to pause my reading of a novel than resent it. But not without asking *why* I want to stop reading. I still aspire to approach strange works, especially those that initially repel or distress me, with curiosity. I remind myself that I have taught students who are initially appalled at being asked to read a particular work, and that I have watched as they came to embrace the reading experience, if not the text, after a sustained struggle or determined encounter (as in the seminar paper). I am one such student, and I often teach the very works that vexed me on first encounter. Deformative fictions may offer few delights, but one of them is that we gain retrospective insight on our reading experience and expand our capacity to find value in even its displeasures. That our altered perspective is hard-won increases its meaningfulness and salience to future reading.

Beyond their nonconformity with the norms of well-made fiction or the qualities expected from a Latin American woman writer, Ocampo's stories reveal and heighten the challenges that are always present, but often obscured, when we read. Ocampo's stories often succeed because of what they are *not*—and because they establish a relationship, through readers, to these disavowed alternatives. Deformative fictions rely on expectations based on readers' more typical narrative experiences. They essentially "talk back" to those works. And just as deformative fictions rely on our previous reading, their peculiar and obstinate qualities have significance beyond the duration of readers' direct engagement with them. Reading deformative fictions returns rhetorical readers to more typical texts with increased awareness of how, and how often, we are accommodated, given emotional access, cushioned by comfortable mimetic effects. Rhetorical readers may become a bit quicker to recall that these are effects among many possible effects, not inherent rights in reading.

If Ocampo rebuffs readers' advances, she also teaches us to notice our appetite for access to character interiority or emotional connection. Certainly, other authors may encourage these appetites and frame narrative experiences to satisfy them. But perhaps we will approach narrative occasions for feeling more cautiously, with greater awareness of the possibility of projection or imposition. Ocampo's deformative fiction offers a unique perspective, particularly on aspects of ourselves and our reading encounters that we might prefer to leave unexamined. In many ways, her intervention becomes more valuable in the face of our reluctance.

CHAPTER 3

Vallejo

Cruelty as Assault and the Entrapment of Readers

If fictional cruelty were a firearm, Ocampo's weapon would be a discreet pistol buried beneath the everyday contents of a handbag. In Fernando Vallejo's fiction, cruelty is on dramatic display, like an automatic weapon in an "open carry" rally. His 1994 novel *La virgen de los sicarios* (*Our Lady of the Assassins*) offers a paradigm of *assaultive* deformative fiction.[1] Eschewing subtlety in favor of more forceful measures to assert dominance, assaultive deformative fictions like Vallejo's novel go beyond arousing readers' discomfort. They create a persistent feeling of being under attack, or of being vulnerable to harm at any moment. In contrast to generalized aggression, assault is aimed *at* someone or something. Assaultive deformative fictions target certain readers, entrapping them in a reading encounter replete with peril and threat. These readers' values come under attack, as do their understandings of the terms of narrative encounter and interpretation. Because you are reading these pages, you likely fit the profile of the readers Vallejo intends to assail with *La virgen*: liberal humanists, critics, scholars, and students, especially those reading from beyond Latin America.[2] This chapter examines how Vallejo conducts a

---

1. Vallejo, *La virgen de los sicarios* (hereafter cited in text as V); Vallejo, *Our Lady of the Assassins*, trans. Paul Hammond (hereafter cited in text as H). Any amendments or changes to the Hammond translation are noted.

2. This characterization is not meant to attribute any virtue to the targeted audience but rather to signal which conventions and assumptions Vallejo seems to target most directly. The deformations of Vallejo's fiction likely distress other readers, with different professions or orientations as well.

multiphase, layered assault on these readers. Vallejo makes some narrative incursions openly, as with the narrator's disturbing diatribes. Other dimensions of his attack are more subtle. It takes cunning, after all, to marshal an offensive without triggering readers' retreat and disengagement. *La virgen* hijacks targeted readers' tendencies and interpretive strategies for use against them to prolong their exposure to the narrator's—and the author's—disturbing ideologies.

La virgen takes place in 1990s Medellín, Colombia, a city that the novel's problematic narrator (also called Fernando) characterizes as "la capital del odio" ("the capital of hate"; V11, H5). The narrative unfolds amid the chaos and violence of heightened drug trafficking, and it focuses on Fernando's parasitic romances with *sicarios,* teen assassins who roam the city. Unmoored from organized crime after the death of a high-profile drug lord, these young men kill casually and without provocation. Fernando temporarily escapes his irrelevance and vulnerability as an aging scholar and gay man through the vicarious potency he gains in the company of his *sicario* lovers—at least until they, too, are murdered. Throughout the novel, the narrator witnesses killings with delight, details his predatory relationships with the *sicarios,* and actively recruits readers as onlookers and accomplices. The events of the novel provide ample occasion for the narrator to circulate his insecurities, fantasies, and ridicule in a stream of relentless invective.

Abrasiveness and assault characterize Vallejo's fiction in general, but they are especially prominent in *La virgen*. The novel is his best known and most internationally circulated work, and its prominence and dissemination in many languages owe much to the success of the film adaptation in 2000, directed by Barbet Schroeder from Vallejo's screenplay. *La virgen* provides a ready example of the literary conversion of local poverty and violence into what Luz Horne and Daniel Noemi Voionmaa call a "spectacle of marginality," one ready for international export.[3] The commodification of suffering in the service of readers' horrified fascination has become one trademark of Colombian and Latin American fiction, particularly as it is read outside the region. At least superficially, *La virgen* may fulfill the expectations of some international readers, namely, those who anticipate violence in Latin American literature and approach the novel as a bloody dispatch from a global periphery.

Murder and predation in Medellín are not, however, the primary source of the novel's deformative assaults on targeted readers. Whereas the *told* in *La virgen* tracks with expectations of hyperviolence, the *telling* vibrates with hostile, even abusive, energy that assails many readers' sensibilities. As I show

---

3. Horne and Voionmaa, "Notes," 38.

in the pages ahead, Vallejo targets liberal humanists, but he simultaneously addresses an audience of like-minded conspirators who delight both in the narrative devaluing of certain Colombians and in the abuse of targeted readers. This tactic of *rhetorical passing* is a cornerstone of Vallejo's approach, and it interweaves many strategies for assaulting targeted readers. I outline those here and address them in detail in the pages ahead. (1) The narrator celebrates the *sicarios*' ruthless murders of ordinary Colombians and weaves a web of hateful diatribe around them. (2) Direct address, narrative positioning, and rhetorical appeals recruit readers to the stance of fascinated onlookers of violence. (3) Readers must weather the narrator's relentless dehumanizing discourse, which attacks the *sicarios*' victims and the *sicarios* themselves. (4) The narrator manipulates language, grammar, and narration to simultaneously (and contradictorily) take credit for violence, refuse responsibility for violence, and demand sympathy. (5) These qualities of the narration encourage targeted readers to misinterpret Fernando as an unreliable narrator, and to presume, mistakenly, the author's disapproval of his attitudes and actions. (6) The narration reveals, by the novel's end, that the narrator's toxic ideologies are not contained by fiction but rather reflect the author's publicly held views. The result is the humiliating revelation to targeted readers that they have been duped into persisting in their reading—or even of being accomplices to this toxic project.

The first strategy becomes evident almost immediately, as readers contend with the scenes of murder that appear by the dozens across the novel's pages, interspersed with harangues about whatever catches the narrator's attention or triggers a memory. Consider one instance of the narrator's delight in the havoc one of his young "angels" wreaks:

> Entonces el ángel disparó. El mimo se tambaleó un instante antes de caer, de desplomarse con su máscara inexpresiva pintarrajeada de blanco: chorreando desde su puta frente la bala le tiñó de rojo el blanco de su puta cara. Cuando cayó el muñeco, uno de los del corrillo en voz baja, que creyó anónima, comentó: 'Eh, qué desgracia, aquí ya no dejan ni trabajar a los pobres.' Fue lo último que comentó porque lo oyó el ángel, y de un tiro en la boca lo calló. Per aeternitatis aeternitatem. El terror se apoderó de todos. Cobarde, reverente, el corrillo bajó los ojos para no ver al Ángel Exterminador porque bien sentían y entendían que verlo era condena de muerte porque lo quedaban conociendo. Alexis y yo seguimos por entre la calle estática. (V77)

> Then the angel fired. The mime tottered a moment before falling, doing a pratfall with his inexpressive mask daubed in white: trickling down from his

fucking forehead, the shot stained the white of his fucking face red. When the stiff went down, one of the crowd commented in a low voice that he took to be anonymous, 'Huh, it's too much, now they don't even let the poor work around here.' It was the last comment he ever made because the angel heard him and shut him up with a bullet in the mouth. *Per aeternitatis aeternitatem.* Fear took hold. Cowardly, reverent, the crowd lowered its eyes so as not to see the Exterminating Angel because they knew for sure that seeing him was a death sentence, since they'd be able to recognise him. Alexis and I continued down the motionless street. (H69, translation modified)[4]

Fernando represents the mime's lifeless body as a puppet or plaything of death through his incorporation of the *sicario* slang for "corpse" (*muñeco,* which also means "doll"), and he luxuriates in the reversal of the performer's former agility. Here and across *La virgen,* the narrator adopts the role of giddy onlooker, relating to murder as if it were a carnival game designed for his satisfaction. His breathless narration discounts any significance to these deaths beyond the momentary delight they provide to him, and he reduces other Colombians to extras, props, or backdrops for his escapades, both in the streets and in the elaborate contortions of the narration through which he performs his power and shores up his insecurities.

The novel's outward-focused narration shifts between depictions of the narrator cruising through Medellín with the *sicarios* and accounts of their more intimate interactions. Many pages turn inward, however, to focus on Fernando's personal grievances and claims to suffering. These include suicidal and homicidal reveries, the injustice of his birth, his incapacitating affection for animals, and other facets of his tortured psyche. Framed within the novel as the writer of the text we read, Fernando flaunts the pen to amplify his privileges; he layers grievance, sentimentality, and self-preoccupation to create a thick rhetorical filter that colors his every anecdote and aside.

These textual features place *La virgen* in a long tradition of first-person, voice-driven fictional narratives anchored in the evocation of a disturbed psyche. This literary genealogy includes the aggrieved antihero of Dostoevsky's *Notes from Underground* (1864), the aggressive but intermittently compassionate Ferdinand in Céline's *Voyage au bout de la nuit* (*Journey to the End of the*

---

4. Hammond mistranslates "estática" ("static") as "ecstatic," which in Spanish would be "extática." Here, the point is that the crowd on the street is unmoving, frozen with fear. I take care to amend the translation wherever possible and to highlight the particularity of the language in Spanish. In an interview with Francisco Garrido, Vallejo disparaged Hammond's translation: "*La virgen de los sicarios* en inglés está muy mal. Es una traducción horrorosa, deformada" ("*La virgen de los sicarios* in English is very bad. It is a horrifying, deformed translation"). Garrido, "La sinceridad."

Night, 1932), and of course Humbert Humbert of Nabokov's *Lolita* (1955). The Latin American tradition offers the capricious narrator of Machado de Assis's *Dom Casmurro* (1899); the solitary and oppositional diarist in José Asunción Silva's *De sobremesa* (*After-Dinner Conversation: The Diary of a Decadent*, 1925); and the bitter, suicidal speaker of José María Arguedas's *El zorro de arriba y el zorro de abajo* (*The Fox from Up Above and the Fox from Down Below*, 1971).

Works with problematic narrators tend to disrupt readers' default approach to fiction. In general, readers presume the ideological continuity (although not identity) of actual author, implied author, and narrator. We may picture the narrator nested inside the implied author, who is in turn nested inside the flesh-and-blood person of the author. Narrators illuminate our understanding of the implied author, who in turn is a partial version of the writer whom we discern from the text. All of this seems quite ordinary in most of our fiction reading, but it creates challenges when we face a narrator like Fernando. In cases of such unreliable narrators, seasoned readers tend to activate a contrasting strategy: we presume *dis*continuity between narrator and implied author, and their respective values.

When approaching *La virgen de los sicarios* in the context of this tradition, trained readers may assume that the implied author's agenda differs substantially from the narrator's, and with good reason. Consider how this plays out in Nabokov's *Lolita*. Whereas the narrator Humbert Humbert rationalizes his sexually predatory behavior, readers find reason to deduce an implied author who contemplates him as a vexing, if fascinating, instance of moral monstrosity. The novel's ending bears out this difference by presenting the evidence that Humbert has destroyed Lolita's life and demonstrating his recognition, as narrator, of this fact. The distinction between unreliable narrator and implied author allows readers to take in Humbert's tale, and even appreciate the artistry with which Nabokov evokes his perversion and charm. For most readers, aesthetic appreciation becomes much more accessible when they believe the implied author shares their negative assessment of a problem narrator.

Vallejo anticipates this approach for interpreting problematic narrators and primes targeted readers to overgeneralize Fernando's unreliability and to imagine, mistakenly, an implied author who shares their disapproval of the narrator. At the same time, he ensures that the novel resonates positively with an audience of readers who appreciate and share the racism, classism, misogyny, and other toxic ideologies that he circulates (and espouses). This conspiratorial audience recognizes and enjoys the ideological continuity between the author Vallejo and the narrator Fernando, as well as targeted readers' failure to recognize it. Rhetorical passing doubles the novel's audiences, creating distinct and overlapping lines of communication between author and readers.

In addition to inducing targeted readers to prolong their engagement with toxic viewpoints, Vallejo's use of rhetorical passing adds additional sites and sources of cruelty in and beyond the narrative. These threads of cruelty tangle and overlap, but I want to lay them out systematically here. I consider them as they pertain to the narrative, to each of Vallejo's main audiences (targeted and conspiratorial readers), and to rhetorical readers. In the *told*, cruelty appears in the representation of 1990s hyperviolence and the narrator's actions, including his interpersonal predation and callous abandonment of his lovers. The narrator's *telling* of these events enacts a further cruelty. His monologues metastasize into diatribes that amplify his indifference to anyone's suffering but his own. On the level of *writing*, cruelty in Vallejo's nonfiction discourses (which present views comparable to those of his narrator) extends through Fernando's speech. Vallejo hybridizes diatribe and fiction, effectively hijacking the practices of "good" close reading of fiction to increase targeted readers' exposure to his dehumanizing stances. Vallejo's deformative assault seeks to entrap targeted readers and make a spectacle of them for a conspiratorial audience.

Cruelty in *reading*, for this conspiratorial audience, is twofold. First, these readers take pleasure in seeing their hatred of certain groups openly espoused and enacted in fiction (e.g., when the *sicarios* murder poor women and their "brats").[5] They also delight in imagining targeted readers' distress, their manipulation by the implied author, and their failure to recognize that Fernando's views are also Vallejo's. This conspiratorial audience essentially amplifies the cruelty of the author's writing, extending it into the extratextual dimensions of the reading encounter.

Targeted readers are, as the name suggests, the focus of this cruelty, but they also may be vulnerable to the outward creep of cruelty. Even as they seek to distance themselves from the narrator's cruel stances, he repeatedly recruits them as onlookers to delight in the suffering. A sense of unwilling exposure to these positions may leave these readers feeling contaminated with cruelty, not just victimized by it.

---

5. As with other discussions of "readers" across the pages of this book, I am hypothesizing here, fleshing out what I believe Vallejo constructs as his audience based on textual particulars. It is certainly the case, however, that there are numerous Vallejo apologists among reviewers and literary critics. Defenders in the academy tend to focus on his stylistic virtuosity, or to interpret his extreme stances as ironic or parodic. Online reviews, YouTube comments, and fan pages offer more direct appreciations of "Maestro Vallejo" and his stances. Gonzalo Maier persuasively accounts for the delight of racist, nonecological, and other conspiratorial readers of Vallejo. "Dogs Don't Vote," 352.

What about cruelty in rhetorical readers' encounters with the novel? For my purposes in this chapter, I think of rhetorical readers as an especially well-informed and supported subset of Vallejo's targeted audience. That is, I assume that rhetorical readers reject the dehumanizing stances of the narrator and author and are likely to be positioned in many of the ways that impact the target audience. But unlike most targeted readers—including me, on my first reading of *La virgen*—rhetorical readers have the benefit of knowing from the outset that Fernando's extreme positions are not a tactical exaggeration but rather reflect Vallejo's stances. Rhetorical readers also have the advantage of additional resources for analysis and modes of provisional engagement with various positions in the narrative. They may be better able to track and reflect on the dynamics of the text without losing track of their agency and ability to reject or detach themselves from positions that are problematic.

The deformative quality of the novel has two main sources for rhetorical readers: the unsettling experience of recognizing Vallejo's rhetorical passing and the challenge of coming to terms with the alignment between Fernando's deeply objectionable stances and those of the implied Vallejo. We find ourselves particularly taxed in the ways that *La virgen* multiplies cruelty in the extratextual realm of the ethics of *writing* and *reading*. There is a core tension between tracking the processes by which *La virgen* accomplishes its deformative effects and withholding our participation in their more distressing implications.

Especially once put on notice about these varied sources of assault, some readers may conclude that the extremes of Vallejo's narrative project render it irredeemable, or at least unworthy of their sincere attention. Although it is certainly reasonable to refuse to read on these grounds, doing so merely bypasses the ethical challenges of assaultive deformative fictions. It also cedes the opportunity for insight we might gain from navigating them. For all their abrasiveness, works like *La virgen* show us something unique about the complex workings of narrative and the ways that textual effects relate to the extratextual concerns of authors and readers. A rhetorical approach to narrative sheds light on the various relationships that *La virgen* establishes between those who tell—the narrator, the implied author, and the writer as "flesh-and-blood person"—and those who receive that telling.

Is this enough compensation for enduring the extremes of *La virgen*? There may indeed be a limit to how far deformation may go before its harms exceed the possibilities it offers. Yet I think we should be wary of a calculus of "worth" or "pay off" when it comes to reading difficult texts, and to consider not only the qualities of the text but the experience of reading it and the altered view we gain on the far side of that reading. Reading *La virgen* carefully—with care for readers as well as care for the text—sheds light on the darker uses of narrative, including how authors of assaultive deformative fictions prey on their targets' vulnerabilities and what choices readers have in response.

DIATRIBE IN THE GUISE OF FICTION: HIJACKING TARGETED READERS' EXPECTATIONS

Rhetorical readers of this chapter come to *La virgen* with the knowledge that it recirculates, in a fictional space, much of the content and ferocity of Vallejo's nonfiction writing and public speaking.[6] Across genres, Vallejo writes with the avowed intent to "molestar a los tartufos" ("get under the skin of hypocrites") and "desenmascarar impostores" ("unmask imposters")—a rhetorical purpose he pursues in his targeting of liberal readers in *La virgen*.[7] His favored topics include overpopulation, forced sterilization and abortion, Colombian political incompetence, lawlessness and disorder, religious hypocrisy, the blight of unauthorized settlements on the outskirts of Medellín, grammar and linguistics, and animal rights.[8] Those following Vallejo's career, or moving in the cultural spaces where his provocative public presence is well known, recognize the proximity between the stances in his nonfiction and those espoused by his fictional narrators. For international readers, especially those confronting the novel in translation, access to Vallejo's nonfiction or biographical and secondary materials is far less likely. In English and many other languages, *La virgen* is the only book by Vallejo to be translated. Limited knowledge of context and other writing by Vallejo still influences the novel's reception today and were even more significant factors in the 1990s, before access to the internet was ubiquitous. The greater readers' distance from information about the Colombian context and the author, the more vulnerable they are to mistaking Vallejo's assaultive deployment of diatribe for a textual effect with a less pernicious explanation.

Diatribe shares many of the rhetorical valences of complaint, which expresses discontent persistently and with significant emotional charge in

---

6. For a representative collection of essays, speeches, and other nonfiction writings, see Vallejo, *Peroratas*.

7. Villena Garrido, *Las máscaras del muerto*, 30.

8. Even this last topic, which initially suggests an affirmative stance, becomes in Vallejo's handling an occasion for provocation. As Maier notes, rather than call for "legislation that attends to a dignified life" for all beings, Vallejo demands "a transposition that takes rights from humans and grants them to wild and domestic animals." Maier, "Dogs Don't Vote," 349.

relation to the grievance.⁹ Diatribe adds animosity toward the recipient of the discourse. Neither primarily rational nor focused on cogency of argument, diatribe relies on the speaker's privilege and sense of entitlement as its justification. Mikhail Bakhtin notes that diatribe addresses an "absent interlocutor,"[10] one whom the speaker imagines must listen even if the discourse is contradictory and lacking in intellectual merit. Diatribe presumes a total claim on listeners (and readers), without any reciprocity, a presumption that characterizes Fernando's narration in *La virgen* as well as Vallejo's public speaking and nonfiction.[11]

Hume describes a range of possible addressees of complaint: (1) *the already converted,* an audience that shares the speaker's views; (2) *the convertible,* those who may be persuaded; and (3) *the intransigently resistant.*[12] Speakers typically direct complaint at the converted or the convertible—at those whom they imagine to be sympathetic to their frustrations. Diatribe, by contrast, presumes an audience that is completely resistant to the speaker's stance. This imagined opposition provides a justification for intensified invective and forcefulness. Diatribe is complaint turned assaultive, a relentless articulation of discontent blasted at a captive reader or listener. In the case of *La virgen,* Vallejo directs diatribe *at* targeted readers while imagining this attack as a performance *for* a conspiratorial audience that agrees with him and approvingly witnesses the harassment of despised humanist readers. (More on this to come in the next section's discussion of rhetorical passing.)

Although this is not an attractive face of literature, it is a recognizable one. But how does Vallejo retain readers who disagree for the duration of *La virgen*? Why do we stay for a novel that announces its project of stirring up vexation and unease almost immediately, then maintains a relentless assault? One answer is that diatribe becomes something else, or at least functions differently and is assessed differently, when deployed within narrative. This difference deepens further when the diatribe in question unfolds in a fictional narrator's voice. The affordances of narrative (as opposed to essay) and fiction (as opposed to nonfiction) shape the options available for readers to interpret Fernando's telling.

Narrative (Story) versus Essay (Argument). For a writer seeking to maximize the range and density of targets for his diatribe, narrative brings practical advantages. These become more evident in contrast to writing in a journalistic

---

9. Hume, *Aggressive Fictions,* 44.
10. Bakhtin, *Problems,* 154.
11. For an illustration of Vallejo's signature nonresponsiveness to interlocutors, see Oliveros Cordoba, "Fernando Vallejo."
12. Hume, *Aggressive Fictions,* 73.

mode, which is met with expectations of focus, logic, and organization, as well as argument (however extreme or faulty). An argumentative essay cues the expectations of order and persuasiveness. There is a limit to the number of topic "switches" or diverging harangues possible before the writing loses coherence. By contrast, a story typically progresses through events, with plot as the organizing principle. (Even a nonlinear account prompts mental reconstruction in chronological order.) Unlike an argument, narratives pair the time of in-the-chair reading with a simulated experience of the passage of story time. They often chart movement through various spaces of the narrative world and track the varied actions of characters.

The temporal and spatial mobility of fictional narrative expands the number of catalysts for diatribe, as we see in *La virgen*. A statue of a politician brings on a litany of state failures. A church visit catalyzes a rant against ecclesiastical corruption and hypocrisy. A glimpse of an attractive young assassin unleashes a critique of the naming practices and (in the narrator's view, pathetic) aspirations of the poor. In choosing a narrative rather than essayistic vehicle for diatribe in *La virgen,* Vallejo gains the rhetorical license to plant as many occasions for vexation as he can squeeze into the novel's scenes and monologues. The *where* and *how* and *when* of these catalysts depend on a further distinction between fictional and nonfictional narrative.

Narrative Modes: Fiction versus Nonfiction. Whereas the range of nonfiction narrative is limited to the particulars of fact, fiction offers the advantage of intensification through invention. When Fernando describes climbing to a lookout point with one of his young lovers, the view's highlight is not the skyline or a fine sunset but rather a corpse-littered hillside, complete with an ineffectual sign: "SE PROHIBE ARROJAR CADAVERES" ("THE DUMPING OF BODIES IS FORBIDDEN"; V53, H47). Fernando describes the gratifying sight of a buzzard unraveling and tugging at intestines "como un niño travieso . . . jalándole la cuerda a un payasito de cuerda" ("like a naughty child . . . tugging the string of a little marionette"; V53, H47). Here, a grizzly setting facilitates the narrator's giddily abrasive narration and delight in suffering.

Practices for Reading Fiction. Our general approach to fiction differs in important ways from the ways we read nonfiction and/or nonnarrative writing. In assessing an essay, for example, we may be quicker to judge the positions asserted, weigh their merits, and dismiss those that come up short. As a reader of nonfiction, I would likely reject the "insights" and discount the credibility of a writer who focuses his sympathies on vultures, with no expression of concern for the human victims on whom they feed. An unfavorable assessment of arguments in nonfiction may prompt a reader to abandon the essay. When reading fiction, however, logical incoherence, dubious argumentation, and departures from normative ethics in a character's narration are factors that lead to a different judgment: that the narrator is unreliable.[13] Once we find a narrator lacking and unreliable, we expend less energy judging the credibility of their specific claims. Our attention goes instead to evaluating the effectiveness of the implied author's *use* of this unreliability to achieve narrative goals. And because the narrator enunciates the text we read, everything in it becomes a potential illustration, or complication, of unreliability. Bakhtin reads the entirety of Dostoevsky's *Notes from Underground* as a diatribe, treating even dramatized scenes as imagined extensions of the narrator's vitriol.[14] Diatribe registers, not as a departure from the story, but as an organic part of it. To think of abrasive narration as serving a purpose (here, deepened characterization of an unreliable narrator) may buffer afflictive scenes and expressive modes, at least during an initial reading. When assuming unreliability, we typically concede continued engagement apart from the merits of the narrator's positions, alignment with our own moral sensibilities, or the degree to which we are persuaded by the credibility of their views.

Anticipation of readers' strategies for handling unreliability plays a particularly important role in Vallejo's circulation of diatribe in *La virgen,* and in his deformative project more broadly. Faye Halpern summarizes the default interpretive process for handling unreliability this way: we "find clues in the text that guide us to infer the presence of an implied author who does not hold the same values or behavioral norms as the narrator. In the implied author's indirect communication with us, we realize that we hold the same values, thus bringing us closer to each other and farther from the unreliable narrator."[15] A critical point here is that readers—who have their own values, knowledge, and practices of interpretation—are the ones who construct a hypothesis about the implied author from the features of the text. Any understanding of the implied author's norms still depends on readers' inferences and judgments.[16] We often have good reason to imagine implied authors who share our values.

---

13. For my purposes in discussing *La virgen,* the narrator is reliable *to the implied author* if there is a general continuity between the expected norms and behaviors of implied author and narrator. The narrator is reliable *to readers* if there is a general continuity between these readers' norms and values and the narrator's. I see unreliability *to the implied author* as a narrator's negative divergence from the norms of the implied author. By "negative," I mean that the narrator is marked as having fewer good qualities (or a given good quality is present to a lesser degree) and/or as having more flaws (or flaws that are expressed more extremely) than the implied author. Unreliability *to a reader* entails a narrator's negative divergence from the reader's norms.

14. Bakhtin, *Problems,* 154.

15. Halpern, "Charles Chesnutt," 53.

16. Shen, "Unreliability."

A sense of alliance with the implied author, *against* the narrator, offers a firewall to protect ourselves from the blaze of the inflammatory attitudes and views circulated in the text. Readers may be forgiven for imagining this sort of protection in *La virgen*, as those unfamiliar with Vallejo's reputation often do. Because they are working with the available information, these readings are not "wrong," so much as incomplete. But they do fall short of capturing the deformative complexity of the interplay between author, textual resources, and audiences in *La virgen*.

RHETORICAL PASSING: UNCERTAIN NARRATIVE TERRAIN

Vallejo's hijacking of fiction in the service of diatribe fits into a broader strategy of selective deception that Peter Rabinowitz calls *rhetorical passing*.[17] To achieve this effect, authors organize the narrative resources of the text to misguide one audience while endeavoring for another audience to recognize their intentions, including the programmed deception of targeted readers. This tactic produces markedly divergent readings of the same text, rooted in contrasting understandings of its implied author and their purposes. In some ways, rhetorical passing represents an extreme expression of Piglia's "two stories" hypothesis. After all, readers of the same text may, and often do, end up imagining very different relationships between its two stories. Rhetorical passing initiates more dramatic deviations from the typical spectrum of author–text–reader dynamics, however. Because the same text addresses itself differently to two (or more) distinct audiences, the usual dynamic of orchestrating the covert and overt content of the narrative is more than doubled.[18] Further, there are important consequences to the fact that one audience recognizes that the other has been misled by the passing into accepting a mistaken reading. This produces a hierarchy of readings, both in terms of how closely they reflect authorial intent, and in terms of relative bonding with the implied author.

A closer look at critics' discussions of three instances of rhetorical passing provides a comparative framework for Vallejo's approach. Rabinowitz coined the term in his reading of Nella Larsen's *Passing* (1929), which probes the impact of color lines and racial dissembling in two women's lives. In Rabinowitz's analysis, the novel also tells the story of lesbian attraction that "passes" for friendship in the eyes of other characters—and in the assessment of many of Larsen's contemporary readers, who would have been scandalized by her

---

17. Rabinowitz, "Betraying the Sender."
18. For a comprehensive treatment of covert and overt progressions, see Shen, *Style and Rhetoric*.

exploration of queer desire had they recognized it. Members of the "discerning" audience recognize both stories of passing—and take pleasure in their superiority over the "gullible" readers who do not.[19] In Larsen's novel, recognizing the multiple *passings* adds to rhetorical readers' understanding of the narrative world and the characters' experiences within it. After sharing in Rabinowitz's analysis of rhetorical passing, we hear the characters' words, and feel the space between them, differently.

In other cases, rhetorical passing plays out primarily in terms of multiple possible conceptions of the implied author and their relationship to the narrative's events and dynamics. For example, the Black fiction writer Charles Chesnutt navigated complex post-Reconstruction racial politics in part by choosing a white Northerner as the narrator for his stories. This led (and may still lead) some readers to presume that the flesh-and-blood author was white, and that the white narrator reflected the implied author's views and dispositions. By contrast, readers aware of Chesnutt's race likely saw the narrator less generously, disapproving of his presumptuous obliviousness to the complexities and injustices of racialized social spaces in the South. As Halpern explains in an analysis of the "The Goophered Grapevine" (1887), these differences lead to starkly contrasting understandings of the narrator and the implied

---

19. Rabinowitz, "Betraying the Sender," 203. For my reading of Vallejo, I prefer "targeted" over "gullible" and "conspiratorial" over "discerning." In addition to opting for terms that reflect the more hostile nature of Vallejo's passing, I refrain from calling these audiences "authorial," as Rabinowitz does. I don't presume to know about what adjustments are called for when speaking about authorial audience in relation to rhetorical passing more broadly, but it seems to me that, although the targeted and conspiratorial audiences are anticipated and intended, it is not quite right to call them "authorial." The case against describing the targeted (or "gullible") audience as authorial is that, by definition, readers in this position fall short of "perfect" understanding of authorial intentions. The novel is no more "for" targeted readers than Fernando's narration is "for" tourists. The implied author's discourse comes *at* the targeted audience but is *for* the conspiratorial audience. If this is the case, why not describe the conspiratorial audience as "authorial"? Although this audience reads in ways that align much more closely with the implied author's goals, can conspiratorial readers appreciate *their* role in Vallejo's broader project? The strongest argument against seeing this as the authorial audience is that the audience serves a *function* in that project (amplifying cruelty by delighting in the targeted audience's humiliation).

I share Phelan's view that "authorial audiences and actual audiences can rarely, if ever, be fully and definitively distinguished" (*Somebody Telling Somebody Else*, 115). Still, if I were pressed to characterize the authorial audience, I would suggest that it consists of a single reader perfectly positioned for appreciation of the implied author's skillful maneuvering of *all* the named audiences: Vallejo himself. To enter the authorial audience means to become as much like Vallejo as possible, attempting to embody the particulars of his sexuality, personal history, and education; his knowledge of and prejudices about Colombia; his preoccupation with language and grammar; his passion for animal rights; his hatred of women, disgust at reproduction, and scorn for the Catholic church and all religion.

author by each audience. In one, the narrator's "equivocal unreliability" as a teller of tall tales "masked Chesnutt's racial critique for post-Reconstruction white readers, who loved realist literature but hated acknowledging their racial prejudice."[20] In the other, readers who welcomed a racial critique imagined an implied author who shared their jaundiced view of the white narrator's actions and conclusions. Even readers among the second group who might have preferred a more direct approach likely also recognized that Chesnutt's reasons for passing included the possibility of being widely read in the first place.

Although an expedient strategy for racially minoritized writers like Larsen and Chesnutt, rhetorical passing also may serve more troubling agendas. Dan Shen's analysis of "La Belle Zoraïde" (1894) by Kate Chopin examines the co-presence of a "feminist and anti-racist overt plot development for an anti-racist authorial audience" alongside "a covert progression mythologizing the relationship between slaves and owners for an authorial audience who is nostalgic for slavery."[21] Shen provides important biographical information on Chopin: her father owned enslaved people, her brother fought for the Confederacy, her husband was a member of the racist White League, and she fiercely opposed Emancipation.

In the analysis of rhetorical passing, consulting contextual information may illuminate how authors and readers imagine the other position.[22] Authors use what they know, or presume, about potential readers as they shape their narratives. To understand those choices, it helps to ask, as Rabinowitz does, "what sort of *corrupted* reader this particular author wrote for: what were that reader's beliefs, engagements, commitments, prejudices, and stampedings of pity and terror?"[23] Particularizing factors include life experiences, identities (e.g., race, ethnicity, nationality, gender, sexuality, class), professional training and literary knowledge, and sociohistorical positioning.

These factors also influence how readers imagine authors, especially when discerning the textual norms and rhetorical purposes of the implied author from the text. Accurate information about authors may serve readers "as a source of inspiration for certain interpretations and an ethical check on others," as Halpern notes.[24] Narratologists emphasize the text as the source of readers' inferences and judgments about the implied author, but discussions

---

20. Halpern, "Charles Chesnutt," 53.
21. Shen, "Dual Narrative Progression."
22. For a discussion of the "feedback loop" among these different positions, and how ideas about the other positions influence narrative choices, see Phelan, *Somebody Telling Somebody Else*, 6.
23. Rabinowitz, *Before Reading*, 26.
24. Halpern, "Charles Chesnutt," 60.

of rhetorical passing highlight the need for attention to biography as well.[25] Given the ways that rhetorical passing multiplies pitfalls for readers, this information holds significant implications for our understanding of how each progression in the text resonates with, or clashes against, the author's views and stances, what Phelan calls "public, textualized intentions."[26]

To be clear, textual details may indeed imply an author who is a better, more principled, version of the flesh-and-blood author. We may even discern, as Booth suggests, an expression of the author's "best self."[27] A person who beats their dog and ridicules their partner nevertheless might mine a vein of empathy in writing, handling the delicacy of human relationships with a tenderness that implies a much more compassionate author. But plausibility depends on there being indications of these qualities in the text, and on the existence of some degree of compatibility with the writer's own asserted intentions and public stances. Unfortunately, there is neither textual detail nor biographical information about Vallejo to support any conception of the implied author in *La virgen* as a "highly moral" avatar sandwiched between a flesh-and-blood author and narrator who each express similarly toxic views. Nevertheless, readers unaware of Vallejo's public positions are especially vulnerable to being duped by rhetorical passing into presuming a gap between the values of the implied author and the narrator.

One five-star Amazon review of *La virgen* by a US-based reader bears the title, "The *Lolita* of the Andes," and credits Vallejo with doing "with Spanish what Nabokov did with English."[28] The review describes Fernando as being "as unreliable a narrator as Humbert Humbert." For the reviewer, both Humbert and Fernando illustrate moral extremes, including "untruthful narrations, youth mercilessly exploited, and the terrible consequences of sexual monomania and spiritual emptiness masked by sophistry." So far so good, but trouble arises in that the reviewer imagines the respective authors of *Lolita* and *La virgen* engaging in an equally emphatic rejection of their narrators' actions and attitudes that enables them to "speak to powerful truths about the human condition." This review illustrates our readiness, when a text creates ethical challenges in the *told* and the *telling,* to imagine an implied author who shares our dismay.

Both in imagining this reviewer's reading and in considering other readers as they first encounter *La virgen,* it is important to remember how fragile the ground appears when we begin to speak of authorial intention, how flimsy

---

25. Shen, *Style and Rhetoric,* 19.
26. Phelan, *Somebody Telling Somebody Else,* 203.
27. Booth, "Resurrection of the Implied Author," 79.
28. Ruiz, "*Lolita* of the Andes."

and inelegant what we say seems in comparison to what might be said about the *narrator's* intentions. Since the narrator is the source of the narrative, examining their unreliability puts us in touch with information that we can relate rather immediately to the narrator's character. Of course, all the information that pertains to narratorial intention also pertains to authorial intention. There is significantly more room for misconstruing the data for authorial intention, however, because it consists almost entirely of indirect indicators. Without context or the supplementation of biographical information, we are more likely to misconnect the dots as the reader of *La virgen* as a "*Lolita* of the Andes" did, construing a thumbs up where a middle finger would be more apt.

NAVIGATING *LA VIRGEN*'S MULTIPLE AUDIENCES

In examples of rhetorical passing that involve a character narrator, as in the case of Chesnutt's stories and Vallejo's novels, biographical information alters how readers imagine the relationship between the implied author and the narrator. For Chesnutt's targeted readers the vital occluded information was that Chesnutt's narrator was *not* a likely expression of the author's views. In the case of Vallejo, the distressing surprise is that Fernando *is*. This creates a cascade of interpretive implications, especially for how we understand the novel's audiences.

1. *The naïve audience* assumes continuity between Vallejo and his narrator. They focus on resemblances that are discernable from as little as the biographical blurb on the back cover. Same name (Fernando), same nationality (Colombian), same profession (writer and grammarian), same avowed ethical commitment (animal rights), same sexual orientation (gay). Further, the tendency to read world literature as a window into the unfamiliar encourages presumptions of documentary or testimonial orientations. The result is a strengthening of the presumption that Fernando reliably reflects his author's general outlook and values. This is a common assumption with respect to the narrator of a memoir or autobiographical novel. (When my students read Ocean Vuong's novel *On Earth We're Briefly Gorgeous*, for example, they track the themes of Vuong's poetry and essays straight into the novel and have to be reminded that the narrator is similar to, but not identical to, the author.) We may further divide the naïve audience based on readers' responses to the idea of Vallejo and Fernando's ideological proximity: (a) readers who share some of these views and/or find the narrator's and author's refusal to pander to liberal beliefs refreshing, and (b) readers repelled by this prospect, who may read under protest or toss the book aside. Because I am interested in how readers

experience rhetorical passing in the context of an assaultive narrative, for the most part, I leave the naïve audience aside.

2. *The targeted audience* is made up of readers—many of them invested professionally in teaching, reading, or writing literature—who tend by default to bracket literary texts from the author's biography. When Nabokov published *Lolita* in 1955, he included the novel's fictional foreword, from the point of view of a psychologist whose framing flags the novel as a cautionary tale. By the time of *La virgen*'s publication in 1994, Vallejo could reasonably rely on readers to locate his novel within the literary tradition of books like *Lolita*. This tradition invites "knowing" readers to separate problem narrator from author. As they adopt what they imagine to be a more sophisticated approach to Fernando's aversive narration, they may experience a sense of superiority to the naïve audience that does not. As conscientious close readers, members of the targeted audience may focus on reading the text well and avoiding a moralizing stance. In targeting this audience, Vallejo counts on their likelihood to give primacy to the text and to postpone any attention to author biography. He also anticipates their recourse to strategies for interpreting unreliability without implicating the author in the narrator's views.

Most important for Vallejo's deformative project is for these targeted readers to imagine, counterfactually, a wide gap between the moral/ethical outlook of the narrator and that of the author. Vallejo's ultimate rhetorical goal seems to be for targeted readers to experience, eventually, a demoralizing discovery: just when they thought they were being "good" readers, they were already entrapped in Vallejo's arena of assault. If targeted readers learn, after reading, of the continuity between the narrator's ideologies and the author's, then they face the humiliation of having been hoodwinked. And if they persist in imagining that the narrator's unreliability envelopes his attitudes and prejudices, then Vallejo has the satisfaction of taking this as a proof of the effectiveness of his con. Perhaps either is a win within the deformative frame of assault.

The wide international circulation of the novel after the success of the film adaptation also increases the likelihood that many targeted readers remain in the dark about the alignment between Vallejo's views and his narrator's. *La virgen* has been translated into Czech, English, French, German, Italian, Hebrew, Polish, Portuguese, and Slovenian. A handful of Vallejo's other works also have been translated into some of these languages over the years, but *La virgen* is the only novel by Vallejo available in English. Access to his complete literary output is limited to those with knowledge of Spanish. Even readers encountering the novel in Spanish often come to it from a significant geographic and linguistic remove from the contexts where Vallejo's extreme views are well known. As someone whose first readings of the novel put her in this last category, I confess that I initially interpreted the abrasive extremes of Fernando's narration as a deliberate exaggeration of toxic attitudes in the service of critique. Surely, I thought, the depiction of Fernando's predatory behavior must be a sustained, ironic treatment of the homophobic pathologizing of queer desire. (The fact that one can come to these conclusions, even provisionally, says something; unintentional self-parody is one reading of the novel.)

3. *The conspiratorial audience* appreciates Fernando's extreme stances and understands that Fernando does not depart substantively from Vallejo's own views.[29] Its readers recognize that those coming to the novel without knowledge of Vallejo's biography and public statements are likely to assume a gap between Vallejo and his narrator and to mistakenly read irony into every facet of the novel. As Vallejo's conspirators, they enjoy a sense of superiority over the duped close readers who do not realize Fernando has hijacked their reading practices to pass his diatribes off as fiction. Perhaps most importantly for Vallejo, this audience recognizes and appreciates his skill as the author who cleverly arranges a multiphase assault on targeted readers and garners his targets' willing cooperation.

As this initial analysis of the audiences created by rhetorical passing suggests, the strategy multiplies the challenges of interpretation. It may especially bewilder or derail readers who lack a clear sense of the audiences involved or who do not have access to sufficient context for parsing the author's likely motives. A solid hypothesis for the general mechanism of rhetorical passing at work in a text can help stabilize interpretation, at least at the level of the text as a whole. It provides a frame for how different audiences experience the same textual elements, and it opens up consideration of how, and why, the author produces this effect.

But considerable challenges persist. It is no small task to track the lines of communication between the text and these audiences, to engage with the distinctive possibilities that each creates, and to consider the interrelations and the counterpoints or tensions between them. We also need to weigh the presence of multiple tellers in the novel, each with potentially different dispositions and goals, including the flesh-and-blood author, the implied author, and the narrator. Organizing these positions as they pertain to *La virgen* might look something like this: (1) Vallejo's (2) implied author creates the (3) narrator Fernando and organizes his (4) description of his affairs with young *sicarios*. The goal seems to be to get (5) targeted readers to focus on Fernando's unreliability and to overgeneralize it to include the ethical/evaluative axis,

---

29. This is the position Rabinowitz describes as "discerning," but given the ways that the target audience of Vallejo's novel *imagines* itself as discerning, I've adjusted the characterizations to fit my case.

not just the axes of reporting and interpreting. Meanwhile (6) conspiratorial readers recognize his views as continuous with Vallejo's *and* see that targeted readers are fooled into thinking otherwise. (7) Rhetorical readers try to keep all of this in view as they analyze the text.

Describing the relationships and intentions embedded in rhetorical passing involves a layered and cognitively taxing feat of "mind-reading" (theorizing the mental states of others).[30] Sustaining this degree of meta-representation may produce an experience of interpretive vertigo. And as Lisa Zunshine notes, uncertainty or ambiguity in relationship to the motives, attitude, or goals in any layer does not remain in that layer. It may shift, or complicate, how we understand other layers, or the whole work. As we try to track the complications of rhetorical passing that ripple through all aspects of the novel, the whole interpretation, and interpretive process, may begin to seem especially speculative.[31] Certainly, the analysis of any work of fiction involves making hypotheses about authorial intention that cannot be proven definitively. But rhetorical passing multiplies the lines of communication about which we might hypothesize. In the case of *La virgen*, this generates uncertainty regarding how Vallejo intends a given phrase or passage to resonate with a given audience, or how he imagines that respective audiences might assess the interpretive activity of other audiences (as in the case of the conspiratorial audience "watching" the targeted audience).

Untangling these relationships becomes even more daunting if we seek to play out their implications in close reading. But careful and conscious exploration of the processes that unfold in the narration, including rhetorical passing, is key to anticipating and interpreting the novel's assaults without being entrapped to the degree that Vallejo intends. To accomplish this, we may begin by considering how a passage likely works for the targeted audience, who incorrectly presumes a gap between Fernando as an unreliable narrator and Vallejo as a disapproving author. We may then consider how the passage resonates for the conspiratorial audience, as well as how this audience relates to the misunderstanding of the targeted audience. And lastly, we may take note of the possibilities open to the rhetorical reader for negotiating between these two readings.

Let's consider a representative passage to see how fiction widens the space of expression for Vallejo's toxic diatribes and how rhetorical passing complicates its reception. Shortly before his *sicario* companion kills a nursing mother

---

30. Lisa Zunshine notes that most people's ability to manage embedded intentionality declines dramatically beyond four levels of mind-reading. Zunshine, *Why We Read Fiction*, 29.

31. For a discussion of the cascading effects and cognitive strain of increased meta-representation in narrative, see Zunshine, *Why We Read Fiction*, 131.

and her two children on a bus, Fernando describes them "en pleno libertinaje: uno, de teta, en su más enfurecido berrinche, cagado sensu stricto de la ira. Y el hermanito brincando, manoteando, jodiendo" ("in flagrante delicto: one on the tit, beside itself with rage, literally shitting itself with anger. And the little brother jumping up and down, banging into people, getting on their nerves"; V116, H109). His disgust quickly veers into diatribe:

> ¿Y la mamá? Ella en la luna, como si nada, poniendo cara de Mona Lisa la delincuente, la desgraciada, convencida de que la maternidad es sagrada, en vez de aterrizar a meter en cintura a sus dos engendros. ¿No se les hace demasiada desconsideración para con el resto de los pasajeros, una verdadera falta de caridad cristiana? (V116)

> And the mother? With her head in the clouds as though nothing was happening, a Mona Lisa smile on her lips, the reprobate, the wretch, convinced that motherhood is sacred, instead of coming down to earth to get her two little freaks under control. An excessive inconsiderateness towards the other passengers, a genuine lack of human charity, wouldn't you say? (H109, translation modified)

Here, as throughout Fernando's narration, complaint quickly escalates into diatribe, and diatribe translates into murder. First, he sees the mother as unacceptably distracted, then delinquent, then disgraceful ("en la luna . . . la delincuente, la desgraciada"; "head in the clouds . . . the reprobate, the wretch"). His indignation reduces the children to less-than-human "engendros" ("freaks" or "spawn"). The transition to murder begins with "¡Tas! ¡Tas! ¡Tas!" (V117, H110), the Spanish equivalent of "Bang! Bang! Bang!" This ostensibly playful onomatopoeia jarringly echoes cartoons, comic books, and playacted violence. The perverse invocation of child's play continues with the diminutives "angelitos" ("little angels") and "corazoncitos" ("little hearts"; V117, H110). Singsong language describes the bullets as if they were cupcakes being doled out at a party: "Una por la mamá, y dos para sus dos redrojos. Una pepita para la mamá en su corazón de madre, y dos para sus angelitos en sus corazoncitos tiernos" ("One for the ma, and two for her two brats. A slug for ma in her motherly heart, and two for her sweet little angels in their tender little hearts"; V117, H110, translation modified).

Targeted readers may imagine authorial critique of Fernando's extreme views in their literalization here. They may trace the speaker's tactics of intensification, such as how he names the bullets' destination twice, rhetorically amplifying his delight in these deaths. They may notice, and resist, Fernando's attempt to solicit their agreement with his dehumanizing assessment of the mother ("¿No se les hace?"; "wouldn't you say?"). They likely experience the uncomfortable tension between the aesthetic appeal of the passage's coarse poetry and the moral distress of its content. By contrast, conspiratorial readers may receive the passage with delight, recognizing the similarity between Fernando's diatribe and Vallejo's published critiques of heterosexual reproduction and overpopulation. The passage offers them a thrilling literalization of racist, classist, and misogynistic impulses, turning private prejudice into (imagined) action. Certain aspects of the passage may hold special resonance with these readers, such as the perverse parallel Fernando forges between murder and impregnation. The word "pepita," which Hammond translates as "slug," also means "seed," so in Fernando's telling, the bullet is a seed planted violently in the bloody soil of the mother's heart.[32] This figure injects another dose of misogyny and antinatalism into the carnage-drenched scene. For the conspiratorial audience, an additional layer of pleasure comes from imagining the targeted audience's queasy response to the celebration of murder. From the vantage point of these readers, the narrative inflicts the "truth" of certain Colombians' inferiority on targeted readers, like the strong philosophers whom Nietzsche imagined "tak[ing] the vivisector's knife to the breast of the very virtues of their age."[33] There is a further satisfaction, for Vallejo's conspirators, at the thought that targeted readers participate, through their reading, in the assault against their liberal values. The conspiratorial audience essentially amplifies and extends Vallejo and Fernando's hatred of the poor and of the hypocritical humanists (targeted readers) who pretend to care about them.

Here, and in reading *La virgen* more broadly, one task of the rhetorical reader is to track these responses and their implications, provisionally identifying with either audience for the purposes of better understanding their experience of the text. For example, although we do not hold the hateful views of the conspiratorial audience, we benefit from considering what reading would be like if we did. And although we do know of Vallejo's similarly abrasive public stances, we better understand the experience of the targeted audience, if we take the time to imagine the experience of lacking this perspective. This allows us to consider what happens for readers whose access

---

32. Joset explores the connection between an anti-reproductive stance and a consistent rejection of the mother figure in the works of Céline and Vallejo (50–51), noting that, in his more autobiographical novels, Vallejo consistently "kills off" his mother, representing her as already deceased well before her factual death (116). Joset, *La muerte*, 50–51, 116. For additional points of comparison and an enumeration of instances of rage against the pregnant in Vallejo's other fiction, see González Espitia, *On the Dark Side*, 189.

33. Nietzsche, *Beyond Good and Evil*, 137.

to this knowledge is postponed until after they read the novel, as is likely the case for most in the targeted audience. Rhetorical readers should also consider the degree to which modes of address may instrumentalize these audiences. This is especially clear for the targeted audience, which the author marks for humiliation—a humiliation that the conspiratorial audience enjoys. But the conspiratorial audience has its function as well, ensuring a delighted reception and witness for an anxious and narcissistically insecure narrator (and author). This audience facilitates the performance of power that Vallejo unfolds through his narrator across the pages of *La virgen*.

In the next sections, I trace the core moves in the rhetorical performance that coalesce in Fernando's narration. Although most narrative strategies in the novel persist across its entirety, certain approaches predominate at different points in the narrative arc. These correspond roughly to the first, middle, and last part of the novel. First, the narrator presents himself to readers as a trustworthy peer as a strategy for securing relevance and importance. Next, Fernando "maxes out" his unreliability through a combination of contradictory rhetorical moves. On the one hand, he denies any responsibility for the harm that comes to others, often resorting to grammatical contortions and elaborate devaluations of victims. On the other hand, he inflates the importance of his lovers' actions and presents himself as the driving force behind them. Fernando extends his aggressive devaluations of others in the novel's final movement through his narration of the deaths of his lovers. This *telling* accentuates his willful abandonment and refuses their originality and humanity. He ultimately turns from his interpersonal manipulations and instrumentalization of his young lovers to focus more fully on narration and language as the essential site of his cruelty and power. Targeted readers and conspiratorial readers experience this progression very differently, an effect I will return to throughout the discussion ahead.

THE *LETRADO*'S LAST STAND: CLAIMS TO AUTHORITY AND POSITIONING FOR POWER

As the novel progresses, Vallejo places increasing emphasis on Fernando's unreliability as a teller and interpreter of events. In the novel's earliest pages, however, the narrator makes a wobbly presentation of himself as a trustworthy local informant who can contextualize the degeneration and lawlessness that prevail in the city of Medellín. The novel opens with a deceptively idyllic line that invites readers—conspiratorial and targeted alike—to identify with Fernando's tender memories of an uncorrupted Colombia: "Había en las afueras de Medellín un pueblo silencioso y apacible que se llamaba Sabaneta" ("There was on the outskirts of Medellín a quiet and peaceful village called Sabaneta"; V7, H1). The first lines activate a nostalgic retrospective stance strongly identified with memoir and autobiography, particularly those focused on childhood. For these genres, readers expect narrative consistency and reliability, if not total accuracy. (Hence readers' outrage and feelings of betrayal when a text presented as a memoir is revealed to have been fabricated significantly.)

Indeed, even as we know Fernando is a character narrator, the opening prompts us to receive him as one who possesses authority over his own story and who offers a competent perspective on the events he observes. Memoirists often acknowledge the incompleteness of their memories, but the idea that they attempt to be accurate is an implicit commitment to the reader, one echoed rhetorically in the opening of *La virgen*. It is important to note that this is (only) a *rhetorical* invocation of the memoirist's attempted faithfulness; the appeal to autobiography is held firmly in a fictional frame. Vallejo's novels are often characterized as *autoficción*. Unlike lightly fictionalized memoir, *autoficción* never claims veracity but rather constitutes a deliberate narrative game using imagined autobiography as its point of departure.[34] "Derailment" might be more accurate. Vallejo begins each novel as if he were writing as himself, then lets "Fernando" veer off the rails of autobiographical experience and into new, imagined terrain. The narrator departs from the Vallejo station—hence the ideological alignment—but takes a nonautobiographical itinerary toward his own singular trainwreck. This enables a tactical extension of Vallejo's diatribe into dramatized action. A fictional "Fernando" can fulfill desires—such as directing mass murder—that might land a flesh-and-blood author in prison.

Genre-based invocations of trustworthiness soon transition to direct bids for attention, admiration, and sympathy. Fernando's directly addressed or implied interlocutors shift frequently, but they are always constructed, grammatically, as male (a reflection of the character's often-expressed hatred of women). He lectures to a "turista extranjero" ("foreign tourist"; V45, H38), someone who "no es de aquí" ("isn't from around here"; V101, H94). Conveniently, the listener Fernando has imagined needs his expertise. Fernando styles himself as an authority on local slang and vocabulary: "gonorrea es el insulto máximo en las barriadas de las comunas, y comunas despúes explico que son" ("*Gonorrea* is the biggest insult in the slums of the *comunas*, and I'll explain what the *comunas* are later on"; V13, H8).

---

34. For a fuller discussion of *autoficción*, see Alberca, "¿Existe la autoficción hispanoamericana?," 115–20. See also Murillo, "Introduction," *El río del tiempo,* 10.

Mimicking a tour guide, Fernando also pretends to revoice his tourists' questions, further anchoring his discourse in a rhetorical exchange. In other moments, he mock-confides in his addressee, bringing him into the bedroom to share the "riches" of his late-life encounters with beautiful young lovers (V19, H13). Fernando's third main strategy is to step outside of events and comment on them from a temporal and spatial remove, like a director pausing a film they are editing to explain a scene to an amateur. Rhetorical gestures such as "wouldn't you say?" position readers, momentarily, as if in agreement (V116, H109). These are not serious bids for persuasion, however. In each case of direct address, the intended effect is to force the positional overlap between actual flesh-and-blood readers and the addressees within the frame of the story's action. If Vallejo succeeds, we end up more fully as recipients of Fernando's carnage-laden sightseeing tours, as well as his acerbic asides and bids for sympathy and collusion.

Conspiratorial readers may find Fernando's frankness refreshing; for them, he says the quiet parts aloud, giving voice to racist vexation and class resentment, among other prejudices. Targeted readers may come to recognize Fernando as a brutally selfish lover and obscenely irresponsible citizen. They may resist or even recoil from his conspiratorial asides and his claims to voice their concerns. They may take stock of the circus-like circularity of Fernando's reasoning and his rhetorical gymnastics. But to navigate the novel, readers must occupy the position of narratees and entertain the narrator's perspective to some degree. Still, we almost instinctively seek a position from which we may judge Fernando and mark out our difference from him.

Perhaps anticipating this, Vallejo does not stop at Fernando's direct address to tourists as visitors. He frames Fernando as the author of the text we read, not just the teller of the story through his narrator's direct address to far-flung "readers," who are explicitly styled as international outsiders (e.g., "lectores japóneses y serbocróatas"; "Japanese and Serbo-Croatian readers"; V126, H117). Fernando also refers to "la mesa desde la que les escribo" ("the table I'm writing to you on"; V19, H14) and periodically mentions his writing task. By thematizing direct address to international readers, Vallejo encourages us to contain the narrator–reader exchange in an envelope of fictionality, inviting reasonable, but false, comparison between the diegetic and extradiegetic roles of readers and writers. Since we know we are "not really" like the distant readers mentioned in the novel, it is a small step to presume, similarly, that Vallejo is "not really" like the diegetic writer, Fernando. Vallejo, who is ultimately responsible for the narrative's composition, makes Fernando a self-conscious composer whose narration expresses his character.

The pretense to authorship intertwines with Fernando's bid for authority as the "last grammarian" of Colombia. His self-identification places him in the Latin American tradition of the cultured intellectual or *letrado* (V58, H52). Although Fernando claims this role to enhance his credibility, the *letrado* is a complex, often suspect, figure in Latin American culture and literature, discussed most famously in Ángel Rama's La ciudad letrada (*The Lettered City*).[35] Rama traces the relationship between writing, institutional power, and the Latin American city from the colonial era through the twentieth century, focusing on how educated urban elites functioned as unscrupulous custodians of cultural capital. Whereas Rama denounces the mechanics of exploitation that form the dark heart of the lettered empire, Fernando expresses nostalgia for this repressive order and clings to his role as the "last" of its representatives.

In the chaotic, violent world of *La virgen*, the *letrado* is an anachronism. Fernando's Colombia is guided, not by so-called men of letters, but by the transnational movement of capital, weapons, and cocaine. The radical curtailment of the public intellectual's role in Latin America corresponds to the failure of revolutionary movements in the 1960s and 1970s and the subsequent rise of neoliberalism in the 1980s and 1990s.[36] Fernando may insist on his testimonial right as a representative *letrado* and his exceptional status as "the last one," the sole witness who can account for the state's failure and express the crisis of his social class. But no one cares about this act of witnessing, at least not in the Medellín of the novel. Vallejo does not conceal or mitigate this fact. Instead, he cultivates the illusion of character autonomy, leaving Fernando to manage his diminished status through narration, especially his diatribes and claims to expertise.

Through direct address and a pretense to orality, Fernando rhetorically guides his narratee on a sightseeing tour through scenes of carnage. In his invocations of writing, he adopts a different strategy. His writing proposes a sort of literary tourism by which distressing local scenes are delivered to rapt readers half a world away, presumably to satisfy an appetite for raw experiences from the margins of modernity. Although they depend on incompatible pretenses, both approaches seek to address Fernando's urgent need to construct narratees whose attention he can captivate—or capture—with performances of power and efficacy.

Many of Fernando's narrative decisions reveal themselves as desperate bids for continued relevance in the face of his diminished status. Fernando

---

35. Rama, *La ciudad letrada*. See also Franco, *Decline and Fall*.

36. These "failures" were all but predetermined by US efforts to strengthen dictatorships and authoritarian regimes that revolutionaries sought to oppose.

acknowledges that, before his relationships with the *sicarios,* no one listened to him. Gonzalo Maier characterizes the defeated but defiant voice that speaks across Vallejo's writings in this way: "this 'final grammarian,' this man who symbolically maintains reason's torch, is abandoned in a world where he has no one with whom to communicate in those terms—nor any way to do so."[37] To circumvent his local irrelevance, at first Fernando imagines addressing international cultural elites who appreciate his expertise and delight in his giddy evocations of harm. He exchanges the *letrado*'s traditionally measured, if morally compromised, discourse and moderate liberalism for virulent diatribe and breathless accounts of murder performed for imagined outsiders. Cruelty—here the casual relation of killing—becomes the narrator's currency in circumstances where his other claims to privilege have been thoroughly devalued.

FERNANDO'S "MAXED OUT" UNRELIABILITY

Despite Fernando's initial pretense to trustworthiness and authority, Vallejo maximizes the narrator's unreliability across the three core domains of *reporting* (facts), *interpreting* (explanations), and *evaluating* (ethics). This unreliability appears across the novel, but it ramps up to new levels of intensity in the middle section. Here, I outline examples of Fernando's unreliability in each of the core narratorial functions and trace some of their implications for readers.

Reporting—the depiction of events, persons, locations, and mental states—is the most prominent and straightforward of a narrator's functions. Fernando frequently refers to memory problems, confuses names and timelines, and makes other technical mistakes. An especially consequential example is Fernando's mistaken reporting that a particular group of *sicarios* has been slaughtered by "las balas con que mi niño Alexis los recibió" ("the bullets my baby boy Alexis greeted them with"; V85, H77–78). His error is revealed later when an assassin from this same group of men returns and murders Alexis (V92, H84).

Interpreting is the process by which narrators "read" the events and situations they report. This may include attaching significance to an event or assessing its connection to other factors such as historical or cultural contexts, family histories, character traits, and characters' past experiences. The knowledge that the audience is presumed to have, or lack, may shape the extent or character of these explanations. Fernando purports to offer clarifications to

---

37. Maier, "Dogs Don't Vote," 359.

benefit addressees who are uninitiated into the particulars of life in Medellín. Rhetorical readers question Fernando's characterizations of events and situations in many instances, rightly discerning the influence of his elitism and the egotism of his interpretations.

His most glaring misinterpretations center on his lovers. For example, he claims the singular ability to interpret the *sicarios'* inner motivations and thoughts, often extracting volumes of devotion from a single word or action. Apart from how these assertions stray from most readers' sense of what interpersonal insight he could plausibly possess under the circumstances, Fernando's own reporting undoes the explanation. On multiple occasions he underscores the inaccessibility of the assassins' inner lives, whatever his wish (or pretense) to the contrary. For example, watching the young men in confession during visits to shrines and churches, Fernando fixates on what he cannot know: "¿Qué pedirán? ¿De qué se confesarán? ¡Cuánto daría por saberlo y sus exactas palabras!" ("What would they ask for? What would they confess? I'd give anything to know their confessions, and in their exact words!"; V60, H54, translation modified). The ready availability of more compelling explanations also undermines the credibility of Fernando's interpretations. On the two occasions when Alexis prevents Fernando from committing suicide, the speaker treats his lover's actions as unambiguous signs of loyalty, ignoring the salient possibility that the young man prefers not to lose his meal ticket (V42, H35; V91, H83).

Evaluating reflects the narrator's intellectual judgment and moral or ethical sensibility, as indicated or expressed in the text. Two explicit expressions of cruelty of the *told*—the *sicarios'* apparent indifference to suffering and Fernando's apparent delight in it—lie within the realm of evaluation. Those who view human life as inherently valuable likely feel distress at Fernando's minimization of the moral significance of random killings. But our dismay at Fernando's inverted ethical compass includes less blatant instances as well, as when he accepts his first *sicario* lover as a "gift" from an older man (V11, H5). Fernando claims, "todo lo mío es tuyo, corazón . . . hasta mis papeles de identidad" ("What's mine is yours, baby . . . Even my identity papers"; V18, H13). Despite this assertion, he makes no attempt to provide his lovers with access to resources—education or noncriminal employment, for example—that might improve their circumstances. He hoards knowledge and insight for himself while goading the *sicarios* toward the violence that puts their lives in jeopardy. Far from sharing his "all," he repeats the exploitation from which he claims to rescue them.

•

What are the implications of maxed-out unreliability for readers? Encountering an unreliable narrator often entices readers to persist in the face of stances they find morally abhorrent. (This is not a problem for the conspiratorial audience, of course, since they find satisfaction in Fernando's extreme views.) But the sustainability of this approach typically depends on hypothesizing an implied author who disapproves of the narrator, and this becomes increasingly difficult. If the implied author were to stand alongside readers *against* Fernando, they might find some shelter from the exposure to his toxic ideologies. Vallejo offers no such protection.

Rhetorical readers meet the challenge of navigating Fernando's unreliability with more perspective and resource. Because his modes of distortion vary across the narration, however, we cannot account for it in any complete or final way. Instead, navigating his narration entails continually fashioning new frames to lend coherence to his perspective and its distressing implications. We strain to see as he sees so that we may understand how he narrates as he does. Fernando's reporting reveals a staggering disregard for "facts." As an interpreter of experience, he spins events to serve his ever-changing project of self-aggrandizement. Fernando's evaluative function might be better characterized as a *de*valuative function: he believes that no victims, other than himself, deserve to count.

MANUFACTURED INNOCENCE, INFLATIONS OF EFFICACY, AND DEVALUATION OF VICTIMS

Although we may track and account for Fernando's attitudes without agreeing with them, doing so still brings us close to them. This is part of the assault of Vallejo's novel. Proximity creates a sense of exposure, as if to something toxic. We may manage to avoid handling the uncertain material leaking from a barrel outside the chemical plant, but closeness is enough to make us feel vulnerable to harm. I want to take a closer look at three expressions of Fernando's unreliability and the functions they serve, both for the narrator and for the author behind him.

Manufactured Innocence. If not for the deadly consequences of his untruthfulness, Fernando's many claims to innocence might be comical in their absurdity. They are like a "100% leak-free!" poster tacked to that barrel dripping with toxic muck. His deflections of moral responsibility often hinge on subtle points of grammar and semantics, and they highlight the degree to which persuasion of his addressees is *not* his goal. Rather, by making such flimsy arguments for his innocence, he ultimately underscores his lack of accountability, the degree to which he can get away with murder, both literally and metaphorically.

A favorite strategy of Fernando's is the performative use of *se inocente*. This Spanish grammatical construction is most common in cases that require or invite delicacy regarding agency; it features prominently in culpable children's accounts of accidents and in the resignation announcements of scandal-ridden politicians. Although *se inocente* has no exact English equivalent, a phrase like "el vaso se me quebró" might be rendered along the lines of the Southern vernacular construction "the glass went and broke on me." Rather than attribute responsibility ("I broke the glass"), *se inocente* announces an accident: the glass was broken, and somebody was the victim of that unfortunate event. Avoiding the designation of blame—whether out of diplomacy or self-protection—is at the core of *se inocente*. The undesirable event simply *occurred*, and any person named in relation to it has been afflicted by a circumstance beyond their control.

Consider Fernando's comparison of Colombia to a car that "se nos desbarajustó" (V8). Hammond translates this phrase as "went all over the place," but a better reflection of the tone in the original might be "went to shit on us" (H2).[38] With this use of *se inocente*, Fernando signals that "we" were innocent victims of the disaster that is Colombia. However, he immediately revises his claim by denying not only responsibility but also connection to this disaster: "Mejor dicho, se 'les' desbarajustó a ellos porque a mí no, yo aquí no estaba" ("better said, it went to shit on 'them' because it didn't happen to me, I wasn't here"; V8, H2, translation modified). He "corrects" the initial expression of already limited connection to Colombia's plight to further distance himself and to assert that, because he was not physically present, the nation's deterioration is not his problem. In another case, Fernando begins with the description—"bastó una chispa para que se nos incendiara después Colombia" ("all it took was a spark for Colombia to catch fire on us after that"), then changes it to "se 'les' incendiara" ("for it to catch fire on 'them'"; V9, H3, translation modified). Through distancing language and performative "corrections" to his own speech, Fernando asserts his conflicted and sentimental identification with Colombia, at least in part, to have the opportunity to then disavow that connection more aggressively. Whatever his disgust at the events around him,

---

38. The Hammond translation frequently softens the speaker's rhetoric. For example, in a passage criticizing power-hungry Colombians, the Spanish reads, "les arde el culo por sentarse en el solio de Bolívar a mandar, a robar" (literally, "their asses burn to sit in Bolívar's seat, giving orders, thieving"), but Hammond translates, "They couldn't wait to sit on Bolívar's throne and give the orders, to line their own pockets" (V105, H98).

he insists that they are not *his* tragedy (except, that is, when he wants to paint himself as a victim deserving of sympathy).

In other cases, Fernando turns to grammatical technicalities as the basis for his denials of responsibility. After Alexis kills a noisy neighbor, Fernando insists that he never asked his lover to act: "Jamás le dije a Alexis: 'Quebráme a éste.' Lo que yo dije y ustedes son testigos fue: 'Lo quisiera matar'" ("I never once said to Alexis, 'Waste this guy for me.' What I said, and you are my witnesses, was 'I'd like to kill him'"; V38, H31–32). Unsurprisingly, the subtle distinction between the imperative ("quebráme a éste") and the past subjunctive used to express a counterfactual wish ("lo quisiera matar") is lost on the uneducated *sicario*. This is a reality that a *letrado* like himself surely could anticipate, as Fernando makes plain in his frequent mentions of the *sicarios'* linguistic limitations. But when it serves him, he maintains the distinction between command and wish with legalistic rigidity. He further attempts to conceal his culpability by styling himself as a bewildered observer of Alexis's next killing in his presence. "¿Cuándo sacó Alexis el revólver? Ni alcancé a ver" ("When did Alexis get his revolver out? I didn't manage to see"; V43, H37, translation modified). Fernando's ludicrous implication is that missing the exact moment of the gun's appearance somehow absolves him of complicity.

Wílmar, Fernando's second lover, also kills upon hearing the smallest complaint from his patron. Yet Fernando still pretends to be taken aback by the deadly consequences of his words: "¡Quién me mandó abrir la boca!" ("I should have kept my big mouth shut!"; V114, H107). After multiple instances that prove the pattern, Fernando knows (as do readers) that his words provoke his lovers' actions. Still, Fernando claims an "horrorizada aversión a las armas de fuego" ("horrified loathing for firearms"; V95, H87) and insists that "Ni nadie, nadie, nadie me ha visto hasta ahora disparar" ("And nobody, nobody, nobody has seen me fire one"; V74, H67, translation modified).[39] Further, readers see that Fernando provides the necessary materials for these killings, including ammunition (V42, H36). Fernando's own accounts overwhelmingly contradict his faux-naïve response to *sicario* violence. His persistence, both in triggering killings and in denying his responsibility for them, saturates the narration with cruelty. In this performed refusal of responsibility, Fernando is his own most important spectator.

Inflated Efficacy. Fernando's self-fashioning through narration also depends, contradictorily, on a highly doubtful assessment of the efficacy of his lovers' violent acts. When he describes the murders his lovers commit in

---

39. For a discussion of emphatic assertion as a "tell" of unreliability and a useful discussion of related topics, see Brütsch, "Irony, Retroactivity, and Ambiguity."

his presence, he claims a separate victim for each bullet they fire. For example, he announces, "¡Tas! Un solo tiro, seco, ineluctable, rotundo, que mandó a la gonorrea esa con su ruido a la profundidad de los infiernos" ("Blam! A single shot, dry, ineluctable, rotund, that sent the *gonorrea* and his racket to the depths of hell"; V30, H24). In the same passage, Fernando repeats his insistence that Alexis needs only one bullet to kill: "¡Tas! Un solo tiro, sin comentarios" ("A single shot, without commentary"; V30, H24). And a few pages later: "¡Tas! ¡Tas! ¡Tas! Tres tiros en las puras frentes y tres soldados caídos" ("Blam! Blam! Blam! Three shots in those unsullied brows and three soldiers down"; V43, H37).

These accounts of deadliness lack any basis in Fernando's broader characterization of *sicario* violence. The *sicarios* are not especially accurate in their firing, and there is no mention of his lovers being exceptional marksmen. So how do we read this insistence on a one-to-one relationship between their bullets and the bodies of victims? Such a claim could be seen as a factual error in Fernando's reporting (e.g., he does not accurately track the number of bullets fired) or confusion about the events he sees (e.g., mistaking passersby sprawled on the ground in fearful self-protection for dead bodies). The strongest explanation for Fernando's insistence on the boys' deadliness is wish fulfillment. Fernando's skewed interpretation of events swells his fragile sense of importance.

Despite refusing to accept any responsibility for harm, Fernando seizes the status-enhancing potential of depicting the *sicarios'* violence as an extension of his speech. When Alexis murders a driver after Fernando shouts at him for abusing his horses (V88, H80), Fernando stresses that the killing "me le remarcó lo dicho" ("underlined my discourse"; V87, H80), as if this pronouncement is all that is needed for the efficacy of the *sicarios* to redound to his credit. An even more aggrandized framing emerges as the novel progresses and Fernando begins to attribute cosmic significance to casual murders. Alexis is now "El Ángel Exterminador" ("Exterminating Angel") who carries an "espada de fuego" ("a sword of fire") through the city to "acabar con su raza perversa" ("finish off its perverse race"; V64, H57). Fernando later describes Wílmar as "el enviado de Satanás que había venido para poner orden en este mundo" ("the special envoy of Satan who'd come to create order in this world"; V117, H108, translation modified). These claims do not square with Fernando's own indications that, for the *sicarios*, killing is a casual activity undertaken with little consideration or intention. Instead, his interpretation of the *sicarios'* actions as "sanctioned" or "righteous" is deeply self-serving. If they are angels (or demons) of death in his telling, surely he is that much mightier as the "director" of their violence.

Devaluation of Victims. Overestimation is not the only source of interpretive unreliability and self-aggrandizement in Fernando's treatment of the killings. Even as he inflates his importance by exaggerating the *sicarios'* deadliness, he undertakes a systematic rhetorical degradation of their victims. Often, he describes deaths in passing, as if the murdered persons do not even deserve to count fully as "victims." The grizzly detail, "les están sacando los ojos para una universidad" ("they're taking out their eyes for university research"), serves as a casual segue between the stabbing of an indigent and a visit to a church (V30, H24).

Fernando also conveys his deliberate devaluation of other Colombians' deaths by performatively "forgetting" the murders in the narration of his adventures with his lovers. Although this resembles a failure of reporting, the practice is too ostentatious to be persuasively read as an accident. After he admits to having lost track of Alexis's killings "cuando llegó a los cien" ("when Alexis reached a hundred"; V88, H81), he feigns concern with providing a complete record and makes a point of correcting himself when he "remembers" a murder. Filling in the murders he has elided, Fernando tells us, "Pero volvámonos un momento atrás que se me olvidaron al bajar del taxi dos muertos" ("But let's backtrack a moment because, while getting out of the taxi, two deaths slipped my mind"; V76, H69, translation modified). Fernando interrupts his own account with another "forgotten" incident: "Ay qué memoria la mía, me quedó faltando un cascado más" ("Ah, my memory! I'm forgetting one more hit"; V77, H70, translation modified). Only the shallowest reading could lead to the conclusion that he sincerely wishes to redress his mistakes and oversights.

This *performance* of forgetting and remembering is a tactic. In "correcting" the record, Fernando is like a dishonest shopkeeper who voluntarily remedies a pricing mistake for a cheap item while pulling off a far more costly swindle. Fernando "steals" the significance of the deaths he pretends to forget, denying them any moral weight, or even the status of memorable "event." He reduces them to a perverse display of local color, as if they were minor details accidentally passed over in a tour guide's spiel. This devaluing of deaths highlights narration's function, for Fernando as a character, as a tool for expressing his newly found power and heightened mobility.

The Wages of Unreliability. As readers move toward the end of *La virgen*, it becomes hard to escape the blatant absence of authorial disapproval in response to Fernando's delight in murder, his predatory relationship to the *sicarios,* his toxic ideologies, and his destructive self-absorption. By the time that targeted readers fully recognize the lack of separation between implied author and narrator on moral terms (often because of contextual information), they already may have proceeded far down the path Halpern describes, cozying up with the implied author. The subsequent discovery that they are alone in their disapproval of Fernando alters the experience of imagined closeness to the implied author. Suddenly, sharing an assessment of Fernando's narratorial shortcomings may feel like a liability or trap—much like the uncomfortable coinciding of the narrator's assessment of Winifred, and our own, in Ocampo's "La furia." The implied author in *La virgen* seems to whisper in the targeted reader's ear, "You already share my view of Fernando's inadequacies. But we have more in common than that. Deep down, aren't we the same? Isn't that why you're reading? Be honest with yourself for once!" The implied author serves as a junction between the narrator's pernicious views and Vallejo's, and an amplifier of their distressing force. Rhetorical readers recognize the moves by which Vallejo entraps and humiliates targeted readers. The shelter they thought they had found with the implied author—behind a firewall to separate them from the narrator—turns out to be another site of assault.[40]

In this respect, we see yet another layer of cruelty in the novel's deformative project. Yet rhetorical readers, at least, are not without recourse. One way of countering the cruelty of the narrative is to liberate our attention from the narrator's direction. By sustaining our attention on precisely those moments and instances that Fernando seeks to hurry us past, we reassert our ability to resist the narrator's rhetorical appeals, even as we recognize their effects. This capacity serves rhetorical readers especially well in the last third of the novel, in which Vallejo further intensifies his deformative assaults.

ILLUSIONS OF EMPATHY AND REFUSALS OF ORIGINALITY: DROWNING DOGS AND DISCARDED LOVERS

In contrast to Fernando's early pretense to trustworthiness, or his claims to grandeur and refusals of responsibility in the middle section, the novel's final movement suggests a deliberate exposure of the desperation that underlies his unreliability. It also emphatically depreciates his storytelling abilities. Among other effects, this establishes cover for the author. It is one way for Vallejo to say, "Don't forget, it's that joker Fernando, not me, who wrote the text you read!" When we encounter flaws, quirks, and errors in a novel that purports to be character-narrated (and character-written), we must decide who to assign

---

40. Building on Booth's introduction of the concept of the implied author in *The Rhetoric of Fiction*, Phelan emphasizes that the implied author is *not neutral*. Rather they are a "partisan" of some agenda, which may or may not align with the narrator's. See Phelan, *Living to Tell about It*, 39.

them to, the fictional "author" of the text (Fernando), or the flesh-and-blood author of the novel. As we approach the novel's end, it is as though Vallejo wants to make sure that the credit accrues to him and that any shortcomings stick to Fernando. At the same time, he lets the narrator's unreliability peak in ways that point to an implied author who is unapologetically complicit, as opposed to discreetly disapproving.

This choice makes sense when we consider it in terms of Vallejo's rhetorical passing. Fully displaying the continuity of values and attitudes between author and narrator, and embracing new extremes of cruelty, provides a satisfying culmination for conspiratorial readers. At the same time, having already secured targeted readers' participation for more than a hundred pages, the author can gamble on their willingness to read a few dozen more even as it becomes increasingly clear that neither the novel's events nor the telling of them will offer redemption.

That does not stop targeted readers from looking, however. One passage near the novel's end appears at first to depart from the circuits of cruelty that so characterize Fernando's actions and narration elsewhere. In it, the speaker seems to respond with empathy to an injured dog drowning in an open sewer (V89, H81). As if preparing for the scene, Fernando claims a page before that "los animales son el amor de mi vida, son mi prójimo, no tengo otro, y su sufrimiento es mi sufrimiento" ("animals are the love of my life, they're my fellows, I have no others, and their suffering is my suffering"; V88, H81). The use of "prójimo" also echoes the often-cited New Testament commandment: "ama . . . a tu prójimo como a ti mismo," rendered in English most often as "love your neighbor as yourself" (Luke 10:27).[41] Fernando, like Vallejo, denies any neighborly responsibility to humans, focusing all concern on animals. Whereas he lambasts racial intermixing in the Colombian population (e.g., V104, H97), he nevertheless sympathizes with the dog he describes as "chandoso" ("mongrel" or "mixed-race") and "criollo" ("creole," "mixed-race"—typically used for people; V89, H82). The dog is the only creature in the novel that Fernando characterizes as "innocent" without irony, imagining its "almita limpia y pura" ("clean and pure little soul"; V90, H83). He insists that the "mirada implorante de esos ojos dulces, inocentes, me acompañará mientras viva" ("the imploring look of those gentle, innocent eyes will remain with me for as long as I live"; V90, H83). He cannot discount canine suffering; this sight interrupts his movements and demands a response.

---

41. Fernando's phrasing also closely parallels Vallejo's public comments about animals, including his self-description in the biographical blurb on many of his books.

But this is not Levinas's radical, asymmetrical encounter with an unrecognizable other. To the contrary, Fernando performs the mercy killing *because* he identifies with the dog as his *prójimo*. Since Fernando himself wishes to be "put out of his suffering," this is precisely the form his expression of "love" for his canine neighbor takes. The primal scene of ethics in Levinas's formulation involves the mute appeal of the other's face, "Do not kill me."[42] But, in Fernando's evaluation, the dog's "llamada muda" ("mute cry"; V89, H82) issues the opposite plea: "Kill me, please." In response to the dog's suffering, and as justification for killing it, the speaker highlights the hopelessness and injustice of the situation. The scene's pathos derives not from the ethical weight of Fernando's act, the one killing he openly claims, but from a skillful miming of responsibility to the other. Conveniently, the dog's plight is Fernando's own; the only call he hears is one he already knows how to answer.

Even as redirected egoism enables this approximation of empathy, it is the closest Fernando comes to substantial recognition of ethical obligation. The passage extends, and intensifies, a general pattern of distortion in Fernando's "concerns" (at least from the standpoint of targeted and rhetorical readers). In the novel's early pages, he displays more distress at the eyesore of soccer fields in the *comunas* than the fact of their residents' illiteracy. Later, he rages over too-small napkins provided by a *sancocho* vendor but then sees the vendor's murder as a source of delight. And here, Fernando treats the suffering of a dog as singular and lamentable, like his own suffering, but he refuses to allow his young lovers to "count" as distinct individuals with unique experiences. Fernando demonstrates his capacity for cruelty, not only to the strangers he watches die in the streets of Medellín but also to the young men he purports to love.

Fernando claims to be bereft when Alexis dies in a shoot-out, but his words and actions suggest instead a logic of replaceability. Fernando registers Alexis's murder with a generic euphemism that echoes his description of a taxi driver's death a few pages earlier in the narrative (V91, H84). After Alexis's death, Fernando refers to him only as "the cadaver" and "it." His haste to be rid of the boy's body, which he now treats as waste, hollows out his earlier performance of distress at the "instante atroz de la muerte de Alexis" ("the awful moment of Alexis's death"; V94, H87). Despite claims to grief-stricken delirium, Fernando is lucid enough to abandon the corpse at one of the for-profit private clinics that arouse his fury: "A estos hijos de puta les voy a dejar el cadáver" ("I'm gonna leave those sons of bitches the body"; V93, H86). The scene ends with Fernando dumping the corpse, then slamming the door in the

---

42. Levinas, *Totality and Infinity*, 84.

faces of the clinic employees. The scene reverberates, not with grief, but with vindictive pleasure. Even more damning, he quickly finds another *sicario* lover to serve as a destination for his desires, an object of narration, and a crutch to prop up his sense of worth and importance.

Fernando's interactions with his second lover, Wílmar, repeat the same activities he engaged in with Alexis, albeit at an accelerated pace: buying new clothes, making love, visiting churches, eating out, wandering the city, and killing at will. Fernando's account of Wílmar's first visit to his apartment echoes the earlier scene with Alexis down to the boys' remarks about the absence of a stereo or television, the scapulars around their necks, and the revolvers that fall from their pockets when they undress. The narrator speaks of sex with each boy as something that might inspire envy in the reader, even recurring to the same expressions of faux discretion.[43] Scenes that initially seem to center queer desire—such as the first time Fernando undresses Alexis—appear empty and staged in retrospect once he repeats them with his second lover.

Fernando even pretends to confuse his lovers' names, as when he takes Wílmar to the same church where he had gone with Alexis and muses, "¿de qué le estaría dando gracias Alexis, perdón, Wílmar a la Virgen?" ("What would Alexis, sorry, Wílmar, be giving thanks to the Virgin for?"; V111, H103-4). As with many of Fernando's performed "errors" and "corrections," this occurs on the level of Fernando's written address to an imagined audience, not in any reported speech directed to another character. We must assess it as an intentional narratorial choice. In terms of characterizing Fernando, the move announces, "I'm the sort of person who claims to be passionately in love with a young killer, only to confuse him repeatedly with a previous lover. Yes, the truth is that I see them as interchangeable—and I want you to know that I do."

The deliberateness of Fernando's devaluing repetition is most striking, and assaultive, in his portrayals of the boys in death. He describes Alexis's corpse in this way:

Cuando **mi niño** cayó en la acera me seguía **mirando** desde su **abismo** insondable **con los ojos abiertos. Traté de cerrárselos** pero los párpados se **le volvían a abrir** . . . **Ojos verdes, incomparables** [eran] **los de mi niño**, de un verde milagroso que **no igualarán jamás** ni siquiera las más puras esmeraldas de Colombia. (V92)

---

43. In both cases, he compares his lavish depictions of his lovers' beauty to counting money in front of a poor person. In the second instance, he comments, "vuelvo y repito: no hay que contar plata delante del pobre" ("I say it again: never count your money in front of a poor man"; V109, H102). "Vuelvo y repito" marks his tacit recognition of his repetitions even as he refuses to reflect on their implications.

When **my baby boy** fell to the pavement he carried on **looking** at me from the endless **abyss with his eyes wide open**. I tried to **close them** but the eyelids **opened** again . . . **Incomparably green were my baby boy's eyes**, of a miraculous green that not even the purest emeralds in Colombia . . . **will ever match**. (H85)

Later, he describes Wílmar in glaringly similar terms, without acknowledging any repetition:

Ahí estaba él, Wílmar, **mi niño, el único**. Me acerqué y tenía **los ojos abiertos. No se los pude cerrar por más que quise: volvían a abrírsele** como **mirando** sin mirar, en **la eternidad** . . . **esos ojos verdes** . . . (V138)

There he was, Wílmar, **my baby boy, my one and only**. I drew close and he had **his eyes open. I couldn't close them however hard I tried: they kept opening** as if **staring**, without seeing, into **eternity** . . . **those green eyes** . . . (H130)

In each case, Fernando fixates on the beauty of the boys' green eyes and laments his inability to close them. He uses the term "mi niño," asserts each lover's singularity, and refers to eternity. These parallels highlight the degree to which the two boys have fulfilled, in succession, the same functions in the narrator's affective economy. Fernando relates to them on the same terms—the terms of his extraction of pleasure and consolation.

What does it mean for Fernando to describe *both* of his boys as his "único," his one and only, even as he makes a rhetorical show of their interchangeability? This contradiction implies Fernando's awareness of the rhetorical power of framing himself as a victim. Insisting that he has suffered two irreparable losses, he styles himself as a bereaved lover. Yes, the duplicated descriptions of the dead boys undermine this posture and render it illogical in the context of the larger narrative. But each claim provides a local justification (with currency in the narrative immediately surrounding it) for expressions of self-pity and bids for sympathy. Fernando's explicit emphasis on the act of writing reminds us that, within the frame of the story, these supposedly accidental repetitions are recorded in the pages that lie before him on the table from which he is writing (V19, H13). In other words, they are available for his examination and amendment, yet the *letrado* refuses to correct his own text.

For conspiratorial readers, Fernando's behavior and narration reinforces the notion that people from the *comunas* are hardly people at all. Even as lovers, they are disposable. This ensures the reversal of any worry among conspirators that Fernando has lost track of his class loyalties. For targeted readers (including rhetorical readers), these dynamics likely intensify the distress in response to Fernando's cruelty, our prolonged exposure to that cruelty across the novel, and the growing knowledge that we are alone in any disapproval of it.

The portrait of cruelty in *La virgen* receives its final touches with the events surrounding Wílmar's death. Beyond echoing Fernando's abandonment of Alexis's body to harass the commercial medical establishment, these final pages make plain the degree to which language itself becomes the most important site of cruelty for the narrator. Fernando does not witness Wílmar's murder, apparently learning of the death only when he receives a call from the morgue asking him to identify a body. (His phone number has been found on a scrap of paper in the boy's pocket.) He treats the excursion as a macabre field trip. Unnoticed by others in the morgue and more concerned with exploring than with locating Wílmar's body, he lingers over a report he finds on the desk of a morgue functionary. In the moments where we expect signs of grief, Fernando enthuses over the document as a great prose achievement: "el lenguaje me encantó. La precisión de los términos, la convicción del estilo . . . no hay mejor novela que un sumario" ("I loved the language. The precision of the words, the conviction of the style . . . there's no better novel than a report"; V136, H128, translation modified). His capacity for distraction and delight signals the lack of significance Fernando attributes to Wílmar's death and, by contrast, the importance he attaches to stylistic decisions. As if drawing rhetorical resource from the report, Fernando offers a detached and stylized description of the naked cadavers of young men laid out in rows in the morgue and "rajados en canal como reses" ("sliced open like sides of beef"; V136, H128). The nudity of the teens no longer spurs his desire; now he speaks disdainfully of "el sexo inútil, estúpido, impúdico, incapaz de volver a engendrar, hacer el mal" ("the stupid, immodest, useless penis, now incapable of begetting children, of doing any more evil"; V137, H129). Locating Wílmar's corpse and the report that accompanies it, Fernando dismisses the death as "nada especial" ("nothing special"; V138, H130).

The scene in the morgue also reprises his performative and contradictory refusal of the harm that comes from *sicario* violence. He crosses out his phone number from the paper in Wílmar's pocket, not once but twenty times. Fernando justifies his action as a preventative measure against investigators who might become wrapped up in "siguiendo pistas falsas" ("following false trails"; V138, H130). But if that were his goal, why not simply remove the paper? The gesture of crossing out his phone number, but leaving evidence of the redaction, enacts a signature of Fernando's narration: memorializing the erasure of responsibility. Fernando accompanies this gesture with a second, stranger justification: "si alguien no lo pudo matar ni mandar matar era yo, que lo quería" ("if somebody couldn't have killed him or had him killed it was me, the one who loved him"; V138, H130). This convoluted and strangely worded denial of responsibility reprises Wílmar's earlier announcement that his patron Fernando is the one person he could never kill. But the addition of "ni mandar matar" ("or have him killed") to Fernando's explanation smacks of oblique confession, an overprotestation that potentially marks the very guilt that it purports to occlude. For targeted readers, this is another distressing instance of a rhetorical tell of cruelty and predation. For conspiratorial readers, it is a wink and a nudge that suggests that the narrator has graduated to a more intentional relationship to violence.

A further detail in Fernando's narration holds open the possibility that he has played a role in Wílmar's murder. After Alexis's death, Fernando announces his wish to find and kill the person responsible, known as "La Laguna Azul." He later learns that "La Laguna Azul" is Wílmar's street alias; his new lover is his former lover's murderer. Fernando announces in narration, "ya sabía que tenía que matarlo" ("I knew I had to kill him"; V130, H123) and imagines killing Wílmar but proves unable to do so:

> El revólver, su revólver, lo había puesto, como siempre, sobre su ropa. Eso él. En cuanto a mí, yo simplemente estiraba . . . el brazo, lo tomaba, le ponía sobre su cabeza la almohada y disparaba, y a ver si alcanzaba a oír el tiro su puta madre que lo parió. Después me iría yendo tan tranquilo, con estos mismos pies con los que entré . . . Y yo inmóvil y él durmiendo y así empezaron a correr las horas y el revólver no venía solo hacia mí volando por el aire ni mi brazo se me alargaba a tomarlo. (V133)

> The revolver, his revolver, he'd placed, as always, on top of his clothes. That was his way. As for me, I would simply stretch out my arm . . . take hold of the gun, put the pillow over his face and fire, wondering if the whore who bore him would hear the shot. Afterwards I'd go off calm as you like, on the same feet I came in on . . . And me motionless and him sleeping, thus the hours began to pass and the revolver didn't come by itself to me flying through the air nor did my arm stretch out to take it. (H125, translation modified)

The English translation obscures the perplexing (a)grammatical choices in this passage, but they stand out in the Spanish. With one exception toward the end of the scene ("iría"), the conjugated verbs are in the imperfect tense, not the conditional mood, which would be the appropriate choice for a fantasy or scenario that has not actually occurred. By contrast, the imperfect normally serves for descriptions of actual past events.

How should rhetorical readers interpret such a basic lapse, especially when it appears in a text supposedly penned by a grammarian? In my view, the strongest possibility is that Vallejo intends to suggest the existence of an obscured or discarded passage in which Fernando, qua narrator-as-writer, describes the killing as a past event that *occurred* rather than was merely fantasized. This does not imply that in some earlier or alternative draft of Vallejo's, Fernando "really" murders his lover. Rather, the implied author imbeds within Fernando's narrative the suggestion that Fernando previously drafted, then incompletely expunged, an account of murdering his young lover. Fernando's expressed wish to kill Wílmar shadows and contradicts his subsequent, equally convoluted, denials of responsibility. It also invites a reversal of his emphatic assertion of innocence in the following form: if anyone could have killed him or had him killed, it was I. For targeted readers, Fernando's casual abandonment of his lovers is one more expression of his broader refusal of responsibility and of his determination to make others' suffering a stage for performing his own importance. Rhetorical readers see more, particularly the implied author's investment in underscoring Fernando's deliberate manipulations of language, as if to make sure their outrageousness does not go unnoticed.

Despite isolated rhetorical gestures feigning empathy or identification, Fernando treats his lovers as accessories in his performance. Their murderous escapades temporarily inflate his sense of significance. By the end of the novel, however, Fernando's experiences with his young lovers, though enthralling, have proven their limited utility to him. Fernando discards his lovers when they no longer offer him pleasure, but he continues to make narrative use of them. The corpus of the narrative itself proves a body that (qua grammarian) he believes he can manipulate even more fully. Readers watch as Fernando discovers how readily narrative absorbs cruelty, and the degree to which a dead lover (or two) brings him a fine opening onto a literary project. (This mobilizes a trope of fin de siècle Hispanic literature that more frequently relies on the death of a woman as a creative catalyst.) Unlike other victims in *La virgen*, the *sicarios* are not simply sacrificed to death. They are first made to live according to Fernando's narrative. Instrumentalized and rendered voiceless, they "speak" only when Fernando acts as ventriloquist or interpreter. The numerous pregnant women, children, taxi drivers, soldiers, hoodlums, and others murdered in passing are victims whose deaths are fortuitous in the narrator's telling. But his *sicario* lovers are necessary victims without whom his narrative loses its logic.

Fernando pivots easily from devotion and delight in his young lovers to an undeniably callous abandonment of them. More telling still is the repeated cycle of use, and its acceleration. With Wílmar, Fernando repeats the activities and narrative gestures he first made use of with Alexis, but he exhausts the affair's satisfactions in half the time. This accelerated depletion of Wílmar's resources (or Wílmar as a resource) highlights the diminishing returns Fernando derives from these dynamics. If he were to continue drawing lovers from Medellín's *sicarios*, the pattern suggests that he would use them up with increasing rapidity. Eventually, Fernando's "relationship" to a lover would resemble the action by which he wipes his mouth with a napkin after sampling a street vendor's *sancocho*.

What matters most here, in terms of what the novel shows us about narrative ethics, is that Fernando's desires cannot be satisfied by the *sicarios* or the experiences they enable. The *told* is not enough. Rhetorical readers recognize that Fernando's bids for relevance must come through his *telling*. He draws on his self-declared legacy as a *letrado* to improvise a new project: the writing of the very text we read. We encounter evidence of this bid for international visibility and significance from the start of the novel; Fernando's references to his writing and to "readers" appear throughout the text. Within the events of the novel, however, the writing begins only *after* the conclusion of Fernando's relationships with the *sicarios*. What seems at first to be a shift from the role of *letrado* to the immediacy of street violence turns out in the final evaluation to be an elaborate redeployment of cruelty, in narrative, as the *letrado*'s birthright. The role of the cultured elite in Latin America has long been tainted by complicity with repression. To the satisfaction of the conspiratorial audience and the dismay of the targeted audience, in *La virgen*, cruelty becomes the *letrado*'s public face, one inscribed in Fernando's narration.

CONCLUSION: CONFRONTING NARRATIVE AS A "CAPITAL OF HATE"

By the end of *La virgen* (and this chapter), rhetorical readers recognize that the novel is no consciousness-raising endeavor. Nor does it make sense as an appeal for humanitarian aid, denunciation of the radical cheapening of life, bid to restore the humanity of marginalized teen killers, or documentation of the grim conditions of their coming of age. The narrator interferes with the efficacy of his own depictions of brutality too often for us to conclude, even, that the goal is to sensationalize violence. Instead, Vallejo takes advantage of language's indifference, its expressivity, its dehumanizing capacity, and the degree to which it can be turned to serve a toxic project of diatribe and self-aggrandizement.

What does it mean to have passed time in a novel that turns out, like Medellín in Fernando's account, to be a "capital of hate"? Rhetorical readers cannot plausibly redeem the values or perspectives expressed in *La virgen*, but we may redeem our reading of it. Attention to the workings of rhetorical passing makes it possible to stand apart from the targeted and conspiratorial audiences that *La virgen* addresses. In so doing, we become more aware of the fuller narrative situation, including the undertow of assaultive works and how quickly we may be swept up into problematic collaboration with narrators and authors more generally.

For much of the novel, Fernando is the main focus of targeted readers' vexation and distress. He is also the locus of readers' (ultimately thwarted) expectations of some partial transformation, remorse, or sign of authorial disapproval. But Fernando is not the only one who turns others into instruments. Vallejo stands behind him, ventriloquizing the character narrator he has created. There is some satisfaction, perhaps, in this irony: Fernando, who has imagined himself to be so powerful, is in fact a thin projection of Vallejo's attitudes, a character whose whole existence is designed to answer to his author's needs and wishes. In fiction, Fernando can carry Vallejo's attitudes and claims to their most dramatic—and deadly—expression, sparing the author physical exertion and legal repercussions. Fernando's instrumental treatment of his lovers mirrors the dynamic by which Vallejo makes use of *him*. If the *sicarios* are the necessary victims of Fernando's narrative, Fernando is the necessary casualty of Vallejo's novel. The strategic benefits of this arrangement bear noting: Vallejo circulates his attitudes and viewpoints while also situating inconsistencies and rhetorical shortcomings as belonging to Fernando's discourse.

Vallejo anticipates and exploits readers' expectations and reading practices. He lays a trap for a targeted audience that does not know at the outset, but will learn, that the novel's cruelty spills out from the *told* and the *telling* to contaminate the various roles of the narrative encounter. He hijacks our reading and makes it serve as a circulator for his afflictive viewpoints, demonstrating his ability to manipulate narrative resources to entice earnest humanists to remaining in the harsh weather of diatribe. All the while, Vallejo performs for a conspiratorial audience who certifies the success of his instrumentalization of Fernando and his layered assaults on targeted readers. *La virgen* seeks to damage our relationship to what we read and how we read it, hollowing out the practices we had relied upon.

Given these layers of use and abuse, rhetorical readers have reason to judge Vallejo a hateful, if talented, author who does not intend persuasion or engagement, but rather to inflict harm vindictively. But we should tread carefully. The greatest ethical risk of reading *La virgen* is not that we will espouse Fernando's or Vallejo's views but rather that we may let ourselves feel righteous simply because we do not. We should beware the pitfalls of virtue by comparison and smug contemplation from a distance. We may refuse to participate in the conspiratorial audience and reject the views nested in the narrator, implied author, and flesh-and-blood author. Yet international readers of *La virgen*, especially in English translation, are likely to be beneficiaries of global structural inequalities. We could stand to reckon with how frequently far-off dysfunction, like that depicted in *La virgen*, underwrites the unjust "functioning" of our relatively comfortable lives. Above all we ought to avoid confusing lack of direct involvement with the absence of guilt. Being targeted readers positions us, structurally, as victims and introduces the temptation to adopt our experience of harm as a cynical proof that we are innocent of harming others. One ethically significant response to an assaultive work like *La virgen*, then, is to decline this pretense to innocence and to embrace our responsibility as readers. Although Vallejo does not set out to awaken consciousnesses, we may awaken them ourselves in how we choose to engage with the novel's complexity.

Vallejo's assaultive deformative fiction displays the vulnerability of narrative to (mis)use and manipulation in ways that refract or amplify cruelty. Narrators make use of characters or narratees; authors make use of narrators, characters, resources, and audiences; and, most prevalent of all, readers make use of what they read. Assaultive deformative fictions wrench us from common notions of readers' virtuous engagement with narrative. To be clear, the goal is not to get "back" to a situation in which we readers have the upper hand in making use of stories and their resources. Rather, assaultive deformative fictions like *La virgen* present an opportunity to become more attentive to our tendency to instrumentalize narrative—and others through it.

With care and intention, rhetorical readers may attend fully to an author's moves while avoiding service as accessories to hatred or amplifiers of vitriol. This experience is deeply distressing and unpleasant, but it does have value. *La virgen* exposes fiction's receptiveness to cruelty as a dark side of making meaning through narrative. Humans recount memories for order and coherence. We construct stories to clarify the course of our lives; we tell jokes that recontextualize circumstances to make them more bearable. We build fictional worlds that make imaginary bets on more loving ways of being, doing, and living. All of this may be true. Yet a character like Fernando—with an author like Vallejo—reminds us of other capacities of narrative, capacities that we may be less eager to discuss. Narrative also allows a teller to distort, omit, tactically reinterpret, and otherwise bend stories to meet emotional and psychological impulses, however destructive or perverse. *La virgen* displays many of the mechanisms by which this bending and shaping occurs, as well as the cruelty that may attend these narrative distortions by the narrator and the author. In *La virgen,* narrative itself proves a surer haven for cruelty than the violent streets of the *comunas,* more a "capital of hate" even than Medellín.

La virgen's lesson for rhetorical readers is this: what Vallejo does with narrative represents one possible use of its resources, not a deviation. How do we contend with this reminder that deformative fiction lies along the spectrum of narrative possibility? And what of the likelihood that some readers might eagerly join Vallejo's conspiratorial audience? I see these realities as part of the rationale for persisting in rhetorical readings of Vallejo, rather than leaving him to rant to his supporters or to assail his unwitting targets. For rhetorical readers, *choosing* to read and engage in attentive analysis of Vallejo begins to reveal a toxic playbook, one we would do well to be aware of. Even when authors weaponize narrative resources, they cannot prevent readers from learning from these attempts at assault. We have the mobility of critical imagination, the capacity to trace the author–audience discourse that unfolds on the page without accepting its terms. And as the next chapter shows, some deformative fictions may appear assaultive but ultimately enable distinctive, if distressing, points of access to ethical reflection and insight. The only way to discern how deformations weigh in the balance of a work is to read the whole thing. We do well, then, to practice navigating treacherous narrative territory when we can.

CHAPTER 4

Bolaño

Cruelty as Anti-Elegy and the Inadequacy of Readers

Chilean expatriate Roberto Bolaño's massive final novel, *2666*[1] exemplifies *anti-elegiac* deformative fiction. Works in this vein activate—then disrupt—elegy's rhetorical triad of lamentation, confrontation, and consolation. Whereas traditional elegy models mourning to resolve a fraught relationship between present experience and past loss, anti-elegy seeks to question the motives for resolution—and the possibility of its achievement. Anti-elegiac deformative fictions raise the stakes even higher. They demand that we grieve even as they block the main avenues by which we might do so, setting continual confrontation with suffering as an unachievable ethical imperative. At more than a thousand pages, with five interconnected sections, *2666* enacts an anti-elegiac deformative project on a large scale, with varied effects. The novel entwines reader, writer, and text in complicated configurations of cruelty while simultaneously suspending any hope of effective mourning.

2666 sets a dystopian vision of contemporary horror adrift in a swirl of conflicting rhetorics of evil, violence, and cruelty. Instances of cruelty in the novel span the second half of the twentieth century, culminating in the 1990s. A character suffering profound mental illness murders his mother and drives a stake into her vagina "para que aprendiera" ("to make her learn"; B492,

---

1. Bolaño, *2666* (hereafter cited in text as "B").

W393, translation modified).² A Nazi bureaucrat authorizes countless deaths yet portrays himself as a distressed victim. A woman fantasizes about Aztec human sacrifice, and may or may not murder the soldiers in a nearby frontier outpost. A carnival atmosphere surrounds the crucifixion of a Romanian general at the hands of his own men. A painter completes his self-portrait by severing his right hand, mummifying it, and attaching it to the canvas. The son of a Mexican university dean subjects his interlocutor, and readers, to a xenophobic, racist, and classist diatribe. This includes his wish to see a military dictatorship that would end the flow of "más muertos de hambre" ("more scum") into his city (B274–75, W215).³ In the streets of London, two European literary critics beat a man unconscious, and possibly to his death.

Despite their intensity, these scenarios pale in comparison to the scenes that anchor the 350 pages of the novel's fourth and longest section. *La parte de los crímenes* (The part about the crimes) incorporates more than one hundred accounts of murdered women and girls whose bodies appear in illegal dumps, abandoned buildings, empty lots, and desert wastelands. The murders of women in *Crímenes* closely resemble events in Ciudad Juárez (El Paso's sister city on the Mexico–Texas border). Similar femicides first registered in Juárez as a disturbing reality in the 1990s and continue into the present. Yet *2666* is not a work of "true crime" or testimony. Bolaño's fictional exploration of murder, corruption, and myriad forms of predation takes place not in Juárez but in Santa Teresa, an invented city that the author locates in Sonora, Mexico, near the border with Arizona.

Bolaño portrays the dramatic cheapening of life in unregulated neoliberal border zones and exposes the grossly inadequate response to the killings. Local and international media scarcely take note. Myriad forces doom investigations to failure, including police incompetence, political corruption, widespread complicity with drug cartels, and deference to the multinational corporations whose business practices capitalize on and intensify the precarity of life in the region. Even as Bolaño draws attention to the ongoing horror of femicide, he rigorously avoids textual effects that would allow readers to feel virtuously separate from the sources of suffering depicted in the novel.

---

2. Spanish quotations of *2666* come from the 2004 Anagrama edition, the pagination of which matches that in the 2009 Vintage Español edition most readily available in the US. For all citations, I give the Spanish followed by the English translation of *2666* by Natasha Wimmer, hereafter cited in text as "W." Any amendments or changes to the Wimmer translation are noted. Unless otherwise indicated, other translations from Spanish sources are my own.

3. In his notes, reproduced as images in an exhibition catalog edited by Juan Insua, Bolaño describes the discourse in question as "un calco del de Fdo. Vallejo en *La virgen de los sicarios*" ("a calque of [Fernando] Vallejo in *Our Lady of the Assassins*"). Bolaño quoted in Insua, 101.

Emotional connection and identification, rational judgment, "witnessing," and grand interpretation: these consolations wither on the tangled vines of our encounter with *2666*.

The disruption of consolation is a hallmark of anti-elegiac deformative fictions. Anti-elegy tactically extends and intensifies what Clifton Spargo describes as "the resistances to resolution or commemoration" already embedded in the elegiac tradition.[4] That is, anti-elegy casts a shadow over the classic expression of elegy, as described by Peter Sacks. Elegy begins with lamentation, proceeds to confrontation with the finality of death, and ultimately arrives at consolation, often through memorialization.[5] The elegiac literary journey culminates in a new vantage point on loss and life, translating grief into self-knowledge or comparable insight. In the twentieth century, elegies increasingly eschew any smooth arc toward relief, however partial or temporary. But they still suggest a lost or deferred promise of consolation. By contrast, anti-elegies express outright suspicion of the longing for relief or release. Instead of seeing successful or "completed" mourning as a discharging of ethical responsibility, anti-elegists typically regard it as a mark of bad faith or complicity with the status quo.[6] Writers working in this vein especially distrust and discredit uses of literature to "recuperate" the dead symbolically by preserving their cultural, if not actual, life.[7] Anti-elegiac deformative fictions signal a need for sincere mourning, even as they bend elegy's consolatory arc to the breaking point and destabilize readers' sense of what constitutes an ethical response to suffering and death in literature and in the world.

These difficult narratives go beyond denying resolution in relationship to an elegized loss. They foreground, via refusal, the moral and ethical problems that attend readers' desire for consolation. If readers expect, even implicitly, that attaining *relief* is a goal of mourning, then mourning ceases to be about experiencing loss and instead becomes a tool for escaping its weight. A desire for resolution becomes still more questionable in the case of ongoing tragedy: femicides remain frequent, and frequently unsolved, not only on the US–Mexico border, but also in other parts of Mexico and in cities across the globe where the pressures of neoliberal policies produce similarly precarious circumstances. The possibility of consolation is doubly foreclosed for readers of *2666*, even upon concluding the novel: mourning cannot end because the suffering continues, and even mourning for "past" deaths becomes contaminated by the probability of self-serving motivations, however reframed. Wrenching

---

4. Spargo, "Contemporary Anti-Elegy," 416.
5. Sacks, *English Elegy*, 1–37.
6. Spargo, "Contemporary Anti-Elegy," 413.
7. Spargo, "Contemporary Anti-Elegy," 416.

the narrative resources of elegy away from resolution, *2666* creates a literary crucible for ethical crisis. On the one hand, Bolaño seems to demand that we respond to death and face our involvement in local and international conditions that devalue women's lives and labor. On the other hand, he consistently denies the consolations that may mediate our encounters with fictional cruelty. By the novel's end, the inadequacy of our response looms larger than any critique of failed social or judicial institutions.

Bolaño's anti-elegiac deformative project unfolds on several levels and in distinct ways at different points in the progression of our reading, interpretation, and rereading. These components demand our close attention: (1) the jarring encounter with accounts of femicide in *Crímenes*; (2) the echoes throughout the novel that create wormholes between scenes of cruelty, compounding their potential for distress; and (3) the traps set for readers as we struggle to read our way out of a sense of responsibility for the suffering at the novel's core. Bolaño's presentation of deaths in *Crímenes*—as well as his activation of intertextual connections that point beyond the novel—intertwine to reinforce the *visibility* of the murders, without facilitating their *legibility* or successful assimilation to interpretation. The idea of visibility without legibility resonates through three instances of altered vision in the novel: sixteenth-century painter Giuseppe Arcimboldo's composite portraits, a device of optical illusion called the thaumatrope, and a recreation of conceptual artist Marcel Duchamp's 1920 *Le Readymade Malheureux* (Unhappy readymade). These visual figures correspond, respectively, to three deformative strategies in the novel: compound composition, indetermination, and dislocation and exposure. Each narrative technique prolongs and intensifies readers' uncomfortable encounter with the murders. Together, they heighten our sense of culpability for the circumstances that cheapen life and enable predation.

As in many other deformative fictions, *2666* alters the implicit terms of encounter in narrative, demoting presumed obligations to readers (especially our comfort or clear path through the narrative) in favor of other commitments. Bolaño's intervention begins with an acceptance of the limits of literature to bring about justice for the Mexican women murdered on the border. He instead focuses on a more possible, if painful, ethical intervention: to correct our vision or, even better, to redirect our gaze so that we must confront the cruelty that neoliberal and misogynist logics otherwise conceal. This confrontation occurs without the relief of consolation. Thus, the femicides persist as a problem for rhetorical readers, both ethically and narratively.

Despite *2666*'s saturation with cruelty of the *told*, as with Ocampo and Vallejo, its most distressing deformations center on cruelty in the *telling*.

Especially in *Crímenes* but also across the novel, Bolaño's narrative tactics suggest indifference to suffering on the part of his narrator. These include "deadpan" narration, extreme detachment, sardonic humor, interpretive traps and dead ends, and (in the femicide accounts) parataxis and a chilling forensic aesthetic. Bolaño's invocations of interpersonal, institutional, and fictional cruelty in *2666* insist that we see femicides as "blood out of place," returning us to Mendieta's tactics in *People Looking at Blood*. (Recall that the blood etymologically linked to cruelty is *cruor*, blood from a wound or blood outside the body. Unlike *sanguis*, blood that circulates inside a body, *cruor* is blood that appears where it does not belong.) As an anti-elegiac deformative project, *2666*'s ethical and narrative force hinges on confronting readers with a persistent vision of the crimes that renders them raw, indigestible, and impossible to adequately process.

POSTHUMOUS CELEBRITY AND *2666*'S SCOPE

As a Chilean-born writer who spent his youth in Mexico and lived in Catalonia for much of his adult life, Bolaño's biography places him at odds with the frames of regional and national literatures. Bolaño identified simply as "Latin American," and he claimed the Spanish language as his only homeland.[8] This refusal of affiliation created practical challenges. Where to shelve his books? How to locate his fiction in syllabi or literary conference panels? Such questions might seem trivial, but they have material consequences in a world literary system often partitioned by nationality. By the end of his life, and increasingly since his death from liver failure in 2003 at the age of 50, Bolaño's rootlessness has come to cement the status of his fiction as *world literature*. Had he lived to see it happen, Bolaño might have been among the most surprised—and not entirely pleased—to read assessments of his fiction in English translation that describe it as "the new face of Latin America" or to see scholars use his career as a line of demarcation in Latin American literary history and criticism.[9]

Bolaño's place in literature and culture, and how it shapes the rhetorical choices in his fiction (and the range of our responses), invites consideration of the *ethics of writing*. Posthumous international commercial success produces

---

8. Bolaño and Maristain, "Last Interview," 99.

9. Jonathan Franzen's remarks at Guadalajara's 2012 Feria Internacional del Libro offer one of many examples. Franzen, "Conversation with Jorge Volpi." For a discussion of the impact of Bolaño's posthumous explosion in popularity and the commodification of his oeuvre, see Pollack, "After Bolaño." See also Medina, "Arts of Homelessness."

powerful forces of commodification that threaten to erode some of the ethical weight of Bolaño's fiction. Some readers fetishize a work like *2666*, skimming it for bragging rights or placing it on their shelf for the status boost of its totemic presence. If sincerely engaged, however, the novel holds up as a powerful, and painful, deformative project. Far from pandering to a "First World" readership, Bolaño endows his aesthetic and ethical interventions with his knowledge of the well-educated European, Latin American, American, and global elites who hungrily awaited his words.[10] Yes, Bolaño makes cynical jabs at academics and self-satisfied liberals. More significant, though, is how Bolaño leads readers into encounters with cruelty and complicity, anticipating in advance what we may try to do to manage that encounter. Bolaño's narrative ethics pivot on his willingness to undermine dramatically the readability of his own novel by multiplying obstructions and curtailing opportunities for the usual satisfactions of fiction. These strategies prevent us from either dismissing cruelty or absorbing it through reading practices and critical moves. Bolaño renders cushioned sites of self-protection unusable, placing tacks on any seat that might offer a "progressive" reader a place of respite from distress or feelings of guilt.

Serial accounts of murdered women in *Crímenes* function as the experiential nadir of reading and the apex of Bolaño's anti-elegiac deformative project. Their resonance depends significantly on how *Crímenes* functions in the full sweep of the novel. Although many critics state the importance of reading the murders in the context of the whole, most criticism of the novel focuses primarily on *Crímenes*.[11] There are practical reasons for this. The novel

---

10. In this chapter, I use the terms "First World" and "Third World" with awareness of their limitations and contaminations. For me, the terms do not serve an analytic function but rather serve to reflect the global disparities that figure prominently in *2666*, as suggested by Fate's description of the piece he imagines writing on the Santa Teresa crimes: "Un retrato del mundo industrial en el Tercer Mundo—dijo Fate—, un aide-mémoire de la situación actual de México, una panorámica de la frontera" ("'A sketch of the industrial landscape in the third world,' said Fate, 'a piece of *reportage* about the current situation in Mexico, a panorama of the border'"; B373, W294–95). Despite the lack of consensus regarding their meaning, I use "First World" and "Third World" as terms that roughly correspond to characters' sense of contrasts between life experiences and possibilities in countries such as the US and the member states of the European Union ("First World") and in spaces where development is uneven, social conditions are unstable, and local economic prospects are dominated by multinationals ("Third World"). Importantly, whereas the notion of a First World space seems to correspond primarily to a national level, Third World designations may be more tied to local spaces. Thus, a space like Santa Teresa—with its grossly inadequate infrastructure—might be marked as "Third World" even when Mexico City would not. My capitalization of the terms follows the Oxford English Dictionary.

11. This is an interesting reversal of the pattern in anecdotal accounts of general readers' responses, which often include a sense that *Crímenes* does not "fit" with the rest of *2666*. In

is enormous. Readers and critics can only tackle so much. The murders, and their challenging presentation, exert an urgency unmatched by other parts of the novel. Further, to deemphasize *Crímenes* might seem to repeat the failure of attention to the murders that the novel addresses as a central problem. The unique mode of deformation in *2666* as a "big" book leads critics to limit their treatment of the rest of the novel. Scenes of cruelty in other parts of *2666* seem to radiate outward from or coalesce around *Crímenes*. This interconnection adds to the weight of *Crímenes*, multiplies distressing resonances, and complicates the prospect of interpretation, much less meaningful mourning. The bidirectional relationship between part 4 and the complex, digressive whole of *2666* tightens the weave of cruelty while also unraveling efforts to make satisfying sense of the crimes.

Limiting interpretive efforts to *Crímenes*, then, may be an act of scholarly self-protection. It is vexing to develop a careful reading of one section only to have it snarled in the tangled weave of digressions and echoes that unfolds across the rest of the novel. Yet this is precisely what happens—and what Bolaño intends to happen—when we read (and reread) *2666*. This second stage of deformation is essential to Bolaño's sophisticated interventions, which include the mobilization of intertextuality as an *ethical,* not merely a narrative or literary, resource. Placing *Crímenes* in relationship to the other parts of the novel begins to reveal the deformative potential of intertextuality in *2666*'s composite portrait of cruelty.

CONTINUITY (AND DISCONTINUITY) OF PARTS IN *2666*

Here, to orient readers unfamiliar with the novel, I offer a summary of *2666* part by part and gloss the basic progression of an initial reading. The first part, *La parte de los críticos* (The part about the critics), follows a knot of self-absorbed European literary critics on their quest to locate the elusive Prussian writer, Benno von Archimboldi. Each critic has built an academic career upon Archimboldi's work, and they share the fantasy of returning to Europe "con Archimboldi de la mano" ("leading [Archimboldi] by the hand"; B142, W105). Their collective obsession furnishes the occasion for a series of erotic entanglements and international adventures that range from academic conferences and celebrity encounters to acts of violence and predation. The critics' hunt ultimately brings them to the border town of Santa Teresa, Mexico, where they

---

other words, those not trained in literary criticism may be more likely to see *Crímenes* as a departure from the novel, as opposed to its center.

meet a displaced Chilean philosophy professor named Óscar Amalfitano. He briefly assists them in their search for Archimboldi, and in the process they also learn about widespread, unaddressed femicide in the city. *Críticos* initiates a theme of contrasting perceptions that repeats across the parts. Focal characters see Santa Teresa in dramatically contrasting ways depending on their outlook and orientation. For their part, the critics view Santa Teresa as a savage periphery, and their response to the crimes vacillates between disturbed incomprehension and suppressed fascination. The critics stand in as unattractive representatives for readers.

In the second part, *La parte de Amalfitano* (The part about Amalfitano), Óscar Amalfitano returns as the focal character. The section traces his decades-long journey from Santiago, Chile, to Barcelona, Spain, to Santa Teresa, Mexico, chronicled amid a number of narrative and thematic off-shoots. The central narrative line, however, focuses on the philosophy professor's brushes with dark, potentially maddening, visions of life on the US–Mexico border. Amalfitano's anxieties about what is happening in Santa Teresa express themselves most clearly in a mysterious voice that addresses him when he is alone. As the father of a nineteen-year-old daughter (Rosa), Amalfitano is obsessed with potential signs of conspiracy or criminality in Santa Teresa, such as black cars parked for hours on residential streets and encounters with mysterious men. These constellations of details appear initially as marks of paranoia or delusion, but in later parts they return in connection with the crimes without the filter of Amalfitano's anxiety and past experiences with political repression in Chile.

The third part, *La parte de Fate* (The part about Fate), centers on Quincy Williams (alias Oscar Fate), a Black journalist sent to Santa Teresa to cover a boxing match for a Harlem magazine. Like the critics in part 1, Fate is unaware of the femicides until he arrives in the region. He meets a journalist from Mexico City who is assigned to interview the man accused of many of the murders and has a chance encounter with Rosa Amalfitano. Their time together propels him into a disorienting and dangerous underworld revealed to be rife with potential for predation. As Fate's confusion grows, it ripples through the narrative as a destabilizing force, leaving the outcome of events uncertain. Nevertheless, Fate shares Amalfitano's conviction that Rosa must leave Santa Teresa, and the section ends with their departure for Arizona.

In the fourth part, *La parte de los crímenes* (The part about the crimes), readers face a chronological series of accounts, each describing the discovery of a murdered woman's body in or around Santa Teresa between 1993 and 1997. The accounts specify the location and condition of each woman's body, the circumstances of its detection, the signs of sexual assault and other violence, and the clothing and personal items recovered in the vicinity. When the victim can be identified, we often also learn her (fictional) name and where she was last employed.[12] The section is not simply an unbroken series of forensic reports, however. Between these accounts, additional plot lines elaborate the failures of police, politicians, and the international community to respond to the murders. Two threads interwoven with the accounts of the crimes are particularly important. One treats the experiences of Klaus Haas, a German businessman who is imprisoned without trial as a suspect for some of the murders. From prison, he holds regular press conferences. Haas implicates the sons of prominent Santa Teresa citizens in the femicides and insists on his innocence while maintaining a mysterious and menacing persona. A second notable thread leads us to a fictional journalist named Sergio González Rodríguez, who, at the prompting of a prominent congresswoman, uses his journalistic influence to investigate and report on the crimes.[13] By the end of the section, Bolaño deflates all expectations that revelations, resolution, or coherence will clarify the crimes.

The fifth and final part of the novel, *La parte de Archimboldi* (The part about Archimboldi), drops readers into a *Künstlerroman* (an artist's bildungsroman) about the Prussian writer whom the critics seek in the first part of the novel. It opens with the story of Hans Reiter's parents. Identified as "el cojo" y "la tuerta" ("the one-legged man" and "the one-eyed woman"), they marry shortly after the First World War. Part 5 traces Reiter's transformation from a barely literate, ocean-obsessed "seaweed boy" named Hans Reiter to Benno von Archimboldi, the European writer of cult renown whom the critics seek.[14] This transformation involves Reiter's service in the German infantry on the Eastern Front during World War II, his strange connection to the writings of a young Russian Jew (likely killed in the death camps), his murder of an SS officer, and his passionate and tender affair with a physically and mentally fragile young woman. The section ends with Archimboldi's departure for Mexico at the behest of his sister, and the revelation that Klaus Haas, who has been accused of several of the Santa Teresa killings, is the writer's nephew. The last

---

12. Maquiladoras or maquilas are factories that operate in free-trade zones around the world, although the model was first pioneered in Ciudad Juárez. Grant Farred notes "how prevalently the maquiladora condition obtains, in economic modality if not in name, in the Third World" ("Impossible Closing," 693). In the fictional Santa Teresa, as in Ciudad Juárez and other border towns, the majority of laborers are women, many of whom come from rural areas in search of work. For a thorough discussion of maquiladora labor practices and their connection to femicide, see Washington Valdez, *Killing Fields*; and Wright, *Disposable Women*.

13. This character shares the name of a prominent, now deceased, Mexican journalist with whom Bolaño corresponded extensively during his writing of the novel. I discuss the influence of González Rodríguez's style in the "Uneven Realism" section of this chapter.

14. Following Bolaño's practice in the novel, I refer to the character as "Reiter" for those portions of the novel that precede the fictional writer's adoption of a pen name and "Archimboldi" thereafter.

line of *2666* announces Archimboldi's departure for Santa Teresa, effectively directing readers back to the beginning, where we meet the critics who have come in search of him.

That the last page returns us to the novel's opening reflects a broader, looping pattern. Bolaño dislocates the order of the parts from the chronology of events they recount while also creating a feeling of distressing return, even déjà vu. Specifically,

- The events in part 1 (*Críticos*) come after those in part 2 (*Amalfitano*).
- The events in part 2 (*Amalfitano*) come before events in part 1 (*Críticos*).
- The events in part 3 (*Fate*) come after those in part 1 (*Críticos*).
- The events in part 4 (*Crímenes*) come before those in part 2 (*Amalfitano*).
- The events in part 5 (*Archimboldi*) begin half a century before the events in part 4, then lead up to the action in part 1 (*Críticos*).

This intercalated structure produces a lurching movement: one step forward (part 1), two steps back (part 2), three steps forward (part 3), four steps back (part 4), a huge leap back (part 5 begins in 1920), followed by a leap and a step forward (the end of part 5). These temporal disjunctions are jarring, but not randomly so. It is as if the narrative were a rubber band anchored to part 4 (*Crímenes*) but stretched to varying degrees in each section. Whatever the movement away from the femicides—temporally, topically, or in terms of reading progression—they remain the essential mooring for all sections. At a structural level, such movement marks the centrality of the Santa Teresa murders to the novel's temporality as well as to its ethical engagements. In fact, Santa Teresa is the only "character" we encounter in all five sections, and the fictional city provides the primary source of unity in the novel. *Crímenes* takes place almost entirely in Santa Teresa, and the trajectories of the focal characters in the other parts take them to the city as well. Santa Teresa reflects the conditions of uneven development across Latin America, particularly in border regions, and the implication of the so-called First World in creating those conditions. Bolaño activates, and then disappoints, expectations that this web of connections to Santa Teresa will provide an explanation or support an interpretation of cruelty in *2666*.

MURDER WITHOUT MYSTERY OR DETECTION

The first three parts of *2666* prepare readers to view the crimes as the cipher of the novel. Narrated conversations and references in these parts signal the patterns of femicide in Santa Teresa. The killings intensify the critics' unease, foment Amalfitano's sense of doom, and foster Fate's concern for Rosa Amalfitano. We encounter many indications, subtle and not so subtle, of the murders' connection to some concealed atrocity. For example, *La parte de Fate,* which directly precedes *Crímenes,* ends with Fate's recollection of these words: "Nadie presta atención a estos asesinatos, pero en ellos se esconde el secreto del mundo" ("No one pays attention to these killings, but the secret of the world is hidden in them"; B439, W348). The oracular pronouncement reinforces the sense that a mystery, and perhaps its solution, awaits us in the fourth part. As we traverse *Crímenes,* Bolaño deflates any hope of successful detection by characters, narrator, or reader. Still, especially on the first reading, readers may anticipate that the discovery of "la primera muerta" ("the first dead woman") will catalyze a collective recognition of a problematic pattern, trigger the labors of investigators, and lead to the apprehension of perpetrators.[15]

By opening with a murder investigation, *Crímenes* activates frames associated with detective fiction. An early description in the section—"La sombra se acercó hacia ella y le disparó un balazo en la frente" ("The shadowy figure approached and shot her in the forehead"; B447, W356)—features the anonymity and the as-yet-unmotivated violence that often catalyzes investigation in murder mysteries. In the classic expression of the genre, the detective's success in solving a crime marks the triumph of a stable and (presumably) just social order. The detached language and intimations of corruption and conspiracy in *Crímenes* situate it more specifically in relationship to *noir* fiction (the *novela negra* in the Spanish-language tradition), where crime erupts as a symptom of a dysfunctional order. The *novela negra* tradition withholds the fuller reassurance presented in classic detective novels and typically illustrates decline and disorder beyond individual crimes. Still, the *noir* detective usually overcomes obstacles and solves at least *some* crimes.

Not so in *Crímenes.* The opening lines initiate a distressing pattern:

La muerta apareció en un pequeño descampado en la colonia Las Flores. Vestía camiseta blanca de manga larga y falda de color amarillo hasta las rodillas, de una talla superior. Unos niños que jugaban en el descampado la encontraron y dieron aviso a sus padres. La madre de uno de ellos telefoneó a la policía, que se presentó al cabo de media hora. El descampado

---

15. The invocation of distinct genres in each of the novel's five parts adds further plausibility to readers' expectation that *Crímenes* fits in the detective genre. Although each part contains considerable variation, there are broad resemblances between the parts and established genres of fiction. *Críticos* resembles an academic satire / campus novel in the tradition of Zadie Smith's *On Beauty,* Amalfitano recalls the philosophical fiction of Milan Kundera, *Fate* blends romance and investigative thriller, and *Archimboldi* fits the pattern of a historical *Künstlerroman.* For an alternative generic classification of the parts in *2666,* see Deckard, "Peripheral Realism," 356.

daba a la calle Peláez y a la calle Hermanos Chacón y luego se perdía en una acequia tras la cual se levantaban los muros de una lechería abandonada y ya en ruinas. . . . Esto ocurrió en 1993. En enero de 1993. A partir de esta muerta comenzaron a contarse los asesinatos de mujeres. Pero es probable que antes hubiera otras. La primera muerta se llamaba Esperanza Gómez Saldaña y tenía trece años. Pero es probable que no fuera la primera muerta. . . . El cuerpo fue llevado a la morgue del hospital de la ciudad, en donde el médico forense le realizó la autopsia. Según ésta Esperanza Gómez Saldaña había muerto estrangulada. Presentaba hematomas en el mentón y en el ojo izquierdo. Fuertes hematomas en las piernas y en las costillas. Había sido violada vaginal y analmente probablemente más de una vez, pues ambos conductos presentaban desgarros y escoriaciones por los que había sangrado profusamente. A las dos de la mañana el forense dio por terminada la autopsia y se marchó. Un enfermero negro, que hacía años había emigrado al norte desde Veracruz, cogió el cadáver y lo metió en un congelador. (B443–45)

The girl's body appeared in a vacant lot in Colonia Las Flores. She was dressed in a white long-sleeved T-shirt and a yellow knee-length skirt, a size too big. Some children playing in the lot found her and told their parents. One of the mothers called the police, who showed up half an hour later. The lot was bordered by Calle Peláez and Calle Hermanos Chacón and it ended in a ditch behind which rose the walls of an abandoned dairy in ruins. . . . This happened in 1993. January 1993. From then on, the killings of women began to be counted. But it's likely that there had been other deaths before. The name of the first victim was Esperanza Gómez Saldaña and she was thirteen. But she probably wasn't really the first of the dead girls. . . . The body was taken to the morgue at the city hospital, where the medical examiner conducted an autopsy. According to the autopsy, Esperanza Gómez Saldaña had been strangled to death. There was bruising on her chin and around her left eye. Severe bruising on her legs and rib cage. She had been vaginally and anally raped, probably more than once, since both orifices exhibited tears and abrasions, from which she had bled profusely. At two in the morning the examiner concluded the autopsy and left. A Black orderly, who had moved north from Veracruz years ago, put the body away in a freezer. (W353–54, translation modified)[16]

---

16. Wimmer's translation omits the narrator's second assertion that other deaths likely preceded this one ("Pero es probable que antes hubiera otras" and "Pero es probable que no fuera la primera muerta"). To remedy the omission, I have added, "But she probably wasn't really the first of the dead girls" as a translation for the Spanish, "Pero es probable que no fuera la primera muerta." I have also modified Wimmer's translation of "apareció." See next note.

I quote the entire account to convey a sense of the language and emphasis that characterizes these cases. How does it land? What responses and impulses arise? What thoughts crowd at the gate of the mind? Imagine now that 110 more such accounts await you in *Crímenes*, each of which will repeat core elements of the series begun here.

The crime scenes vary, and elements in the description are sometimes presented in a different order or degrees of development, but a remarkable consistency unifies the accounts. The narrator specifies the location of the body and the features of the local geography, which in turn often serve as subtle indications of local conditions. In the first account, the "lechería abandonada y ya en ruinas" ("abandoned dairy in ruins") signals the state of decline in the area where the body is found. The accounts also identify the placement of the bodies, the likely age of the victims, and the distinguishing physical features. The specific mutilations suffered by the women receive detailed, forensic attention. Some forms of damage (signs of vaginal and anal rape, for example) are present in all but a few of the corpses. Other patterns unify subsets of the killings, as in the case of the total or partial severing of a nipple, bound hands, clear signs of strangulation, stabbing, or peculiar arrangements of the victim's clothing. Accounts typically end with a summary of the autopsy results, if one was performed, and a note about any attempts at identifying the victim, finding family members, or otherwise closing the case (usually without resolution).

The first words of the account, "La muerta apareció," ("The girl's body appeared") introduce the insistent trope of *appearance* in relationship to the murdered women. Similar constructions occur at least twenty-three times across the section, or in about 21 percent of the murder accounts.[17] This

---

17. Bolaño's use of *aparecer* ("to appear") is as deliberate as it is insistent. In multiple cases, though, Wimmer makes choices in translation that obscure the repetition, rendering it as "turned up" or other, less direct phrases (e.g., W353, 413, 419, 456, 468, 495). For reference, here are the first nine instances of "appearance" in *Crímenes*. "La muerta **apareció** en un pequeño descampado en la colonia Las Flores" ("The girl's body **turned up** in a vacant lot in Colonia Las Flores"; B443, W353); "dos semanas después . . . **apareció** otro cadáver" ("two weeks after . . . another body **turned up**"; B488, W390); "En octubre **apareció**, en el basurero del parque industrial Arsenio Farrell, la siguiente muerta" ("The next dead woman **appeared** in October, at the dump in the Arsenio Farrell industrial park"; B489, W391); "su cuerpo había **aparecido** en el parque industrial Arsenio Farrell" ("her body **was found** in the Aresenio Farrell industrial park"; B489, W391); "Una semana después **apareció** su cadáver" ("A week later her body **turned up**"; B506, W404); "Su cuerpo **apareció** dos días después" ("Her body **appeared** two days after"; B515, W412); "La siguiente muerta **apareció** en agosto de 1994" ("The next dead woman **turned up** in August 1994"; B521; W417); "la muerta **aparecida** en el edificio de la calle Alondra" ("the dead woman who had **turned up** in the building on Calle Alondra"; B531; W425); "El quince de enero **apareció** la siguiente muerta" ("On January 15 the next dead woman **turned up**"; B563, W449).

recurrence to the notion of bodies "appearing" subtly underscores two important aspects of Bolaño's presentation of the killings. First, it minimizes the active role of the killer or killers (no one "leaves" the bodies; they "appear"). Second, it obscures the specific circumstances of the deaths. *2666* is not exceptional in concealing, at least initially, the details or dramatization of the murders from which it derives narrative energy. Particularly in detective fiction, the occlusion of murder scenes often provides the impetus to reconstruct the crime. This enables legal justice (in the classic detective novel) or revenge (in the *noir* tradition). The inaccessibility of the death scene in *2666*, however, serves as a site of indetermination rather than an engine for investigation.

In the first account, the narrator acknowledges that "antes hubiera otras [muertas]" ("it's likely that there had been other deaths before"). The construction "la primera muerta . . . no fuera la primera muerta" (the first victim . . . probably wasn't really the first") further highlights the contingency of the girl's placement as the first of the many *muertas* discovered in the section, suggesting that inattention, not absence of harm, accounts for the failure to recognize the pattern sooner. The belatedly established Department of Sex Crimes has a single employee (B704, W563). The police department expends far more resources in the search for "el Penitente," a disturbed "profanador de iglesias" ("desecrator of churches") who urinates in Catholic churches across Santa Teresa and sometimes turns violent (B453, W361). At the height of the mobilization of forces in response to the Penitent's desecrations, an officer is stationed in every church in the city (B465, W371). The police extend no such protective presence to the neighborhoods or dumps where the bodies appear. Nor do they exercise care in investigating the murders. The accounts in *Crímenes* frequently end with the implication of police incompetence, as in "el examen balístico . . . se perdió definitivamente" ("the ballistic analysis . . . was later lost for good"; B447, W356) and "las muestras de semen enviadas a Hermosillo se perdieron" ("the semen samples sent to Hermosillo were lost"; B713, W570).[18]

Familiar types from the detective tradition hold some promise for a break in this pattern. Juan de Dios Martínez, a taciturn, middle-aged detective tries to solve the murders, but his superiors insist that he focus on his assigned case (tracking the Penitent). We also follow the efforts of Lalo Cura, a teen sharpshooter turned phlegmatic police officer who brings us closer to the *novela*

---

18. Other common phrases include, "el caso se cerró" ("the case was . . . closed"; B524, W488), "dejó de pensar en [el caso]" ("he didn't think about [the case] anymore"; B532, W425), "el caso quedó sin aclarar" ("the case remained unsolved"; B579, W462), "no tardó en clasificarse como caso no resuelto" ("the case . . . was soon filed as unsolved"; B630, W504), and "el caso no tardó en ser archivado" ("the case was soon shelved"; B658, W526).

negra tradition. In his former role as a cartel bodyguard, Lalo murdered not only the men who tried to kill his boss's wife but also the other bodyguards who did nothing to stop it. (It is worth noting that "Lalo" is often short for Eduardo or Gonzalo, and "Cura" is a plausible last name, but together they pun on "la locura," or "madness." This almost mocking naming suggests Bolaño's ironic, lightly derisive engagement with detective fiction tropes.) Another investigator, the US sheriff Harry Magaña, fits in the frame of the *noir* tradition. Magaña gets farther than the Mexican police by employing extralegal tactics and violence but is murdered before he solves any crimes. A political novelist turned investigative journalist briefly pursues the cases. In the last third of *Crímenes*, Klaus Haas, a German business owner accused of some of the crimes, begins to hold press conferences from prison to offer evidence of his innocence.[19] *2666* makes plain that the crimes exceed the capacity of all these investigators. Despite their many successful precursors in detective fiction, no one manages to reconstruct the circumstances of the murders, much less bring a single perpetrator to justice.

DISTRACTED NARRATION AND ABSENT AFFECT

The narrator demonstrates a clear recognition of police incompetence and the tendency toward obstruction of justice by pointing out oddities in the crime scenes that generally go unquestioned by the police. He notes, for instance, that a dead woman found with "una cajetilla de cigarillos" ("a . . . pack of cigarettes") does not have a lighter (B446, W355). In several other passages, the narrator appears to speak from a position of greater investigative prowess, as when he enumerates the investigators' missteps (e.g., B631, W504) and poses the many questions that the police leave not only unanswered, but also unasked: "¿Qué hacía allí? ¿Cómo había llegado allí? Eso no lo dijeron" ("What was she doing there? How had she come there? That they didn't say"; B627, W501). Although we might hope for the narrator to respond with judgment or emotion, he simply observes the failings.

---

19. Bolaño's portrayal of Haas in *Crímenes* combines the trope of the falsely accused victim who must clear his name with the trope of the brilliant, incarcerated detective, as in Borges and Bioy Casares' parodic detective stories, *Seis problemas para don Isidro Parodi* (Six problems for Sir Isidro Parodi). German by birth but a naturalized US citizen, Haas turns out to be Archimboldi's nephew. This connection is not confirmed until the last pages of *2666*, but most attentive readers will intuit some link between the two men. In addition to their nationality, both are described as being astonishingly tall.

Even this noticing seems to be a strain. Often the narrator's attention strays, and digressions abound. Most evade all but the most whimsical notions of relevance to the crimes. Long after it has become clear that the Penitent cannot be responsible for the murders, for example, the narrator continues to describe the search for him in excruciating detail, often for dozens of pages at a time.[20] Meticulous attention to the breakfast habits of a US forensics expert drifts into a discussion of how modern food science can produce microwavable frozen bread that tastes "recién salido de un horno europeo" ("straight from a European oven"; B727, W582). Another passage lingers on a character's fantasy of liquidating her assets to fund plastic surgery by a famous Parisian surgeon (B668–69, W534–35). Despite occasional echoes of other parts of *2666*, many of these digressions are irrecuperable to any investigation of the crimes. The mismatch between the urgency of the crimes and this unrelated narration signals that our narrator will neither analyze the evidence he offers nor attempt to reconstruct the crimes. As rhetorical readers persist through the murder accounts and endure the digressions between them, the narrator's distraction and susceptibility to digression emerge as further obstacles to efforts to make sense of the killings.

In the absence of successful detection, some sign of affective response might bring coherence to our encounter with this challenging content. This is what Rei Terada describes as the self-consoling character of emotion: "When we don't know what to think, emotions give us something to feel; they make our unstable perceptions and sensations seem more stable and nameable."[21] The consolation of emotional insight is *possible* in *2666*; in many passages not focused on the murders, the narrator dives into character psychology and interiority. Extensive, detailed descriptions of characters' dreams, sexual fantasies, and thoughts contrast sharply with the narrator's treatment of the murders—and others' responses to them.[22] The refusal of interior access pulls most of *Crímenes* far beneath the already low base level of emotional resonance in *2666*.

---

20. See, for example, B453–66, W361–72; B470–86, W376–89.

21. Terada, *Feeling in Theory*, 49.

22. For detailed accounts of dreams and fantasies, see the following (dreamer/fantasizer in parentheses): B67–69, W45–47 (Morini); B107–9, W78–79 (Pelletier); B116, W85 (Espinoza); B154, W115 (Norton); B165–66, W123–24 (Norton); B173, W130–31 (Pelletier, Norton, Espinoza); B202, W155 (Pelletier); B202, W155 (Norton); B264, W206 (Amalfitano); B290, W227–28 (Amalfitano); B484, W386–87 (Pedro Negrete); B484, W387 (Epifanio Galindo); B560, W447 (Harry Magaña); B590, W471 (Juan de Dios Martínez); B610, W488 (Klaus Haas); B633, W506 (Florita Almada); B668, W534 (Elvira Campos); B920, W736 (Ansky); B921–22, W737–38 (Reiter); B1096, W875 (Lotte); and B1103, W881 (Klaus Haas).

Since literary fiction generally indicates characters' emotions and guides our feelings in response, readers likely experience these as instances of the *withholding* of an expected narrative resource. But subtraction of emotion is, itself, a narrative resource, what Susan Sontag calls a "technique of avoidance."[23] We need, then, to look closely at how Bolaño wields this resource to raise the stakes of readers' encounters with cruelty.

The absence of emotional resonance increases the number of occasions for us to register cruelty in the *told*. One scene near the beginning of *Crímenes* juxtaposes a raucous birthday celebration at a police station with the arrival of a shrouded body of a murdered woman, as seen by inspector Juan de Dios Martínez. The police officers' casual disregard becomes even more potent, as drunken dereliction of duty grates against the somber reality of femicide, which prompts the narrator's observation, "Nadie se fijó en [el cadáver]" ("Nobody noticed [the cadaver]"; B466, W372, translation modified). Bolaño withholds clarity as to whether the "nadie" (nobody) of the final line includes Martínez (which would mean it is the narrator's observation) or whether it is Martínez's assessment of the scene, relayed in the narration.

The narrator's flat affect causes the most distress when it describes the cruelty of characters we may have hoped would serve as avatars of justice. This is the case with the boy detective Lalo Cura, whose righteous vigilante streak raises expectations that he may remain outside of police complacency and corruption. But scenes that illustrate his passivity—and possibly pleasure—in the face of others' suffering ultimately disappoint these expectations. In one scene, Lalo stands idly by, watching with a colleague as "en las otras celdas los policías estaban violando a las putas de La Riviera" ("In the other cells policemen were raping the whores from La Riviera"; B502, W401). Lalo refrains from participating, but we must contend with his failure to intervene—and the fact that he and his companion turn away only when "se cansaron de mirar" ("they got tired of watching"; B502, W401, translation modified). Only later does he ask what these "whores" have done. His question conveys a vague sense that he presumes them to be guilty of something, but he remains silent when his companion notes that they may have murdered another sex worker. Are we to assume he accepts a moral equation in which suspicion of murder warrants sexual assault? What does it mean to "get tired" of beholding rape? Does it mean that his satisfaction diminishes to the point at which the activity is no longer appealing? Or has Lalo watched all he can bear? Even without the answers to these questions, we must attribute some degree of cruelty to Lalo's behavior and his silence.

---

23. Sontag, *Against Interpretation*, 36.

Although the likelihood of Lalo's cruelty vexes, our inability to calibrate our judgment troubles still more. The description at the end of the scene intensifies the sense that the narrator actively blocks our access to the information that would make judgment possible. In a descriptive flourish rare in Bolaño's prose, the narrator observes, "La brisa que soplaba a esas horas por las calles de Santa Teresa era fresca de verdad. La luna, llena de cicatrices, aún resplandecía en el cielo" ("The early morning breeze along the streets of Santa Teresa really was fresh and cool. The scarred moon still shone in the sky"; B502, W401). Instead of delighting the reader, this nuanced sensory detail intensifies a feeling of affront. *Why*, we may feel, *does the narrator withhold this sensitivity when it comes to Lalo's emotions and thoughts? Is the impassive telling of this cruelty itself cruel?*

THE ELOQUENCE OF SILENCE

The ethical implications of the narrator's reticence intertwine tightly with the challenges and possibilities it presents to readers. The temptation to attribute cruelty to the narrator, or to the implied author, increases with the discomfort of withheld affect. This builds dramatically, even excruciatingly, across *Crímenes*. At first, the narrator's placid recounting of investigatory and empathetic failures aligns him with the problematic unresponsiveness of the characters. At the least, he appears "morally imperceptive," failing to register—or express—the weight of his telling.[24] Considering silence as a form of emphasis offers a different accounting for the narrator's reticence, however. Novelist and critic José Ovejero argues for the ethical impact of "call[ing] attention to that which is not said" so that the "silenced aspect becomes laceratingly present."[25] Perhaps the narrator restricts his own expressivity because silence draws more attention to the crimes and widespread indifference more effectively than commentary would.

Reticence is one tool by which Bolaño manages our response to the crimes—and to the telling of them. Here, rhetorical readers benefit from distinguishing between the communicative efforts of the narrator and the implied author (who shapes the narrator) and attending to the two main pathways of communication that unfold in the novel (and in most fiction).[26] The first pathway connects the narrator and narratee. The second connects the

---

24. Phelan, *Experiencing Fiction*, 2.
25. Ovejero, *La ética de la crueldad* (The ethics of cruelty), 70.
26. Rhetorical passing, the effect examined in *La virgen*, adds a pathway from the implied author to a conspiratorial audience.

implied author and authorial audience. Withholding commentary, *2666*'s narrator makes no appeal for the narratee to judge the violence against women. By managing the narrator's allocation of attention (the lingering narration of the shrouded body, the recounting of Lalo Cura's lack of response to the rapes), the implied author conveys to the authorial audience that *we* should view instances of indifference and inaction as serious moral concerns even if characters do not. This strategy—making use of the differences between the dual lines of communication to guide the authorial audience toward judgments not stated by the narrator or characters—is not unique to Bolaño.[27] The explicit separation of the dual lines of communication is fairly common (and therefore familiar to readers) as a feature of character narration, as in Ocampo's stories: as the narrator tells one story, another (or more than one) is being told by the implied author. Fernando's *La virgen* takes the differentiation of address still farther through rhetorical passing. Part of the challenge of reading Bolaño is that this separation occurs in a noncharacter narration where the narrator is accurately reporting but refraining from interpretive and evaluative commentary. There is an experience, then, of the narrator actively *withholding* affective response.

Strategic departures in the narration contribute to an especially distressing experience for readers of *2666*. When Bolaño's narrator illustrates police indifference with a heavy hand while refraining from judgment or emotional response, our desire to catalog and condemn these local failures spikes in intensity. The narrator's unemotional language creates an experience of *loneliness,* even hollowness, in our indignation. Whom does our feeling serve? If silence invites judgments of unresponsiveness and inaction, it also raises uncomfortable questions for readers who feel their own capacity for emotional response, or meaningful action, called into question. Stopping the murders lies outside most readers' locus of control. By contrast, indifference to suffering—specifically to violence against women—is a moral issue that narrator, implied author, and reader *can* address. The absence of narratorial judgment, even when narrative attention focuses on inadequate response, seems to ask for our judgment. Like a dry sponge, the narration opens the space for the "water" of our moral and ethical responses to fill its cells. When that response feels difficult for us, we likely experience discomfort and anxiety about the possibility of cruelty in *reading*.

Readers of *2666* may be tempted to compensate for the text's emotional poverty, a tendency that crops up as well in response to the flat affect of

---

27. See Phelan, *Experiencing Fiction,* for several examinations of narratives that engage readers in this way, from the relatively straightforward, such as Ambrose Bierce's "The Crimson Candle" (8–15) to the morally labyrinthine, such as Nabokov's *Lolita* (138–39).

Ocampo's narrative world. Perhaps we imagine melancholy or discouragement in Martínez and Lalo Cura's responses, or we assign some other redemptive narrative ("he feels overwhelmed by the impossibility of doing anything about it"; "he's just caught up in the system"). But this compensatory impulse may lead to further implication in the violence and indifference depicted in the narrative. In the case of Lalo Cura, for example, what does it mean to witness ourselves becoming more generous toward a man-boy who does not intervene in violence, whereas the women whom the officers rape and brutalize remain nonpeople, a backdrop for this illustration of indifference?

Crímenes constricts the potential routes for feeling, providing little access to empathy for the women, dead or alive, who endure violence.[28] One consequence is that the rare expressions of emotional response to violence against women catalyze retrospective awareness of the backlog of emotions that we do *not* feel in relation to the murders. In one scene, a local Mexican healer named Florita Almada appears on a television talk show as a guest psychic. But her impassioned "vision" about the murders only reaffirms what we already know: "niñas asesinadas, mujeres asesinadas. . . . ¡Es Santa Teresa! ¡Es Santa Teresa!" ("girls killed, women killed. . . . It's Santa Teresa! It's Santa Teresa!"; B546–47, W436). She continues, "Matan a mis hijas. ¡Mis hijas! ¡Mis hijas!" ("They're killing my daughters. My daughters! My daughters!") as she throws an imaginary *rebozo* over her head (B547, W436). The narrator opens the possibility that Florita is a charlatan, but more signs point to her sincerity. Still, her shrill exclamations seem to reverberate with embarrassing emotiveness in the postmodern cool of Bolaño's prose.

Is her response excessive? Does it seem overwrought because she is alone in it? Florita enacts the distress that the deaths of the "daughters" of Santa Teresa *should* cause the public. Psychic powers are hardly needed to identify crimes that are already in the open. Florita's most important role is not prophetic but pedagogical. She models the response that is missing, as if to say, "This is how you mourn; now join me in mourning." Like other elegiac appeals, her performance operates in a testimonial vein. As Ross Chambers notes, the goal of this mode of expressivity is to shift responses to the elegized plight from "delegation, disdain, or dismissal into empathy and involvement."[29] This is a bid for the reader to embrace the mourned loss as their own, recognize their "historical responsibility," and reorganize their response toward

---

28. In a few instances, still maintaining a rigid exterior view, the narrator depicts failed expressions of feeling, as when an investigator covers his head with his hands and moans, "como si llorara o pugnara por llorar" ("as if he were weeping or trying to weep"), but his face remains "seca, sin el más mínimo rastro de una lágrima" ("dry, and not the slightest trace of a tear"; B668, W534).

29. Chambers, "Attending to AIDS," 385.

conscience.[30] Despite the absence of a full resolution, this elegiac stance seems to hold out the consolation of meaningful participation.

Not so in Bolaño's anti-elegiac deformative fiction. The narrator implies that there is something unsavory, even suspect, to Florita's presence on stage. She is put on display to do the emotional labor that the wealthy elite and powerbrokers of Santa Teresa will not. In contrast to this morally dubious delegation of the work of feeling, Bolaño refuses to offer emotional resonance or otherwise lubricate First World readers' encounters with the extremes of cruelty. To do so would be to perform the narrative equivalent of Florita's cries, but Bolaño has no interest in making his text or characters into surrogates for readers who are unwilling to feel these losses for themselves. When an author provides us with access to characters' emotional and ethical responses to suffering, we may feel virtuous, as if we have discharged some obligation by following along. The discomfort of having this access reduced, or denied, reveals the often-self-serving nature of empathetic responses to literature from the global periphery. Bolaño denies this consolation, instead drawing on the ethical power of silence.

OVERDETERMINED PRECARIOUSNESS AND THE TRAP OF JUDGMENT

Bolaño breaks the detective genre frames, leaving us without longed-for solutions to the murders, and withholds the relief of emotional connection. In the absence of explanation or consolation, readers may shift their focus to the "crimes" of exploitation and local dysfunction that create the conditions for victimization. *2666* illustrates misogyny, corruption, and complicity. It also hints at ways that politicians, journalists, US diplomats, coroners, and businessmen in Santa Teresa may bear direct or indirect responsibility for the crimes. Still greater suspicion falls on the role of the maquiladoras. Most of the murders have a connection to at least one maquiladora, either through the victim's employment history or because the bodies are found in spaces connected to the factories. These include industrial parks, the routes women travel to the maquiladoras, and the dumps where they discard their waste.[31]

---

30. Chambers, "Attending to AIDS," 385.

31. The narrator notes that El Chile is the largest of the illegal dumps and the most frequent destination for both maquiladora waste and the bodies of the murdered women (B752; W602). Larger even than the largest (legal) municipal dump, it materially represents how the structures and pathways of illegality are more firmly established in Santa Teresa than the corresponding legal pathways.

The Santa Teresa murders constitute a disturbing continuation of the logic of female disposability that drives the maquiladora model. Starvation wages, a mostly female workforce, poor working conditions, high turnover, and nearly frictionless firing and replacement of workers who attempt to unionize stand out among the features of this distinctly exploitative economic arrangement.[32] Melissa Wright documents the bad-faith claims of maquiladora managers and executives that women workers are "impossible" to train, promote, or retain long-term.[33] Those in power use this characterization to justify implementing practices that "de-skill" labor to ensure that little training or technical proficiency is needed to accomplish a task.[34] By refusing to invest in training workers, maquiladora management removes any economic consequence to the rapid depletion of each woman's capacity for labor. This hastens the end of her employment, which Wright characterizes as "corporate death."[35] Short-term, strenuous labor in maquiladoras reduces laborers to a form of industrial waste. Maquiladora managers casually discard these "spent" workers—the vast majority of whom are identified as women—to make room for the continual supply of "fresh" migrant workers whose labor is more profitable.[36] The narrator locates the fictional victims as part of this factual pattern. For example, Sofía Serrano "había trabajado como obrera en tres maquiladoras y como camarera y últimamente hacía de puta en los baldíos de la colonia Ciudad Nueva" ("had worked at three maquiladoras and as a waitress, and most recently as a whore in the vacant lots of Colonia Ciudad Nueva"; B566, W452). The appearances of the bodies in the desolate areas

---

32. *Crímenes* names these circumstances repeatedly. For maquiladora labor practices, including starvation wages, see B474, W379; and B710, W568. For the mostly female workforce, see B363, W286; B449, W358; and B470, W375. For deplorable working conditions, see B449, W358; and B474, W379. For the threat of firing and replacement for workers who attempt to unionize, see B516, W412; B634, W507; B710, W568; and B721, W577. *Crímenes* documents how justifications for low pay lean on entrenched notions of women's work as supplementary (since their "primary" role is as mothers in the home). Reality defies these justifications both in *Crímenes*, as in actual US–Mexico border spaces, for women are often the primary breadwinners in their households. The economic realities of Santa Teresa strain the dual notions of *machismo* and *marianismo* that have long defined the ideals of domestic life in Latin America. *Machismo* often connotes misogyny but has a range of further implications; one can imagine, for example, a "benevolent" *machismo* that expresses masculinity through protectiveness and dutiful breadwinning. Conversely, *marianismo* offers a vision of femininity deeply rooted in the unattainable ideal of the Virgin Mary: women are to be consummately maternal yet not sexual, and their sphere of activity is expected to be limited to the household. Within these frames, the working woman is the antithesis of the masculine fantasy of a docile, dependent partner.

33. Wright, *Disposable Women*, 1–19.
34. Wright, *Disposable Women*, 86.
35. Wright, *Disposable Women*, 74–87.
36. Wright, *Disposable Women*, 96.

FIGURE 4.1. Two views of *Summer* (1573) by Giuseppe Arcimboldo. The image on the left shows the full canvas of *Summer*. The image on the right is a detail of the face.

surrounding the maquiladoras give the narrator occasion to document the conditions endured by women on their way to work. To reach the factories, they must walk long distances through empty fields, isolated desert spaces, and unlit, unpaved terrain. These journeys often take place early in the morning or during the night, depending on the women's ever-changing shifts. Even when the women can take the buses to the distant maquiladoras (rides they must pay for), many still must walk more than a kilometer in total darkness.

In literalizing and accelerating the women's demise, the murders represent the logical end point of the trajectory of exhaustion established by the maquiladora model. *2666* also demands attention to the misogyny, economic precarity, and social instability that ripple through domestic life in Santa Teresa. This multifaceted portrayal of the many factors affecting the crimes has discernible ethical implications. Exposing the conditions of the global periphery to a broad readership amplifies the appeals of activists and scholars who argue that the border femicides are crimes against humanity and should fall under international jurisdiction. But even as *Crímenes* seems to call for righteous indignation in the face of outrageous predation, Bolaño deploys multiple strategies to obstruct the satisfactions of judgment.

A reference to sixteenth-century painter Giuseppe Arcimboldo on the first page of *2666* offers a valuable, if surprising, visual analogy for the strategy by which Bolaño complicates readers' involvement with the sources of cruelty in Santa Teresa. Arcimboldo's best-known paintings combine the pictorial particularity of still life painting with the codes of portraiture (see figure 4.1).

The visual syntax of *Summer* invites multiple competing readings. Distance, or a focus on the whole image, enables the reader to see the profile of a man (figure 4.1, image on left). Proximity, or a narrowing of focus, makes the individual fruits and vegetables stand out distinctly (figure 4.1, image on right). The more we move in or focus our attention on any part of the portrait, the more we see an assemblage of harvested food or, at the closest range, the details of each fruit or vegetable. The farther we move out, the more we see a portrait in which these components together suggest aliveness (that robust frame and strong neck), emotion (the sly smile), and intelligence (the keen eye).

For a painting like *Summer,* both distance and proximity promote meaning and potential viewing pleasure. But what of the zone in between? When moving from proximity to distance (or vice versa), we confront a problematic middle space as well as the intellectual uneasiness and aesthetic ambiguity it arouses. In this zone, the composition of inanimate objects reminds us that what we see is an approximation that relies on our seeing to produce the effects of "life," "emotion," and "intelligence." In other words, the represented components draw attention to the composite character of the image and its relative rejection of norms for representing reality (in particular, the notion that the artist will strive to enchant their creation, concealing the composite and approximate character of the narrative world they create). The discomfort of the middle zone creates an urge to flee toward one extreme or the other.

Reading *Crímenes* is like being forced to engage with an Arcimboldo portrait from *only* a middle distance. We crave the relief of a position that might resolve the parts into a coherent whole or, conversely, that would let us focus attention and emotional resources on the specificity of the individual components. Instead, *Crímenes* suspends us between a composite portrait of overdetermined precariousness and the specific accounts of the murdered women. Bolaño refuses to allow readers to see the murders (or the victims) up close, as individual losses. Nor does he allow the relief of distance, a vantage point from which they might serve as cautionary tales about globalization in which impersonal forces like "transnational capital" and "neoliberal structures" by themselves are ultimately responsible. Instead, *Crímenes* presents an aggregate of cruelties that implicates readers. The paths from the maquiladoras in the novel lead also to readers' doorsteps. Commercial goods and "savings" generated in the free-trade zone are likely the most direct connection between many readers and the murders. Electronics, clothing, home furnishings, and other items flow from the maquiladoras into the US, Canada, and other world markets. *2666* suggests that, through banal purchases, unwitting consumers become contributors to border femicide: cheap jeans on the shelf here, the "wasting" of women workers there. Even as Bolaño exposes and denounces the deplorable conditions that accompany neoliberalism, the misogyny that fuels predation, and the resource drain driven by globalization, he ensures that readers feel the insufficiency of judging these sources of cruelty. Instead, he calls us toward examining our complicity and, above all, presses us to *see* the murders, rather than allow them to recede into a pattern of dysfunction.

INDETERMINATION AND THE MULTIPLICATION OF HORRORS

If Bolaño's goal is to increase the visibility of the murders, why not use the resources of fiction to dramatize individual instances of suffering? Treating an individual death as paradigmatic or exemplary of many others is a staple of literary representations of suffering, after all. But as Adam Kirsch notes, a signature of *2666* is Bolaño's "refusal to imagine his way into the murders. He does not take advantage of the novelist's privilege of going anywhere—into the mind of the victim as she suffers or of the killer as he kills."[37] Instead, Bolaño recounts the "appearance" of bodies after death, leaving the possibility of sadistic pleasure or excruciating suffering distressingly open. This exemplifies Bolaño's strategy of indetermination, but its reach extends beyond the portrayal of the femicides.

A narrative and stylistic cornerstone of deformation in *2666*, indetermination appears at the scale of individual sentences, images, and events as well as in the relationship between larger narrative units, such as the novel's five parts. Indetermination creates an unresolved vacillation between discrete, and often incompatible, possibilities that are articulated with comparable clarity, or can be inferred with equal plausibility. Whereas literary ambiguity typically invites some resolution or hints at connections, Bolaño's indetermination undermines attempts at establishing the relationship between narrated events or interpreting their significance.[38]

Bolaño provides a literal instance of indetermination in the "disco mágico" ("magic disc") displayed by Amalfitano in part 2 of the novel (B421, W334). The device (more technically referred to as a *thaumatrope*) uses an optical illusion to establish a unique relationship between two drawings rendered on separate sides of the same disc. When the disc is rotated rapidly by twirling

---

37. Kirsch, "Slouching towards Santa Teresa."
38. Literary ambiguity is, of course, far more complex than I can show here. For an exploration of the relationship between ambiguity, textuality, and reading desire, see Brooks, "Ambiguity."

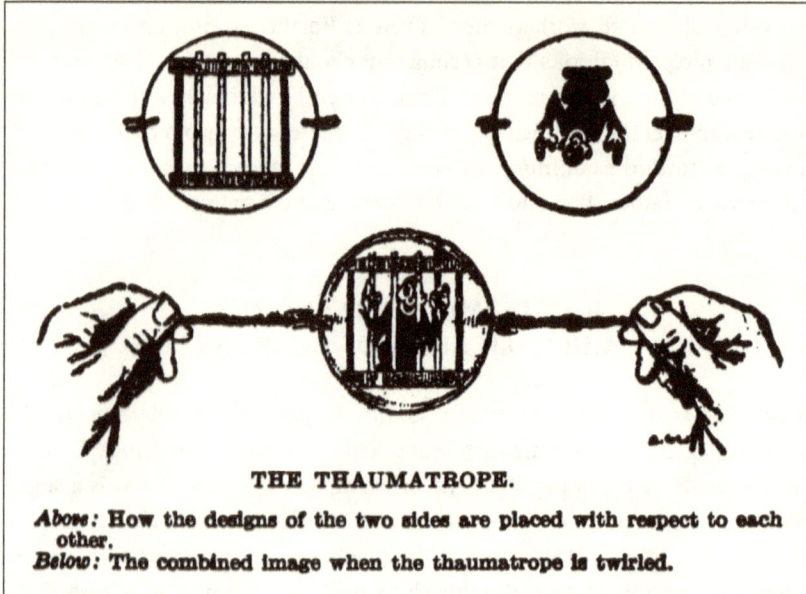

FIGURE 4.2. Illustration of a thaumatrope. The bottom half of the image shows how, when the strings of the thaumatrope are twirled, the two sides of the disc (depicted in the top half) appear combined to create the image of a monkey behind the bars. Lutz, *Animated Cartoons*, 17.

the attached strings, the drawings appear combined into a single image (see figure 4.2). The effect results from the persistence of vision. This is the delay that allows a new image to be inscribed on the retina before the previous image has completely faded, which takes about 1/25 of a second. Any two images may be combined in this way; common thaumatrope pairings include a horse and rider, a bird and tree, a hanged man and gallows, or, as in figure 4.2, a monkey and a cage.

In *2666*, the two images described on the magic disc are a laughing "borrachito" (a caricature of a "drunkard") and a set of jail bars.

Seemingly separate elements of *2666* interrelate or overlap in the reader's mind in much the same way that the two sides of the thaumatrope combine in perception. This is especially the case in relation to menacing elements. Black cars, snuff films, maquiladoras, unlit alleys, sexual predators, and other disturbing figures may be superimposed upon the bodies of the dead women, producing a bewildering and contradictory simultaneity. This effect thickens the intertextual weave of the novel. But most importantly, the connections we see—which seem so persuasive—reside first and foremost in our "vision" and do not inhere in the novel itself. The thaumotrope's rapidly alternating combination of discrete possibilities illustrates both the uncertainty of representation and the degree to which this uncertainty undermines interpretive confidence.

Amalfitano, the exiled Chilean philosophy professor whose name provides the title for the novel's second part, illustrates this point in a mock Socratic exchange with his teenage daughter's friends. Is the drunkard laughing because he doesn't know he is in prison? Or does he laugh because, even though he appears to be in prison, he knows he is free, safely inscribed on the opposite side of the disc? Amalfitano then suggests a different conclusion: the *borrachito* laughs knowingly at "nuestra credulidad, es decir se ríe de nuestros ojos" ("our credulity, you might even say at our eyes"; B423, W335). This recalls Ocampo's insistence in "Informe del Cielo y del Infierno" that our eyes are the source of whatever beauty, deformity, or cruelty we behold. In terms of our reading, the credulity Amalfitano speaks of corresponds to the expectation that close examination of the superimposed images and passages will yield interpretive convergence. Instead, rhetorical readers face the "laughter" of a text that will not let them establish the relationship between competing possibilities.

A minor example of indetermination appears in the passage that closes *La parte de Amalfitano*. Amalfitano dreams that he meets the last Communist philosopher (in the dream, this turns out to be Boris Yeltsin) on a patio's expanse of marble, which is interrupted by "una especie de cráter o de letrina" ("a kind of crater or latrine"; B290, W227). The phrase appears four times in only a few lines, and this emphasis helps turn it into a thaumatropic image. We may *try* to picture a crater or a latrine, but we must also countenance the presence of *both* even as we know that only one is possible. At the end of the dream, Amalfitano watches as Yeltsin disappears into the hole, swallowed up by what is described once again as "el cráter veteado de rojo o por la letrina veteada de rojo" ("the crater streaked with red or by the latrine streaked with red"; B291, W228). Does it matter if Yeltsin falls into a crater or a latrine? More to the point, why doesn't Bolaño resolve the image? What does he gain by emphatically *not* specifying one or the other?

This strategy imposes an uncomfortable vision, a rapid alternation between contrasting possibilities. After all, although they might appear similar from a certain angle, the differences between a latrine and a crater are significant. A latrine is a human intervention on a landscape to create a destination for bodily waste, whereas a crater is a geographic feature with origins unrelated to whatever uses it might come to serve. Like the spinning disc, Bolaño's "crater or latrine" produces a combined configuration that differs fundamentally from either of the options. This instance of indetermination implies several questions: is the abyss an inherent part of the world (crater), or is it a human addition (latrine)? How potent is scatology in this narrative world? Does the philosopher fall into a geological formation of unknown dimensions or into a vessel of human excrement? Like the novel more broadly, the dream reflects not only uncertainty on the level of the *told* (crater or latrine?), but also the narrator's refusal to specify what a character sees, although he has done so in other instances. Indetermination is not an aberration in the narrative fabric, but rather a feature that belongs to the project of *2666*. This local instance creates a gravitational pull that brings many of the novel's other examples of holes, abysses, voids, and subterranean spaces into a flickering assemblage of images.[39] In this way, indetermination multiplies possibilities and gestures at the exhausting prospect of trying to track them down and account for them. And that is not to mention the possible effort of considering the many instances of their co-presence in our reading, as in Amalfitano's dream. Even when indetermination is less extravagant, our attempts to interpret a particular passage in *2666* often reverberate, cascading through the novel's network of images and scenes and generating still more connections and counterpoints. This intra- and intertextuality complicates rhetorical reading. It shakes our confidence in our readerly instincts and destabilizes our sense of direction as we navigate the narrative.

2666's most dramatic, and distressing, instances of indetermination are the obscured death scenes in *Crímenes*. A tension persists between the evident, even overdetermined, vulnerability of women in Santa Teresa and the inaccessibility of the scenes of death. Potential sources of cruelty and death abound: the maquiladoras, narcotraffickers, psychopathic killers, politicians and their patrons, and other predators. But Bolaño strategically withholds specific causes, scenes, and circumstances for most of the deaths in *Crímenes*. In response to the question of how the women die, a resident of Santa Teresa explains, "Eso no está nada claro. Desaparecen. Se evaporan en el aire, visto y no visto. Y al cabo de un tiempo aparecen sus cuerpos en el desierto" ("Nobody's sure. They disappear. They vanish into thin air, here one minute,

---

39. To give just a few examples: early on the indeterminate "bulto en el fondo del agujero" ("mass at the bottom of the hole") on the beach in Pelletier's dream (B109, W79). In *Crímenes*, one of Klaus Haas's dreams involves sleeping at the edge of an abyss after finding his mouth sewn shut with a piece of flesh inside, which he ultimately discovers to be someone else's severed penis (B610–11, W488). While attempting to investigate the Santa Teresa murders, Albert Kessler dreams of a crater and a man "que daba vueltas alrededor del cráter" ("pacing around it"; B742, W594). Demetrio Águila describes a vagina as "un puto agujero. Un puto ojo. Una puta rajadura, como la falla en la corteza terrestre" ("a goddamn hole. A goddamn hole. A goddamn gash, like the crack in the earth's crust"; B553, W441). Crypts, trenches, and other subterranean spaces also abound in *La parte de Archimboldi*.

gone the next. In time, their bodies appear in the desert"; B363, W287, translation modified). As they track the femicides narrated in *2666*, readers often confront a lacuna between the disappearance of a live woman and the appearance of a dead body. This gap in *telling* underscores the inaccessibility of the specific circumstances of the deaths and occludes the violent actions of the killer(s). In the world of *2666*, the women become most visible in death, an appearance that lasts only until it stimulates the grossly inadequate response to "clean up" the evidence.

The inaccessibility of the events between the disappearance of a living woman and the appearance of a dead body incubates imagined scenes of cruelty. The effects of violence may be enumerated (as the repetitive accounts with their catalogs of wounds and violations attest). The suffering each act inflicts, however, remains unknowable. A chilling array of possible scenarios accompanies any given set of wounds. The narrator often stresses the indeterminacy of the pain that may have been involved in a death, multiplying possible scenes of cruelty. For example: "en el informe forense se indica que fue violada, acuchillada y quemada, sin especificar si la causa de la muerte fueron las cuchilladas o las quemaduras, y sin especificar tampoco si en el momento de las quemaduras Emilia Mena Mena ya estaba muerta" ("The medical examiner's report stated that she had been raped, stabbed, and burned, without specifying whether Emilia Mena Mena was already dead when the burns were inflicted"; B466, W372). For imaginative readers susceptible to envisioning literary descriptions, the uncertain order of afflictions overlaps and multiplies images of possible suffering. The result is a virtual *trauma*trope that comes from, but exists beyond, the novel.

Horrifying, equally possible, and mutually exclusive nightmare scenarios alternate before the mind's eye, superimposed in grisly simultaneity: Emilia Mena Mena is raped, then stabbed to death; her dead body is burned. Emilia Mena Mena is stabbed and burned, and the agony of these horrors is intensified by rape. Emilia Mena Mena is stabbed to death, then her dead body is raped and burned. In the case of a girl who "había muerto debido a un fallo cardiaco mientras era sometida a los abusos" ("had died of a heart attack while being subjected to the abuses"), we do not know when her heart attack occurred in relation to the chain of tortures and mutilations inflicted by the perpetrator(s) (B506, W404). Depending on our receptiveness to suggestion—or our propensity to compensate for narrative reticence—these configurations may proliferate further. This indeterminacy intensifies and extends a strategy evident in Ocampo's stories, where ambiguity prompts readers to activate potential cruelty and enact distressing scenarios. By maintaining the indeterminacy of the specific death scenes, Bolaño raises the stakes, amplifying the already high index of cruelty in *Crímenes*. Visualization and extrapolation from narrated particulars, practices that serve us so well in much of fiction reading, become liabilities here. Phrases like "sangrado profusamente" ("bled profusely") and "hematomas en las piernas" ("bruising on her legs") are trapdoors into scenes of horror that we populate with grisly possibilities (B444, W354). When it comes to femicides on the border, *2666* seeks to make them *persistently* visible to readers. The degree to which we sustain attention to the crimes, without relieving ourselves of responsibility, is one measure of Bolaño's success.

UNEVEN REALISM: DISRUPTING THE CONSOLATION OF "WITNESSING"

Given Bolaño's emphasis on the sources of vulnerability in these women's lives, one might conceive of reading *Crímenes* as a way of bearing witness to suffering. The circumstances represented in *2666* also exist in Ciudad Juárez. (Juárez is the Mexican border city most infamous for its high rate of unsolved murders targeting women, although these are prevalent in other border towns as well.) Many readers and critics assume that Bolaño's Santa Teresa stands in for Juárez. Even the jacket copy of the Anagrama edition of the novel, which describes Santa Teresa as a "trasunto de Ciudad Juárez" ("mirror image of Ciudad Juárez"), encourages this conflation.[40] But these characterizations elide Bolaño's important dislocation of the murders from their more obvious historical location.[41] A skeptical reader might presume that Bolaño, who had never been to Juárez, chose "Santa Teresa" to avoid scrutiny of the accuracy of the novel's spatial and historical detail. But his notes include a careful diagram of his invented city that marks its substantial difference from Juárez.[42]

Santa Teresa has a definite presence as an invention within Bolaño's narrative world. It also appears in *Los detectives salvajes* (*The Savage Detectives*) as a sleepy Sonoran backwater.[43] Even a cursory examination of the physical,

---

40. Jean Franco writes that the novel "situates the murdered women within the chaotic conditions of Ciudad Juárez, which, though renamed Santa Teresa in the novel, is surely meant to be identified by the reader." Franco, *Cruel Modernity*, 214.

41. Among others who stress the significance of Santa Teresa's *dis*location in terms of geography and other factors, see Pelaez, "Counting Violence"; and Levinson, "Case Closed."

42. Bolaño quoted in Insua, 106–7.

43. The 1970s Santa Teresa in *Los detectives salvajes* has a distinctly uncertain location; the narrator sleeps through the journey to the town, noting only that "cuando despierto estamos en Santa Teresa" ("when I wake up we're in Santa Teresa"). Bolaño, *Los detectives salvajes*, 568. Also, the famed Mexican healer Teresa Urrea (1873–1906) was often referred to as "Santa Teresa." Urrea lived in Sonora before moving to Nogales, Arizona, later in life.

cultural, political, and economic landscape of Bolaño's Santa Teresa makes its differences from Juárez plain.[44] Whereas Ciudad Juárez is surrounded by El Paso, Texas, on three sides because of the curvature of the Río Grande, the invented Santa Teresa floats like an island in a desert.

Inventing Santa Teresa reflects a broader strategy in 2666: a combination of direct reference, oblique reference, pseudo-reference, and flat-out invention that generates great variation in the relationships between the narrative and the external world. The degree of realism in one passage offers little reliable information about the terms of narration elsewhere in the novel. In these ways, Bolaño disrupts the expectation that we can reasonably estimate the relationship between 2666's narrative world and the world "out here." Most of the time, we manage to co-create the mimetic illusions of texts without overthinking the process. In the background of our reading, we gather and arrange what we take as signals of the intended degree of proximity between fictional world and reality. We generalize that sense of the narrative's referentiality to the entire text. The illusion of a consistent relationship between the external world and the novel's world derives from author and reader working together. But not all novels reward collaboration in this way, as becomes clear in Bolaño's determined disruption of any consistent relationships between the fictional world of 2666 and the actual world.

Bolaño deliberately destabilizes referentiality and cultivates unevenness. The effects of unevenness work in both directions, at times making inventions seem plausible (as with the murder accounts), and at other times making actual references seem unbelievable. For example, when Amalfitano reads a book called *O'Higgens es araucano: 17 pruebas, tomadas de la Historia Secreta de la Araucanía* (O'Higgens is Araucanian: 17 proofs, taken from the secret history of Araucanía), the implausibility of the title seems to suggest invention, but this book by Lonko Kilapán does exist outside the novel. Meanwhile, following the tradition of Bolaño's invented encyclopedia of right-wing writers, *La literatura nazi en América* (*Nazi Literature in the Americas*, 1996), 2666 presents many examples of pseudo-references. Among other inventions, Bolaño fabricates names for the tunnels of the Maginot Line (the failed French defense against Nazi invasion) as well as for the illegal dumps, neighborhoods,

---

44. Juárez is the largest city (population 1.5 million) in the Mexican state of Chihuahua; Bolaño describes Santa Teresa as a smallish city in the state of Sonora, Mexico, about 200 miles west of the actual Juárez (roughly where Nogales, Mexico, is located). The description of Santa Teresa as having only a handful of hotels and tourist attractions (B158–59, W118–19) more closely reflects the profile of Nogales, Mexico (population 200,000), than a sprawling city like Ciudad Juárez. Adobe, the fictional US city Bolaño places across the border from Santa Teresa, is a small, economically depressed town, more like Nogales, Arizona (population 20,000), than the booming economy of El Paso, Texas (population 672,538).

and maquiladoras of Santa Teresa. The names and circumstances of the murdered women are also carefully fictionalized.

Accounts of reader response to the wealth of testimonial literature suggests that readers are adept—too adept, Bolaño might say—at assimilating representative suffering. Bolaño's choices in *2666* suggest his determination to obstruct any efforts on readers' part to process or "witness" these murders. Santa Teresa is not Ciudad Juárez, and the invented crimes of Santa Teresa do not *represent* the Ciudad Juárez murders. Instead, Bolaño feeds forensic and journalistic language into the machine of his novel, reconfiguring scenes, dislocating circumstances, and flattening out a range of investigative registers, rather than reproducing investigative reports or creating fictional facsimiles.

Although the first description of a body's appearance likely registers as a shock, what becomes most notable as the murder accounts accumulate is their narrative *consistency*. Counterintuitively, Bolaño's studied use of forensic language calls attention to its departures from literal representation. Bolaño extensively researched the accounts of femicide in *2666*, including extensive correspondence with Mexican journalist Sergio González Rodríguez about the particulars of the murders. González Rodríguez, now deceased, dedicated decades to reporting on the femicides, and Bolaño pays tribute to these efforts by including a character in the novel, also a reporter, who goes by the same name. Even as *2666* bears clear marks of González Rodríguez's influence, Bolaño's portrayal of the crimes departs significantly from the journalist's approach, and these differences shape the ethical contours of *2666*.

González Rodríguez's essay "La vida inconclusa" ("Unfinished life"), consists of a series of factual accounts of femicide in Juárez, narrated in reverse chronological order without further context.[45] Although many of the characteristics observed in *Crímenes* are also present in "La vida inconclusa," there are significant, if not immediately apparent, differences between these seemingly homologous treatments. Consider this representative passage:

> 29/01/00, María Isabel Nava Vázquez, 18 años de edad, canal de irrigación en el poblado de Loma Blanca, a unos 500 metros de la carretera Juárez-Porvenir, asesinada a cuchilladas, calcinada, se la vio por última vez viva cuando fue a solicitar trabajo en una maquiladora cerca de la estación Aldama de la Policía Judicial del Estado (PJE). 19/01/00, osamenta de una mujer, 28 o 30 años de edad, a 2 kilómetros del cuartel de la Policía Montada Ejido Adolfo López Mateos, al parecer estrangulada, 6 meses a la intemperie, cabello castaño claro y largo, anillo de plástico en el dedo pulgar izquierdo, otro más

---

45. González Rodríguez, "La vida inconclusa."

se encontró en su pantalón vaquero color negro, playera blanca, desgaste de dientes que quizás indique padecimiento de epilepsia.[46]

29/01/00, María Isabel Nava Vázquez, 18 years of age, irrigation canal in the Loma Blanca settlement, about 500 meters from the Juárez-Porvenir highway, stabbed to death, burned, last seen alive when she went to look for work at a maquiladora near the Aldama Judicial Police Station. 19/01/00, skeleton of a woman between 28 and 30 years of age, two kilometers from the headquarters of the Ejido Adolfo López Mateos Mounted Police, apparently strangled, body exposed to the elements for six months, long, light brown hair, plastic ring on her left thumb, another in the pocket of black denim pants, white T-shirt, corrosion of the teeth that might indicate an epileptic condition.

The murder chronicles in "La vida inconclusa" display uniform compression. Exposition pertains strictly to the victim or the circumstances of her death. By contrast, the descriptive density is far more varied in *Crímenes,* and the narrator's attention sometimes strays from the particulars of the crimes. Instead of a narrow focus on facts, Bolaño's narrator offers vignettes and slips into free indirect discourse that often focalizes witnesses and investigators, as in the forty-fourth account of a murdered woman:

En los primeros días de septiembre apareció el cuerpo de una desconocida a la que luego se identificaría como Marisa Hernández Silva, de diecisiete años, desaparecida a principios de julio cuando iba camino a la preparatoria Vasconcelos, en la colonia Reforma. Según el dictamen forense había sido violada y estrangulada. Uno de los pechos estaba casi completamente cercenado y en el otro faltaba el pezón, que había sido arrancado a mordidas. El cuerpo se localizó a la entrada del basurero clandestino llamado El Chile. La llamada que puso sobre aviso a la policía la efectuó una mujer que se había acercado al basurero a tirar un refrigerador, al mediodía, una hora en la que no hay vagabundos en el basurero, sólo alguna partida ocasional de niños y perros. Marisa Hernández Silva estaba tirada entre dos grandes bolsas de plástico gris llenas de retales de fibra sintética. Vestía la misma ropa que en el momento de su desaparición: pantalón de mezclilla, blusa amarilla y tenis. (B580–81)

---

46. González Rodríguez, "La vida inconclusa," 260.

Early in September, the body of a girl later identified as Marisa Hernández Silva appeared. She was seventeen and had vanished at the beginning of July on her way to the Vasconcelos Preparatory School, in Colonia Reforma. According to the forensic report, she had been raped and strangled. One of her breasts was almost completely severed and the other was missing the nipple, which had been bitten off. The body was found at the entrance to the illegal dump El Chile. The call that alerted the police was made by a woman who had come to the dump to dispose of a refrigerator, at noon, a time of day when there were no tramps, just the occasional pack of children or dogs. Marisa Hernández Silva was sprawled between two big gray plastic bags full of scraps of synthetic fiber. She was wearing the same clothes she'd had on when she disappeared: denim pants, yellow blouse, and sneakers. (W463–64)

For all the lexical influence of forensic reports and journalism on Bolaño's treatment of the crimes, his narrator does not remain strictly within this frame. Narration drifts from the specificity of a police report and is imbued with lengthy indirect quotations from witnesses' accounts. The narrator focalizes the woman who finds the body, registering the scene from her perspective and adopting the scope of her concern. This includes her reasons for being at the dump and the habits of children, dogs, and vagrants in the area. This narration exceeds the frame of González Rodríguez's accounts, which maintain a tighter focus on the crime scene.

González Rodríguez's essay includes marks of its composite construction. To produce the descriptions, he condenses actual documents composed by a range of investigators. Their presence is indirectly suggested by differences in register, parenthetical references, and variation in terminology. For example, in one account compiled by González Rodríguez, "violencia sexual" ("sexual violence")[47] suggests the recording investigator's tendency toward euphemism, while other reports document rape with clinical precision: "violada por vía anal y vaginal" ("anally and vaginally raped")[48] and "dilatación anal y vulvar" ("dilation of the anus and vulva").[49] By contrast, *Crímenes* directly mentions investigative and forensic documents, undermining any implicit claim that the account is itself such a document.[50] Bolaño mixes voices and perspectives, but the phrases he uses to describe forensic particulars in *Crímenes* are far more

---

47. González Rodríguez, "La vida inconclusa," 258.
48. González Rodríguez, "La vida inconclusa," 262.
49. González Rodríguez, "La vida inconclusa," 269.
50. For mentions of the findings of police forensic reports and of coroners' comments in autopsy reports, see B490, W391; B506, W404; B514, W411; B562, W449; B576, W460; B580, W463; and B626, W500, among other instances.

consistent than in González Rodríguez's nonfiction account. The paltry findings of the revolving circuit of investigators and coroners assigned to Bolaño's invented cases are filtered through the consciousness and lexicon of a single narrator.

Bolaño's careful language alludes to emotional detachment and objectivity, but the uniformity of his method—the degree of "evening out"—exceeds even nonfiction accounts of the murders. The tone and terminology are *too* consistent, so uniform that we sense a narratorial or authorial presence carefully applying what Mikkel Krause Frantzen calls a "forensic aesthetic," rather than imagining "real" source documents filtered through a narrator's rendition.[51] Consistency of phrasing becomes afflictive when it intensifies the monotony, lack of variation, and *lack of imagination* in the accounts. By "lack of imagination," I refer first to the murderers: the same violations, wounds, and indignities appear repeatedly. But this characterization also applies implicitly to the narrator, who—we realize based on the narration elsewhere—*could* adjust the scope, vary the rhythm, or alter the granularity of the accounts. The determined consistency in the femicide accounts is a choice, a deliberate deformation.

A refusal to summarize, compare, vary the focus, or otherwise relieve our discomfort prevails across the murder accounts in *Crímenes*. The narrator recounts the particulars of the forty-fourth, sixtieth, ninetieth, and one hundred eleventh murders with the same detachment, limited range of expression, and closely controlled level of detail as the first.[52] There is neither coordination nor subordination of victims. The acts of violence appear with serial insistence and consistency, whether they are against children or older women, sex workers or factory workers, foreigners or Mexican nationals. Even when wounds are the same as in previous accounts, they are described as if for the first time. Each repeated location is detailed as if no other woman has been found there. The narrator details each instance of police failure as if we might have reason to expect otherwise. That the effect is repetitive and tedious is itself the point. Parataxis in the accounts and across *Crímenes*—one murder after another—resists sense-making and closure.[53]

---

51. Frantzen, "Forensic Fiction."

52. As Sol Pelaez notes, however, the *narrator* never provides "a final progressive list" and avoids the "most conventional cumulative mode of counting." Pelaez, "Counting Violence," 41. See writing on *2666* by Marcela Valdés, Carlos Walker, and Alexis Candia Cáceres for critics who, like Pelaez and me, count these crimes, which total 111. Valdés, "Alone among the Ghosts"; Walker, "El tono del horror" (The tone of horror); and Candia Cáceres, "Todos los males el mal" (Of all evils, the worst).

53. For a compelling reading of parataxis as part of an "aesthetic of poverty" or "sobriety," see Herlinghaus, *Narcoepics*, 213–14.

Bolaño's insistence on readers' prolonged, unresolved encounters with suffering contributes to a coherent anti-elegiac deformative project in *2666*, which imposes a mode of vision that obstructs any conclusive mourning. Considered as an aesthetic and ethical intervention, the disruption of a dysfunctional pattern or way of seeing (our relation to suffering in peripheral spaces) is an effort to restore proper sight. This may be. But what about the perspective of the recipient of the intervention? An eye surgeon's conviction that an operation is necessary does little to lessen an unwilling patient's sense that the "procedure" she undergoes constitutes a mutilation. By the same token, Bolaño's deformative agenda will register for some readers as a withholding of literary satisfactions to which they feel entitled—or even as an instance of cruel disregard for their distress.

Or perhaps we hypothesize that Bolaño deploys the monotony of the murder accounts as a lesson or test of our endurance and commitment. Narration (ethics of *telling*) in *2666* creates a sense of boredom and fatigue in the face of narrated suffering. This, in turn, heightens our vulnerability to the feeling that *we* are cruel (ethics of *reading*). Literary critic Shaj Mathew poses the question this way, "Do you have the courage to read—and finish—this chapter?" He adds, "if not, it is possible to feel implicated—and complicit—in the crippling indifference" that also characterizes "the public's real-life relationship to the violence in Ciudad Juárez."[54] The act of "turning away" from the novel—or skipping over the accounts—can produce a sense of complicity and active indifference (ethics of *reading*). Bolaño insists that we notice the failures of attention represented in *Crímenes* and in the three parts that precede it.

By the time rhetorical readers reach the accounts of femicide, they cannot recoil without repeating the problematic reactions of discredited characters. The critics function here as our most disconcerting "stand-ins." Unlike the maquiladora workers driven by economic necessity to migrate to the Mexican border or Amalfitano, whose Chilean citizenship complicates his professional and immigration status, the critics' visit to Santa Teresa is voluntary. They have the luxury of distance from its problems and the European Union passports to facilitate their retreat when they have met their limit. They respond to the conditions in the city with a mix of disgust and fascination—Norton repeatedly describes Santa Teresa as "esa ciudad horrible" ("that horrible city")—before turning away from it completely.[55] *2666* may not tell us what we should do in response to the network of horrors it illuminates, but the critics clearly offer one model of what *not* to do. Still, Bolaño's deformative

---

54. Mathew, "Ciudad Juárez," 409, 408.
55. For representative instances, see B189, W143; B196, W149; and B199, W152.

sights are not fixed (only) on those who would spare themselves the challenge of uncomfortable reading or seeing. His goal is to ensure that even readers who persist will not be able to shake off their responsibility, no matter their "faithfulness" or thoroughness in reading. Bolaño doesn't want us to turn away from the reports. He wants us to have the *experience* of wanting to turn away. *2666* insists that we recognize the impulse to stop looking, even if we do not follow it. And Bolaño incorporates his knowledge of that impulse into his broader deformative project.

These narrative encounters need not be tests of endurance (or, some might say, of masochism). To turn away—perhaps by taking a break from reading—may be part of the broader unfolding of a rhetorical reader's relationship with the novel. The ethical implications for readers hinge primarily on an awareness of how we relate to narrated suffering, and why, as well as of the other ways of responding that might be possible. As we confront these reports, or as we seek a reprieve from them, might we inquire into the factors that shape our typical protocols of response to depictions of pain? Could we ask ourselves how staying with, or returning to, painful material matters even when doing so seems to yield few rewards? And might rhetorical readers distinguish between this mode of uneasy perception and the more self-serving mechanics of "bearing witness" as a mode of unburdening?

ILLUSIONS OF INTERPRETIVE ESCAPE

In reading *2666*, we find ourselves in a tightening net of inadequacy, unease, and even guilt. Bolaño weaves it from the strong threads of his deformative strategies, especially his treatment of the femicides in Santa Teresa, the responses to those murders, the circumstances that make the murders (seem) likely, and the broader logics of disposability and unaccountability that condition the deaths. Readers respond in their own ways, according to their own set of protocols, past reading experiences, and specific textual responses. Still, the most likely reaction for experienced readers is to try to contain their distress through interpretation and consideration of theme.

To feel our own guilt causes more distress than to contemplate a *theme* of readers' guilt in *2666*. Interpretation feels like "doing something." And it is, in fact, doing something. Bolaño presses us further, insisting that we consider who that "something" serves. In fact, the "better" our reading of *2666* in a traditional sense—the more effectively we find themes and patterns or chart constellations of meaning—the greater our potential sense of failure. The deformative character of the novel exposes interpretation as a self-serving act, focused not on sincerely discharging a moral responsibility but on eluding that responsibility's unpleasant hold on us. Each time we attempt to assess the novel at a farther remove, we still get ourselves tangled in the insinuations of guilt that Bolaño patterns so insistently in the novel. Writing this chapter itself remains vulnerable to critique as an instance of this frame-broadening move.

Faced with this quandary, readers may see a perverse determination, on Bolaño's part, to make them suffer. We should be careful, though, of too quickly declaring ourselves victims of cruelty. We may notice the structural similarity—the feeling *as if* we have been treated cruelly—while staying present to the difference between actual suffering and the construction, by an author, of the warranted occasion for readers to feel a sense of persistent inadequacy and guilt. Perhaps we can remake interpretation as a contemplation of guilt, as a sustained act of mourning. First, we need to understand the traps laid for us as we conclude the novel—and as we reread it, whether that rereading is a literal return to the first part of the novel or an imagined rerouting through textual details.

The fifth and final part of the novel, *La parte de Archimboldi*, features prominently in *2666*'s invitations to interpretive release. In the progression of our readings, we attend to "endings" as a rich site for creating retrospective coherence. Even Bolaño, famed for his aesthetics of inconclusion, ties up some loose ends. The problem is that they are not the loose ends we are most concerned about, those that pertain to the femicides, or our responsibility for harm. To the contrary, Bolaño provides us with intimate access to Archimboldi, the mysterious writer whom the critics lionize and pursue in the first part of the novel. Moving back to the 1930s and then working forward to the 1990s, when Archimboldi departs for Santa Teresa, the last part of the novel explores instances of individual and historical cruelty that reverberate the lines of connection to the murders in *Crímenes*. Part 5 tantalizes readers with the possibility of reading deaths in Santa Teresa as the strange fruit of a tree whose roots extend deep into human atrocities, from Aztec human sacrifice, to crucifixion, to the Holocaust. I write "tantalize" because I think Bolaño establishes *Archimboldi* as a test: Will readers use these final 350 pages to improvise consolations, retreat into theme, and "unburden" themselves of *Crímenes*?

Part 5 offers many temptations to flee the "middle zone" of indetermination in favor of a more distant position from which the details catalogued in *Crímenes* would be less vexingly prominent. Does a thematizing shift outward in scope *work*? Do the Santa Teresa femicides contribute to a broader interpretation of *2666* in ways that alleviate their afflictive potential? Not unless we read forcefully against the grain of the narrative. Thematic readings only intensify the potential scenarios of cruelty, heighten the challenge of interpreting the murders, and effectively discredit efforts to assimilate the femicides as part of a series of humanitarian catastrophes. Consider the contrast between the casual abandonment of corpses in Santa Teresa and the disposal of victims' bodies in other historical contexts addressed in the novel.

The unconcealed disposal of murdered women in dumps in Santa Teresa so prevails that it emerges as a norm, even to the police.[56] But it contrasts sharply with the logic that governs a Nazi bureaucrat's "handling" of Greek Jews in part 5. What most disturbs Sammer, the Nazi bureaucrat, is not the mass murder itself but the inability of his men to hide the bodies. Each time they attempt to dig graves for the Jews they murdered, the Nazi soldiers discover that, where they dig, "había algo" ("there was something there"; B955, W764). Although Sammer never identifies human remains as the "algo" ("something") that the men uncover, the implication is plain. The site is already saturated with corpses. With each failed attempt to find space for the victims, Sammer turns more rancorous, shouting, "Recuerde que no se trata de encontrar sino de no encontrar" ("Remember the idea isn't to find things, it's to *not* find them"; B956, W764, emphasis in original). The urgency of Sammer's intent to conceal the results of violence attests, not to shame or regret, but to a perverse sense of decorum, an impulse to bracket violence off from the "normal" operations of society. Although comparisons of magnitude of suffering collapse under the weight of the Holocaust, Bolaño ensures that the singular horror of the casual disposal of women in Santa Teresa stands out in its callousness even in comparison with Nazi concealment.

The Holocaust is not the only point of comparison dangled before readers' eyes. Describing the Santa Teresa women as "desaparecidas" recalls the widespread use of the term "los desaparecidos" ("the disappeared") to characterize the abductions, torture, and murder of citizens (often students) under the US-supported dictatorships in Chile (1973–90) and Argentina (1976–83). References in 2666 to feminist protests on behalf of "las desaparecidas" recall the efforts of Las Madres de Plaza del Mayo, the group of mothers who marched daily outside Argentina's presidential palace to protest the disappearances of their adult children and demand action. Given that the "long arm of justice" finally brought down the Argentine dictatorship, to place the Santa Teresa

---

56. At one point, an investigator finds a body abandoned on a construction site and wonders, "por qué ir a arrojar el cadáver allí . . . cuando lo más lógico era tirarla en el desierto o por los alrededores de un basurero?" ("why go to the effort to leave the body [there] . . . when the logical thing would be to dispose of it in the desert or at the edge of a dump?"; B532, W425). The few bodies that the investigators find buried are only "semienterrados" ("half-buried"), as if the killers "no se esmeraron" ("didn't try very hard"; B684–85, W548).

murders in a broader Latin American context that includes *los desaparecidos* offers the comfort of imagining a future reckoning. But during the Southern Cone dirty wars, those who were "missing" far outnumbered those who returned, whether alive or as corpses. By contrast, in Bolaño's Santa Teresa, there are significantly more bodies recovered than women reported missing.[57] Often, officials dismiss unidentified Santa Teresa victims as prostitutes, migrants passing through on their way to an illegal crossing into the US, or others without family or known only to people too disenfranchised to contact the authorities. In other cases, however, the lack of response even baffles the police, as when no one comes for the body of a well-dressed young teen (B584, W466–67). Bolaño makes plain that concealment is not at issue in Santa Teresa, where dead women are openly discarded and their absence from the living fails to register as a concern.[58]

The tentacular whole of *2666* tugs at our attention with intertextual references—and a felt sense of urgency to follow the connections. We may imagine that charting constellations of meaning allows us to discharge our duty, or, alternatively, positions us at enough of a remove to appreciate Bolaño's strange portrait from a safe distance. But Bolaño systematically subverts narrative's thematic functions. Instead, any effort at focusing primarily on theme intensifies the ambivalent, afflictive potential of intertextuality to reinscribe and underscore our culpability. Attempts to map themes onto *Crímenes* make us vulnerable to the charge that we are unwilling to look, or that we are driven by a desire to stop seeing what the novel demands that we see.

READERS' DISTRESSING DOUBLES

In *2666*, suggestion is all it takes to activate distressing echoes. As we progress through the novel's layers of cruelty and harm, new horrors force the

---

57. The narrator notes that many of the murdered women's bodies "iban a parar a la fosa común del cementerio pues nadie reclamaba sus cadáveres" ("ended up in the common grave at the cemetery because no one claimed their bodies"; B328, W258). When an unidentified body of one of the murdered women is made available to families, "nadie lo reconoció como el de una de sus hijas, hermanas, primas o esposas" ("no one recognized her as a daughter, sister, cousin, or wife"; B684, W547). Elsewhere, the narrator observes of a murdered woman that "nadie la echó en falta" ("no one had reported her missing"; B450, W359). See also B584, W466; B618, W493–94; B631, W504; and B635, W507.

58. Other instances of thematic patterning threaten to trivialize the femicides. For example, in part 1 the critics meet a circus performer whose stage magic act consists of a series of disappearances of increasing magnitude. He begins with "haciendo desaparecer pulgas" ("making fleas disappear") and leading up to the disappearance of doves, a cat, and a dog before the finale in which "finalizo mi acto haciendo desaparecer a un niño" ("I end my act by disappearing a kid"; B176, W133). The discussion of the act makes no mention of making anything reappear.

reassessment of instances elsewhere in the novel. Growing awareness of the implication of First World leisure in the suffering in Santa Teresa magnetizes our attention to characters who abuse privileges conferred by class, nationality, and other accidents of identity.[59] These characters serve as an unflattering, distorted mirror for international readers. What does it mean to identify, initially, with the literary critics of part 1, only to see them emerge as figures of First World criminality and predation? What changes when we see how their criminality and predation contribute to widespread patterns of harm? We may disavow this connection. We may insist that, whatever positional similarity exists between the literary critics and ourselves, we cannot be guilty of fictional crimes. Still, this sort of insistence or disavowal has a hollow ring. Bolaño endeavors to keep us entangled with his portrayal of professional readers who capitalize on the vulnerability of Third World bodies. When those responsible for harm are sufficiently like readers to evoke feelings of responsibility or complicity, Bolaño ensures that we recognize both their perpetration and their guilt.

In particular, Bolaño encourages readers—many of whom he anticipated would be students and professors—to see something of themselves in these academic characters. Whatever their myopic and self-serving tendencies, the critics consider themselves sensible liberals. Any identification with them becomes intensely uncomfortable, however, when the two men, Jean-Claude Pelletier and Manuel Espinoza, berate and beat a Pakistani taxi driver "hasta que dejarlo inconsciente y sangrando por todos los orificios de la cabeza, menos por los ojos" ("until he was unconscious and bleeding from every orifice in the head, except the eyes"; B103, W74).[60] Their colleague and lover, Liz Norton, does not participate, but neither does she render aid to the driver, whom they abandon on a London street. The narrator's observation of the intense sexual arousal that accompanies her apparent distress at the men's violence effectively undermines the sincerity of her intermittent pleas for the men to stop the beating.

This passage stands out among the many treatments of cruelty in the novel. Most instances stress the grizzly effects of violence while withholding the specific scene of harm. Here, by contrast, we know precisely what prompts the

---

59. Earlier novels express Bolaño's disgust with Latin American intellectuals' complicity in state repression. Both *Estrella distante* (Distant star) and *Nocturno de Chile* (By night in Chile) suggest that literary aspiration and violent repression are frequent bedfellows. In 2666, a Mexican character named "el Cerdo" ("the Pig") is ostensibly a novelist and essayist but is more obviously an agent of the state, fat from the perquisites of his position and the power it confers (B136–40, W100–104).

60. Note the echo of the accounts of the murdered women in Santa Teresa and the cataloguing of how many orifices in their bodies had been raped.

attack and how it unfolds. The Pakistani's "crime" is that he disparages the critics' civilly negotiated three-way romance (B102, W73). The men see his comment about whores and pimps as an unjust attack on their (and Liz's) honor. Their sense of themselves as *victims* of an imagined cruelty (that is, cruelty in the story they tell themselves) catalyzes their abusive behavior. Beyond their implicit claim to victimization, the critics experience the Pakistani as "cruel" in the etymological sense: he is raw, uncooked, out of place, insufficiently prepared for access to *their* London. (Although only Norton is British, as European Union citizens, the male critics move freely across borders.) Before the attack, the narrator notes the Pakistani's outsider status in the critics' eyes. Although they esteem their own "civilized" multilingualism, they devalue the driver's departures from English as instances of a "lengua incomprensible" ("incomprehensible tongue"). His navigational error further demonstrates, to them, his lack of belonging in London (B102, W73).

The affective benefits of this violent episode accrue to the perpetrators. Afterward, each is immersed in "la quietud más extraña de sus vidas" ("the strangest calm of their lives"; B103, W74). Given the narrator's recounting of their internal states at the time of the beating (pleasure to the point of orgasm) and their indifference to the fate of the driver after, there is no escaping their cruelty. As in *La virgen*, the significance of the event is articulated solely in terms of its impact on the focalized perpetrators. They relate to the (potentially) wasted life of the victim as if it were irrelevant except as it affects them, whether positively, by enabling their affective release, or negatively, by complicating their trip. We witness the Pakistani driver's physical vulnerability—he crumples in on himself like "un ovillo en el suelo" ("a ball on the ground") while the blows rain down on him (B103, W74). But his internal experience remains inaccessible, and his humanity recedes into his narrative function as the recipient of their cruelty.

Jean Franco reads the beating as evidence that, in Bolaño's fiction, "the perpetrators are not always criminals."[61] But the critics *are* criminals—criminals who have not been apprehended. The morning after the beating, Pelletier and Espinoza confide to each other that they wiped their fingerprints from the taxi before fleeing the scene (B105, W76). The narrator describes this revelation as a "confession." But what do they "confess," given that both know what transpired? They reveal their shared knowledge that they *should* be punished, and that they knew as much in the moments immediately after their crime of "passion." As EU citizens, the critics can leave the country quickly, further limiting the likelihood of detection or accountability. Shortly after beating

---

61. Franco, "Questions for Bolaño," 213.

the Pakistani, they return, "frescos como lechugas" ("as fresh as daisies"; B117, W85) to their circuit of literary conferences and seminars. They face no consequences.

The critics' smooth transition from perpetration to renewed participation in academia underscores a disconcerting, bidirectional relationship between the two. On the one hand, the indeterminate character of the exact causes of the murders in Santa Teresa holds open multiple potentially guilty parties. On the other hand, Bolaño leaves no room for doubt regarding the critics' crimes of direct violence (Pelletier and Espinoza) and of complicity (Norton). During the beating, Espinoza and Pelletier deliver each kick to the Pakistani taxi driver in the name of a particular icon of cosmopolitan liberalism: "esta patada es por Salman Rushdie . . . esta patada es de parte de las feministas de París . . . esta patada es de parte de las feministas de Nueva York" ("this one is for Salman Rushdie . . . this one is for the feminists of Paris . . . this one is for the feminists of New York"; B103, W74). The situational irony is thick. The alternation between these "dedications" and raw violence powerfully dramatizes, and magnifies, what Idelber Avelar calls "the limits of well-meaning first-world liberalism in dealing with ethical questions in an international context."[62]

We see repeatedly the critics' refusal to deal with ethical questions at all, at least not when they pertain to bodies other than those of fellow Europeans. The men display a knowing willingness to extract the energy of "Third World" laborers—whether "here" or "there"—and translate it into their First World pleasure. In addition to the dramatized transgressions, both Espinoza and Pelletier frequently buy sex from immigrant women living in Europe.[63] By giving a face to First World criminality, Bolaño forestalls the temptation to locate responsibility for violence only behind the blank walls of the maquiladoras, or in the executive suites of multinational companies, armored cars of drug cartels, or thorny brambles of misogyny.

If the critics are unlikely to face consequences for harming a "Third World" person in London, the possibility of accountability recedes almost completely in the context of Santa Teresa. The critic Espinoza's relationship with a teen-aged girl during their visit appears not merely opportunistic, but positively predatory to readers who hold in view the desperate situation of Mexican

---

62. Avelar, "Ethics of Interpretation," 90.
63. A narratorial aside provides some insight into Espinoza's disregard for the dignity of sex workers. When Pelletier appears to have become too interested in the inner life of a North African prostitute, Espinoza chastises him, as if to reground him in the "proper" relationship of extraction: "a las putas . . . hay que follárselas, no servirles de psicoanalista" ("whores are there to be fucked . . . not psychoanalyzed"; B115, W84).

working-class women depicted in *Crímenes*. And for a reader who has completed the novel, this relationship shimmers with distressing resonances of the circumstances hypothesized to explain some of the murders.

As Espinoza's pursuit of Rebeca unfolds, several details mark the high school student, like Amalfitano's daughter Rosa, as a potential future victim of femicide. Espinoza notices that her house is located "en las zonas en donde . . . se cometían los crímenes" ("[in] the area where . . . the crimes were committed"; B193, W147). Rebeca informs Espinoza during a date at a club that "al salir de aquella discoteca habían secuestrado a dos de las muchachas que tiempo después aparecieron muertas" ("two of the girls who later appeared dead had been kidnapped on their way out of the club"; B198, W151, translation modified). But whereas the journalist Fate "rescues" Rosa, transporting her across the US border at her father's urging, Espinoza capitalizes on Rebeca's vulnerability.

The narrator's descriptions of Espinoza's interactions with Rebeca's family highlight the precariousness of her circumstances. Her parents' "approval" surprises even Espinoza, and the mother's strained assertion that Espinoza "tenía cara de hombre responsible" ("had a responsible look") appears more an expression of desperate optimism than an accurate assessment of his character (B201, W153). The obvious rationale for the family's tolerance of Espinoza is that his sexual interest in Rebeca comes with the paltry benefits of additional meals for the girl and her younger brother, small gifts of money, and the Spaniard's purchase of numerous rugs. The narrator stresses the transactional dynamic by connecting gifts and sexual activity: "le entregó los otros regalos que le había comprado y después volvieron a follar hasta que empezó a amanecer" ("he gave her the other gifts he'd bought her and then they fucked again until the sun began to come up"; B201, W154). As with Fernando and his lovers, Espinoza's repeated purchases from and for Rebeca position these sexual encounters within the realm of exchange.

The narrator also stresses the impossibility of meaningful consent from Rebeca. Before their first "polvo rápido" ("quick fuck") in a car parked outside Rebeca's home, for example, Espinoza "le preguntó si quería hacer el amor y ella asintió con la cabeza, varias veces, sin decir nada" ("asked if she wanted to make love and she nodded, several times, without saying anything"; B198, W151). How meaningful can a nod of the head be, given the difference of power and age between Espinoza and Rebeca, and the fact that the teen has had enough drinks to smell of alcohol? After a few more cheap lunches and generic gifts, Espinoza dresses Rebeca up in lingerie and takes her to his hotel room where "la folló hasta que ella no fue más que un temblor entre sus brazos" ("[he] fucked her until she was no more than a tremor in his arms"; B201,

W154). The language of expenditure ("until she was no more than . . .") figures this sexual encounter as a variation on the extraction of energy and labor from young women in the maquiladoras. The distance between predatory sexual acts and deadly violence narrows in the case of Espinoza.

On a first reading, readers likely disapprove of Espinoza's behavior and find his unethical opportunism disturbing. But the full deformative potential of the scenario emerges only as we come to understand its resonances with other scenes and situations, especially those we encounter in *Crímenes*. From there, our reassessment opens up the possibility of actions far darker than manipulation. One way of reading Espinoza's "affair" with Rebeca is as a preview of the sort of dynamic that makes young women's bodies appear in the desert. Espinoza's distressing behavior becomes overlaid with, and intensified by, the scenes of horror we encounter elsewhere. This thaumatropic effect also heightens the discomfort of readers' relative positional similarity to the critics. By characterizing a literary critic like Espinoza as culpable, Bolaño connects readers to the sources of suffering, both immediate (the hands that strangle and mutilate) and structural (the maquiladoras, neoliberal policies).

READY-MADE DISTRESS, DISLOCATION, AND EXPOSURE

With Espinoza's predatory interest in Rebeca, Bolaño makes plain the harms of First World pleasure-seeking, but he leaves it to us to extrapolate her possible dislocation from her family and potential exposure to cruelty. *2666* offers a figure for this progression from vulnerability to exposure: Amalfitano's impromptu readymade, a backyard conceptual art piece inspired by Marcel Duchamp's *Le Readymade malheureux* (*The Unhappy Readymade*, 1919, Buenos Aires [original lost]). Upon arriving in Santa Teresa, the Chilean philosophy professor unpacks a geometry book he does not recognize. His inability to recall how he acquired it proves distressing, and he is preoccupied by the book—even obsessed—until he hangs it from the clothesline in the backyard of the house he shares with his daughter Rosa. The book is the poet Rafael Dieste's *Testamento geométrico* (Geometric testament, 1975), and Amalfitano's description of *Testamento* applies equally well to *2666* itself. He describes the volume as several books, "con su propia unidad, pero funcionalmente correlacionados por el destino del conjunto" ("each independent, but functionally correlated by the sweep of the whole"; B240, W186). In response to Rosa's objection that exposing this "innocent" book to the elements is madness, Amalfitano explains: "la idea es de Duchamp, dejar un libro de geometría colgado a la intemperie para ver si aprende cuatro cosas de la vida real" ("it's a

Duchamp idea, leaving a geometry book hanging exposed to the elements to see if it learns something about real life"; B251, W195). The narrator provides a fuller account. During his stay in Argentina in 1919, Marcel Duchamp sent a book of geometry to his sister as a wedding gift with instructions that she hang it out on a clothesline (B245-46, W190-91). The result, *Le Readymade malheureux* (*The Unhappy Readymade*), consists of a book disfigured by the weather. Its remnants were photographed but not preserved (see figure 4.3).[64]

When Amalfitano initially finds the *Testamento*, he believes that he is seeing it for the first time. Its very presence signals that there must have been other encounters, namely, when he purchased it, or at least when he packed it upon leaving Barcelona for Santa Teresa (B241-43, W187-88). The book cannot account for how it arrived among Amalfitano's things any more than the murdered bodies of women can explain their deaths. But it did not simply *appear* among his things. We know this intuitively, just as we know that, whatever the narrator's choice of words, the murdered women's bodies do not simply *appear* in dumps and abandoned fields. Someone left the bodies; someone purchased and packed the book. Still, Amalfitano's inability to locate any memory of the book distresses him. His discomfort makes the book an uncanny, problematic object for him. Without knowing why himself, he associates it with the trauma of the Chilean dictatorship he fled, and a sense of urgency marks his expulsion of the book to the backyard. He feels "mucho más aliviado" ("much calmer") once the book is exiled to the outdoors (B245, W190). The condition for "disowning" the book seems to be the inability to tolerate having it belong to him.

From that point on, Amalfitano insists, "no es mío" ("it isn't mine") and "no lo siento como un libro que me pertenezca" ("I really don't have the sense it belongs to me"; B251, W196). His comments anticipate (if it is our first reading) or echo (if we are rereading) the words of several women upon finding a murdered victim in *Crímenes*: "Nunca la habíamos visto. Esta criatura no es de aquí" ("We've never seen her before. She isn't from around here, poor thing"; B443, W353). But disavowal, no matter how insistent, does not accomplish separation. After Amalfitano hangs the book on the line, he remains obsessed with the patterns in its pages, scribbling its diagrams on student work and in notebooks. When Rosa protests, "lo vas a destrozar" ("you're going to destroy it"), Amalfitano retorts with a legalistic refusal of responsibility: "Yo no . . . la naturaleza" ("Not me . . . nature"; B251, W195). *Nature* is responsible; Amalfitano does not acknowledge that exposing the book to the elements implicates

---

64. While the original artwork was not preserved, it was documented in an anonymous photograph, attributed to Suzanne Duchamp and Jean Crotti, now at the Philadelphia Museum of Art.

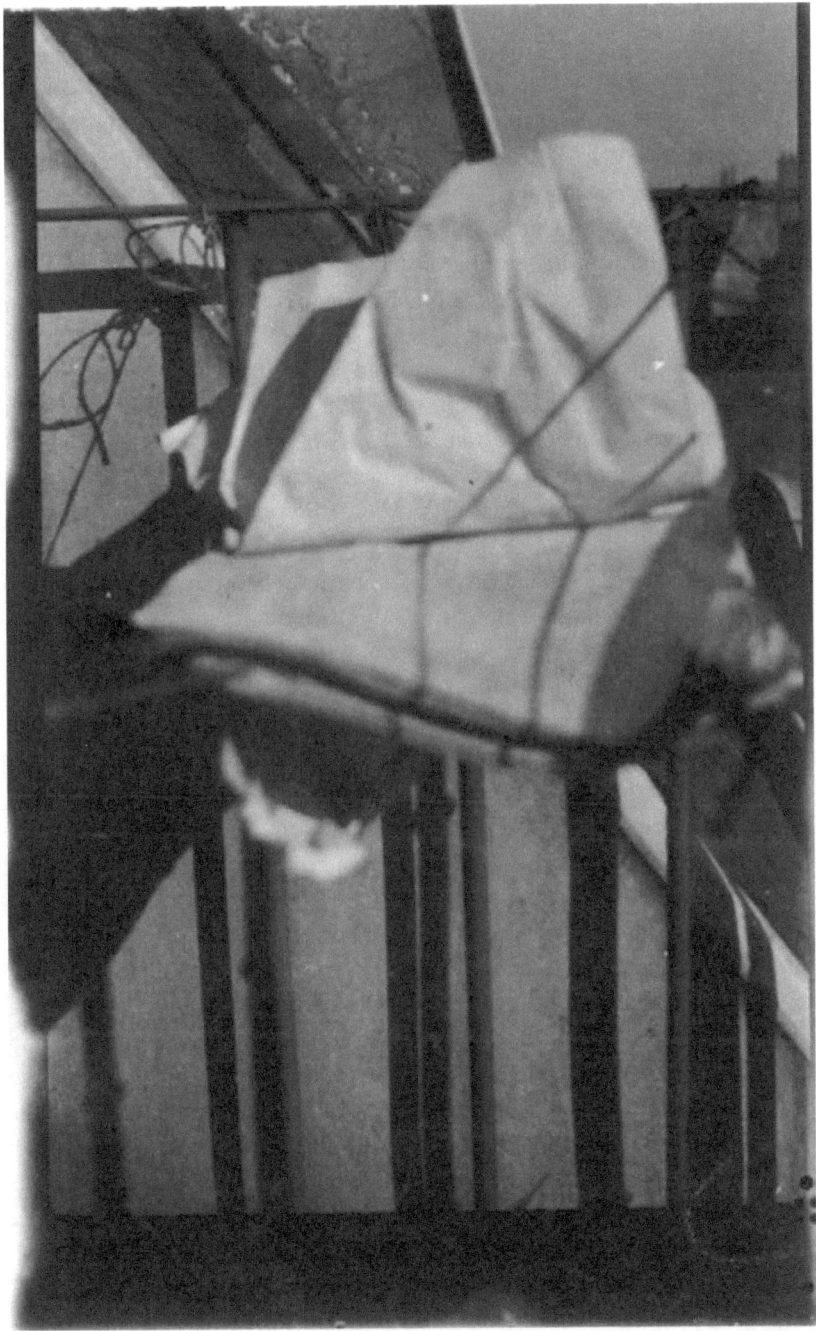

FIGURE 4.3. Photograph of *Le Readymade Malheureux* (1919–20) by Marcel Duchamp. The high-contrast, black-and-white photograph, attributed to Suzanne Duchamp and Jean Crotti, documents the fulfillment of Duchamp's instructions to create the artwork. Gelatin silver print, image: 10.7 × 6.9 cm, sheet: 11 × 7 cm. Philadelphia Museum of Art. © Suzanne Duchamp and Jean Crotti /ADAGP.

him in its destruction. He supplements his defense by noting, "en esta ciudad están pasando cosas mucho más terribles que colgar un libro de un cordel" ("much worse things are happening in this city than a book being hung from a cord"; B251–52, W196). Instead of creating distance between his readymade and the Santa Teresa murders, Amalfitano emphasizes their connection. The procedure by which exposure accelerates the book's deterioration and diminishes the usefulness of its resources recalls the extraction of energy from the workers of Santa Teresa as well as the disposal of murdered women in plain view.

Distancing and disavowal have a paradoxical effect. Even as they reflect an *intention* to break a connection, they ultimately signal relationship with greater emphasis. Amalfitano watches the book from inside the house, as if to monitor its continued separation, but Rosa insists, "ahora [el libro] es tuyo," ("[the book] is yours now"; B251, W196). Responsibility and connection accrue to Amalfitano through the very gesture he intended to achieve separation. Once displaced from its "home" as an object, a book among other books, the readymade's dislocation alludes to its former status. The book belongs to Amalfitano even more emphatically, much as the femicides "belong" to Santa Teresa even in the absence of local recognition of the victims. In the context of *Crímenes*, the feature that would seem to distance us from the events—the dislocation of the murders from conclusive explanation or emotional coherence—forcefully implies our connection to them. Responsibility, even guilt, haunts the reading of *Crímenes*, and *2666* more broadly. These effects remain undiminished by our disavowal. Ultimately, there is only the reader to account for the murders.

Creating the readymade, like Bolaño's writing of *2666*, depends on a forceful dislocation that may seem cruel and unwarranted. Once the book is out on the line, it troubles Rosa, who objects, "Nunca te había visto hacerle una cosa así a un libro" ("I've never seen you do a thing like that to a book"), and "no somos bárbaros" ("we're not barbarians"; B251–52, W195–96, translation modified). But she would likely be unaffected if Amalfitano were to leave the book to molder in a basement or to toss it in the trash. The dislocation that produces the readymade is not the sole source of distress, nor is it that its *appearance* reminds Rosa of the object's former location. The challenge comes from the indeterminate relationship between the two.

Rosa objects to the hanging geometry book because she can neither "read" the book nor ignore it. Even as she wishes to blame the book's fate on Amalfitano, the "author" of this readymade, she, too, cannot *not* feel responsible for it (like the reader of *2666*, made to see the femicides). As what Duchamp called "a work of art without an artist to make it," the readymade's character as art stems from the viewer.[65] Whether book, urinal, or wine case, the readymade's inevitable question, "What makes *this* art?" opens a more fundamental question, "How does my seeing make what I see into art?" We must reckon with the conjunction of the readymade's past as functional object and its present dislocation from that function. Like examples of indetermination, this produces a mental thaumatrope through the co-presence of ordinary object/art, book/victim, and worker/slain woman. These fleeting reversals, and combinations, occur in our seeing. The readymade, composite portrait, and thaumatrope underscore the challenges of looking. They also draw attention to our wish to gain relief from this relentless confrontation with our inadequacy and implication.

CONCLUSION: LITERATURE AS AFFLICTION AND ANTIDOTE

For Bolaño, literature is both a contaminated category and one of the few human endeavors that retains value. Literature often facilitates the procedures by which we expel, cloak, or pretend to redeem our darkness. Yet literature can also disrupt these procedures. In *2666*, as in *La virgen,* the abject character of literature—its outrageous receptivity to scenes of cruelty—becomes another burden for readers to carry. This is not only a burden of knowledge, of injustices in the global periphery, for example. Nor does it reside primarily in being forced to endure the serial accounts of murdered victims. Instead, Bolaño asks us to *continue seeing* the suffering at the heart of *2666*, to refrain from processing, interpreting away, feeling past, or otherwise "cleaning up" the cruelty. We are to avoid reenacting, in our reading, the morally ambiguous conclusion of Mendieta's *People Looking at Blood.*

2666 is two interventions at once. One is very specific: to tactically portray femicides and the broader harms along the border in ways that will entangle and encumber readers with their responsibility for and to these conditions. The other intervention runs through Bolaño's career: to confront, and perhaps temporarily disable, what Michael Bernstein calls literature's "self-delight, the inevitable accents of mastery and joy in its expressive powers . . . [its] limitless capacity to transform anything, including the death camps, into an 'occasion' for the display of its potency."[66] Literature cannot *not* be expressive. Even the most deformative or subtractive narrative choices have their aesthetic effects. The murdered women in *Crímenes* blend together. The horror of their wounds

---

65. Duchamp, "Interview with Marcel Duchamp," 47.
66. Bernstein, *Foregone Conclusions,* 144.

becomes blunted by repetition. Monstrosity stuns with its sheer monotony. I am ashamed to admit that I thought, more than once during my readings of *Crímenes*, "Anal rape? Again?," as if variety would have made the crimes bearable. A thought like this, which erupts unbidden onto the scene of reading, takes us to the crux of the matter, the confrontation with a suppressed desire for relief, even at the cost of ethical attention. Variety *would* make the crimes more bearable—for readers. The chance to identify with the murdered women *would* ease our burden. But Bolaño wants to increase the weight of that burden, not relieve us of it. Maintaining his anti-elegiac stance, he rejects our appetite for literary redemption, the consolatory notion that art can repair experiences that are traumatic or damaging in such a way as to give meaning or value to them.[67]

Interweaving multiple threads of deformation, Bolaño makes the murders distressingly visible while also curtailing their legibility. In the absence of identifiable perpetrators, and in the face of a proliferation of causes, the most relevant guilty party is the reader. Bolaño centers readers, and himself, as part of the international community that not only tolerates the deplorable circumstances in Santa Teresa, but also derives material benefits from their continuation. *2666* insists on foregrounding readers' participation in the global circuits that direct the benefits of precarity and extraction of labor to the First World. We cannot evade awareness of our implication in the narrative, nor can we redeem interpretive tactics that we regularly use to read *past* this knowledge or otherwise dismiss it. Bolaño exposes and disarms the consolatory practices that keep the ethical weight of others' suffering from registering. He insists, not just on answerability, but also on guilt. Above all, we are guilty of longing to return to the lie of our innocence. We may insist that the murders in *2666* are fictional or that the telling of them precedes our reading. But this does not lessen our implication in the circumstances that render some bodies especially vulnerable to harm, nor does it diminish the inadequacy of our response.

2666 afflicts us with an unassimilable encounter. It demands that we uncover and regard horror, be wounded by it rather than compartmentalizing it as "bad news" from a distant and dysfunctional space. This sustained, unspectacular visibility emerges as an alternative to the absorption and digestion that follow from legibility. Bolaño directs our attention to the contexts of the invented killings. He also challenges us to consider what it means to sustain or abrade the visibility of cruelty through interpretation. He makes us

---

67. For a full exploration of this expectation and its more problematic ethical implications, see Bersani, *Culture of Redemption*.

uncomfortably aware of the implications of absorbing the appearances of the murdered women into grand readings that, rather than completing mourning, attempt to evade it.

Taking *2666* as a biography of evil diminishes human responsibility. Seeing Santa Teresa as a cautionary tale about globalization reduces the women to the waste of capitalist modernity. Relating to an individual death as the paradigm of suffering obscures the extent of the crisis. Bolaño also denies the consolations of identification, empathy, or imagined relation with the murdered women. This central cruelty in the novel remains resistant to interpretation and understanding.

Like Amalfitano's exposure of *Testamento geométrico* to the Santa Teresa elements, *2666* may fade in the weather of our memory as we continue reading and living. A deformative fiction cannot ensure that its intervention persists. But when rhetorical readers do think of *2666*, it may assert itself more insistently than books more easily closed and returned to a shelf. If Bolaño has succeeded, then the novel appears again, distressing in its dislocation from the telling we prefer. It resumes its deformative project. It confronts us. It demands that we take up the incomplete labor of seeing and mourning as a duty that cannot be discharged. Bolaño's central ethical intervention appears in *Crímenes*, but its suspension on the long clothesline of the novel ensures the duration of the crimes' visibility to readers and the multiplication of distressing resonances across the book as a whole. Ultimately, we may look away. We may stop reading *2666*. But we cannot *finish* reading. There is no satisfaction that would pair ending the book with a sense of accomplishment or attainment. There can be no completion of elegy's arc. Obstruction of lamentation, and confrontation without consolation: this is the core contribution of Bolaño's anti-elegiac deformative fiction.

CHAPTER 5

Strategic Hospitality in World Literature

Bridges from Deformative Fictions to Responsive Readings

Deformative fictions help rhetorical readers see more clearly the relationships integral to narrative encounters and the ethical complexities that attend them. In chapter 1, I examined "deformative fiction" and "fictional cruelty" as concepts that advance our understanding of a category of difficult texts and of the ethical challenges they raise. Chapters 2, 3, and 4 refined these ideas through closer examination of three paradigmatic deformative fictions. Across these case studies, I have argued that deformative fictions are worth close consideration, not despite their challenges for readers, but because of them. But what do these experiences mean for our other reading? Deformative fictions function differentially in relationship to other works of literature. We need not—in fact, likely *should not*—read deformative fictions in isolation. Because deformative fictions reveal our sometimes narrow and ethically problematic expectations as readers, we benefit from bringing our experiences with them to works that seem to ask little of us.

Here, I examine how serious engagements with deformative fictions matter to the reading, interpreting, and teaching of popular contemporary world literature, especially what I call "hospitable fictions."[1] As I will discuss in

---

1. In this chapter, when I speak of world literature without quotation marks, I mean the body of work readers constitute when they intentionally approach literature in a global context and with particular attention to the crossing of borders, whether national, linguistic, racial, ethnic, or otherwise. I use scare quotes any time I am referring to a specific conception of world literature.

greater detail, hospitable fictions satiate many of the appetites that deformative fictions leave unsatisfied. They also pose unique ethical challenges for the readers they cater to. I explore how we may extend the insights of our encounters with deformative fictions to respond more fully to less disruptive works. Strategies we have developed already for engaging with deformative fictions point the way to approaches for cultivating greater sensitivity to other kinds of fiction.

In this chapter, I examine the implications of strategic hospitality as a strategy that minoritized or otherwise nondominant authors use to appeal to privileged readers in other parts of the globe while simultaneously embedding reminders of inequalities. I also consider the options available to rhetorical readers, especially the practices that better position us to navigate the ethical complexities of these encounters with world literature. I discuss these matters in relation to the privileged readers of world literature I have witnessed most closely: my undergraduates. I argue that consideration of strategic hospitality provides one path through debates on contemporary world literature. In the second half of the chapter, I expand on these insights and illustrate some paradigmatic workings of strategic hospitality through a final case study of *Daytripper* (2011), an award-winning and best-selling graphic novel by the Brazilian comics creators Gabriel Bá and Fábio Moon.

BRIDGES FROM DEFORMATIVE FICTIONS

What happens when rhetorical readers shift attention from deformative fictions to texts that conform more closely to expectations and usual experiences? Do we return to these "ordinary" writings with relief, like weary travelers who are finally home? Are we eager to rest, to forget the hardships of our journey with deformative fictions? Many fictions lull readers to sleep with songs of innocence, goodness, and ordinariness. We may find it noticeably harder to be soothed after our encounters with deformative projects like those by Silvina Ocampo, Fernando Vallejo, and Roberto Bolaño. In the wake of *2666*'s relentless reckoning with the degradation of human life in border spaces, most books seem obscenely Pollyanna-ish.

There is nothing inherently wrong with preferring reading that encourages playfulness, enlightenment, emotional depth, or tangible personal growth. If we engage texts with the purpose of forgetting or evading deformative fictions and their challenges, however, our reading may well feel less "ordinary" and more like a flight from responsibility. What if we choose instead to let our experiences with deformative fictions matter to our other encounters with literature? How might keeping them in mind influence our assessment of other texts as occasions for unique experiences, and of ourselves as readers? Deformative fictions reform reading practices even as they deform satisfactions and expectations. One of the benefits of reading deformative fictions is that we develop a capacity for proceeding carefully that can be useful even in contexts of reading where this level of care might at first seem unnecessary. What we learn under the stress of reading deformative fictions points the way to more productive approaches to a wide range of texts.

Among the works that benefit from the counterpoint of deformative fictions are accommodating works I call "hospitable fictions." Hospitable fictions often remake what we experience as sites of disruption in deformative fictions into sites of cushioned ease. They offer the warmth of invitation, not the rebuff of refusal; the reassurance of comfort and security, not the abrasions of assault; the story of innocence, not the demonstrations of guilt or responsibility. They sit far from deformative fictions on the spectrum of literary difficulty. I paint these works in stark contrast to deformative fictions in the interest of drawing a distinction, but within the range of literary hospitality, too, there is variation. In particular, texts of *strategic* hospitality evince varying degrees of a double agenda (explicit ease and implicit challenge).

Arguably, hospitable fictions most often anticipate and accommodate readers of English in the United States. Such readers may be so accustomed to the privilege of feeling "at home" that they may not notice to what degree all has been arranged for their comfort, or at what cost. By contrast, if we attend to the constraints of authorship as experienced by writers in much of the world, we may recognize that what looks like a warm welcome may in fact be a command performance for "foreign" readers. Authors of popular world literature may bring the desired tourist destination to readers' familiar shores. They maintain readers' comfort during manageable excursions, recirculating images that often confirm existing assumptions about conditions and experiences far from home. They then nudge readers back into their lives unchanged.

Unchanged, that is, unless we resolve to alter our relationship to these texts (ethics of *reading*) and the contexts of their authorship (ethics of *writing*). Those of us who approach world literature with a degree of privilege, as so many US-based readers of English do, also have a responsibility to resist complacency and consider the cultural, literary, and economic factors that influence the choices of authors who must navigate marginalized positionalities and the expectations of foreign audiences. Rhetorical readers may choose to pursue actively the experience of what *is* present in the text, not only what we *expect* to be present. This effort matters most when reading those works that seem to endorse our ways of seeing, as hospitable fictions often do. If we instead learn to welcome what Paul Ardoin describes as the unsettling of our "seeing,"[2] we are more likely to recognize that the hospitality in question is often *strategic*. Far from spontaneous generosity, *strategic hospitality* is adopted intentionally and tactically by authors who address distant, privileged readers with a rhetorical performance that layers overt invitation and inclusion over textual elements that disrupt this ease.

Here and beyond, the skills and dispositions cultivated through reading deformative fictions offer a foundation for navigating the complex ethics of writing and reading works that circulate as world literature. When we draw on our experiences with deformative fictions, we may attend more closely to the contextual and textual particularities of hospitable fictions rather than rest in their accommodation of our privilege. A more self-aware relationship to a text's strategic hospitality invites us to abandon the tourist's stance and instead notice how textual elements complicate the broad welcome they appear to offer. In these encounters, strategic hospitality emerges as a narrative approach that pretends to offer intimacy and connection, but at the same time invites scrutiny of these "gifts." Because deformative fictions prevent us from taking any feature of a text as solely or primarily for our pleasure, they also help us to recognize how the apparent generosity of a hospitable text like *Daytripper* opens onto greater demands for close attention. We need this help. As I show in the pages that follow, the path of sincere engagement with hospitable fictions in world literature is surprisingly narrow.

STRATEGIC HOSPITALITY IN STUDENT ENCOUNTERS WITH LITERATURE

Many of the works that I teach in my undergraduate world literature courses have deformative qualities. An intentional reading progression increases the opportunity to engage sincerely and sustain attention when reading texts that do not offer the experiences that students might expect or prefer. My thinking about deformative fiction preceded my use of it in the classroom. By contrast, my concept of strategic hospitality developed as a way of talking with

---

2. See Ardoin, *Not a Big Deal*. Ardoin argues that "we have an ethical responsibility to put in the cognitive effort to unsettle our settled sight and learn to see better, to allow categorical flexibility, and to be willing to engage with unfamiliar or unfriendly ideas" (48). Ardoin qualifies this "we" as I seek to in this chapter: "the *obligated* 'we' that I am often constructing or imagining in this book is one that benefits in some situation from a culturally privileged mode of seeing that has costs for others" (85).

my students about how some nondominant writers respond to the challenges of reaching an international audience.

Like deformativity, strategic hospitality is a differential quality, one that exists in relation to other possibilities. Understanding authorial choices at either end of a spectrum from deformativity to hospitality begins with considering factors that facilitate, or obstruct, the circulation of a text beyond its place of authorship. My students and I take up this inquiry as it pertains to world literature in English, beginning with the circumstances that shape whether a text ever appears in translation. We consider the very small percentage of works translated into English in the first place and the correspondingly vast quantities of work that are completely inaccessible to monolingual English speakers.[3] We ask, what factors influence the selection of those works that do get translated? Readers and critics coming to translations in English prioritize ease and fluency at the level of prose; as Lawrence Venuti has argued, this amounts to an expectation that the translator render the fact of translation invisible.[4] Even setting aside critiques of this erasure of textual difference for any work, we can imagine how it excludes much non-English literature from candidacy for translation. Then there is the relative challenge a work poses to readers' conceptual maps and its relationship to their expectations of style and theme in world literature (e.g., the dominance of magical realism in popular understandings of Latin American literature). Although works of world literature need not aim for a US readership, they often do, and authors employing strategic hospitality tend to presume a cosmopolitan middle-class reader as the default.[5]

The conceptual domain of strategic hospitality lies far from the generosity of a host welcoming an old friend or other scenarios rooted in equality and reciprocity. Think instead of compromise, financial entanglement, power imbalances, or exposure to exploitation. The relevant connotations are conveyed by such euphemistic terms as "hospitality industry" and "hospitality worker." Like well-trained hotel staff, the implied authors of hospitable fictions preemptively smooth away sources of difficulty. They encourage privileged audiences to enjoy ease and pleasure in the moveable "resort" of the

---

3. In the US, only about 3 percent of books published annually are translations. The percentage drops still more for translation of works of literature (versus textbooks, reference works, and the like), where the number is about 0.07 percent. See Three Percent, "About."

4. Venuti, *Translator's Invisibility*, 1–34.

5. Here, it is useful to remember the gap that exists between authorial audiences and actual readers. For example, readers in diasporic communities may share the author's heritage, ethnicity, or other identity. This may make them more sensitive than most to the *strategy* of hospitality, sometimes leading to frustration at what seem to them to be pandering gestures where they would prefer to see the author issue direct challenges.

narrative. Often, this comfort depends on the fact that hospitable fictions are "born translated," to borrow Rebecca Walkowitz's term. For a text to be born translated means that it is written in anticipation of the needs and preferences of audiences across cultural, national, and linguistic borders.[6] This translation may be stylistic, linguistic, and/or cultural. Authors of world literature may write to facilitate translation from the original language into English or another language with a greater potential for circulation. Or they may write preemptively in English (or French or Spanish) even when it is not the language of their daily lives.[7] In either case, the author also may include or exclude information, events, cultural context, and/or "local" literary references with an eye to encouraging the comfort and satisfying the appetites of a culturally dominant foreign reader.

Whereas the deformative fictions in our case studies defy readings that neglect their deformative qualities, close attention and inquiry may seem optional when reading hospitable texts. Our host may insist that there is *no problem at all* with our wearing muddy boots into the clean foyer. She may even reassure us repeatedly that we do not need to take care with the delicate carpeting. We should be most cautious when the assurances we receive conflict with reasonable levels of responsibility, however. Electing to accept the host's invitation to trample over the floor coverings fails to acknowledge, much less attempt to address, how power differences limit direct communication. The host may be keenly aware of the potential repercussions, financial and otherwise, of *not* accommodating a Western guest's mud tracks.

Strategic hospitality echoes Gayatri Spivak's notion of strategic essentialism. Even as Spivak demands that we take a "stand against the discourses of essentialism," she recognizes, and provisionally embraces, essentialism's potential as a temporary tool for coalition building and subversion of dominant orders.[8] Engaging in strategic essentialism is a tactical choice to proceed *as if* identities were stable while maintaining awareness that they are not. As a corollary, strategic hospitality describes how an author orchestrates a text *as if* the pleasure and comfort of the reader were its central concern while also maintaining elements within the text that undermine that ease. In this way, authors increase the possibility for their writing to circulate without abandoning the possibility of other literary, cultural, or political agendas. Of course, strategies may be used for any number of ends, and writers' goals for strategic hospitality may be linked to less noble ends than the solidarity that Spivak

---

6. Walkowitz, *Born Translated*, 3–4.
7. Walkowitz, *Born Translated*, 11–14.
8. Spivak, "Criticism, Feminism and the Institution," 184.

suggests as the goal of strategic essentialism.[9] Regardless of agenda, hospitality should be approached as a critically significant dimension of a text, one that calls for interpretation.[10]

Hospitable fictions predominate in contemporary world literature, in part because many writers do not have the privilege of challenging their audiences to the degree that deformative fictions do, at least not if they want their work to be published, translated, and read. It is just as important that readers learn how to engage responsibly with works of world literature that anticipate and accommodate foreign readers' limitations, expectations, and capacities. These hospitable texts are the face of world literature that those in the United States are most likely to stumble upon, whether on an endcap display in an airport bookstore, at a comics conference, or in a film festival. Certainly, we can engage them as part of a broader menu that includes literature across the spectrum of reading and viewing choices we might make. But to ignore them is to turn our noses up at the literary expressivity of many authors writing outside the literary power centers of the world, writers for whom accommodation of foreign readers is a prerequisite for access to the global literary market.[11]

Our understanding of what we read shifts over time and in relation to everything else we read. Each reading of each text informs the horizon of expectations we bring to our next reading. To set the terms for students in my world literature courses, I begin with (relatively) deformative works that present obstacles where they may expect to find open doors. I teach my students first to accept the discomfort of reading deformative fictions and to find ways to value their experience when familiar rewards are withheld. Then, with the last text of the semester, I challenge them to apply the skills and dispositions they developed with deformative fictions to reading hospitable fictions. I move in this direction along the spectrum of difficulty—from deformative

---

9. See, in particular, Sánchez Prado, *Strategic Occidentalism*. Sánchez Prado speaks of "strategic Occidentalism" to characterize the tactics of Mexican writers who "adopt a cosmopolitan stance to acquire cultural capital within their national tradition" (19). Whereas strategic hospitality helps a text circulate outside its context of authorship, strategic Occidentalism helps texts achieve greater acclaim within the Mexican publishing context. For a related discussion of strategic engagement with Orientalism, see Hassan, *Immigrant Narratives*.

10. Doris Sommer points to the importance of attention to the whole range of rhetorical accommodations that writers may make to manage the inequalities of the reading encounter, including the strategy of inhospitality. Sommer, *Proceed with Caution*, xiii.

11. For an assessment of the peripheral or semi-peripheral statuses of some authors and the implication of considering this status as a factor in reading, see Fisk, *Orhan Pamuk*, 189–201; Brouillette, "World Literature and Market Dynamics"; and Sánchez Prado, *Strategic Occidentalism*, 3–24. These writers update the now-classic, but distinctly Eurocentric, perspectives of Franco Moretti and Pascale Casanova. Cf. Moretti, "Conjectures on World Literature"; and Casanova, *World Republic of Letters*.

to hospitable—so that students grapple with a seemingly "easy" book like *Daytripper* only once they have developed their analytical and intercultural competence in ways that support recognition of the complex dance with constraints that underlies this apparent ease.

Set primarily in São Paulo, *Daytripper* tells the story of a well-to-do white Brazilian writer named Brás de Oliva Domingos. Unlike Moon and Bá's previous comics collaborations, penned in their native Portuguese, *Daytripper* was written in English and first marketed to a US-based audience. This makes it a prime example of a "born translated" text. Publication in English meant bypassing, at least initially, Moon and Bá's Portuguese-speaking Brazilian audience.[12] The book was translated into Portuguese only after its success in English. Thus far, it has been translated into eight other languages. *Daytripper* first appeared in US markets in 2010 as a full-color ten-issue series published by Vertigo, an imprint of DC Comics. It later won the prestigious Eisner Award for best limited series.[13] In February 2011, it was released in a single volume with the original cover art for each issue serving as chapter dividers in the graphic novel format. *Daytripper* then claimed the number-one slot on the *New York Times* bestseller list for paperback graphic books and stayed on the list for four weeks.

Such a commercial and critical breakthrough is no small feat for an introspective graphic narrative set in Brazil, especially in a market awash in superheroes and big-name US-based creators. In a 2009 interview, Moon credits his and Bá's success in securing a major contract with a US publisher to "the way all the stories we told show how 'Brazilian' we are, or at least how interestingly 'foreign' all these seemingly ordinary stories come out on paper."[14] The ironic use of "Brazilian" and "foreign" reveals Moon's awareness of both the possibility of leveraging a marginal position as a tactical asset and the managed risk of exoticizing and essentializing Brazil. The paratextual elements and marketing for *Daytripper* certainly present it as a destination for literary tourists and, consequently, position its creators as hospitality workers who cater to these guests. As with many works of contemporary world literature,

---

12. Nor is the choice of English exclusively, or primarily, about the audience's mother language. As Pascale Casanova points out, a language's world dominance is measured less in how many people speak it as a mother tongue than in the number and variety of people who *choose* to use it as a secondary or tertiary language. In the contemporary context, English thus offers access to the markets of the US, Canada, Britain, Australia and so on, but it also enables a work to reach Nigeria, Russia, Brazil, China, and other nations. Casanova, *World Republic of Letters*, 67–75.

13. The Eisners are awarded at Comic-Con International: San Diego and are considered the "Oscars" of the comics world.

14. Bá and Moon, "Bá and Moon Go 'Daytripping.'"

publishers (and their marketing departments) appeal to readers' desire to be able to feel at once "transported" and at home in their reading. A back cover blurb from Paul Pope, a *Batman* cartoonist, calls the book "a glimpse into an exotic yet believable world. It makes you want to be there with them . . . !"[15] Acclaimed American cartoonist Craig Thompson's visual introduction to *Daytripper* offers such generic praise that it could come from a travel guide. "They call Brazil 'the country of the future'—thriving, vibrant, bursting with energy and life—just like the stories of Brazilian twins Moon & Bá," he notes, before pivoting to his description of the novel as "an honest meditation on mortality" that "infus[es] reality with the sacred" by "pondering the past, wishing for the future, but existing foremost in the experience" (7). Building on this bid for universality, *Daytripper*'s back cover copy shouts in all capital letters, "WHAT ARE THE MOST IMPORTANT DAYS OF YOUR LIFE?" preparing us to identify with the main character's quest for self-discovery and to find in each chapter's "day trip" a framework for reflecting on our fleeting attentiveness to the world around us. These messages promise novelty, while reassuring us that we can readily convert what we encounter into a resource for understanding our own lives.

Despite these invitations to tread the broad path of literary tourism, rhetorical readers may chart alternative itineraries. We may choose to analyze, rather than uncritically accept, the offered hospitality, treating it as a textual feature that merits attention. How do we prioritize attentiveness and responsiveness in our reading *even when the text seems not to require it*? Reading deformative fictions may help rhetorical readers attune themselves to the subtler signs, disruptions, and challenges of hospitable fictions. Whereas deformative fictions meet readers with the literary equivalent of stinging slaps, hospitable fictions signal subdued resistance through a forced invitation or pained smile.

For example, *Daytripper* offers occasional bits of dialogue that, although spoken to the main character, also pertain to the reader. These often contain a subtle criticism. For example, one scene figures Brás conversing with a young woman he meets during his travels who cautions, "If you travel too fast, all you're gonna see is a blur and you'll never really meet anyone interesting" (44). This is hardly a damning indictment, nor even the faintest echo of *2666*'s insistent critique of our stand-ins, the critics. Still, this sort of reproach seems to fly over Brás's privileged head and at the reader. If we attend to it, and take it as relevant to our own readings, it prompts us to consider what lies off the most plainly marked path. It demands that we consider the tendency to

---

15. Moon and Bá, *Daytripper*, back cover. All subsequent citations in text.

treat cultural content as a source of pleasure, entertainment, distraction, and self-enrichment.

WHY CAN'T WE IGNORE DEFORMATIVE FICTIONS?

If ethical readings of hospitable fictions are possible, why can't we simply bypass deformative fictions? Consider a clinical story from Oliver Sacks's *The Man Who Mistook His Wife for a Hat*. Sacks describes a group of patients with severe aphasia, people whose brain damage removed their ability to understand language. What made these patients remarkable was not their degree of impairment, but the extent to which they comprehended what was communicated *despite* their complete loss of access to the meaning of words. They were so effective that friends and family struggled to believe that their loved ones truly could not understand the words spoken to them. As Sacks notes, these people with aphasia learned, out of necessity, to attend closely to "an expressiveness that transcends the verbal," that is, to all the subtle nonverbal cues of tone, facial expression, pacing, and emotion. They achieved a "preternaturally enhanced" sensitivity to aspects of communication that others might see as secondary.[16] The deprivation of meaning—words no longer make sense—prompts cognitive, social, and emotional compensation. The result is an enriched relationship to the nonverbal elements of their communicative encounters.

Imagine what it might be like to have accomplished, laboriously and out of necessity, this degree of attunement to nonverbal communication. Having developed these skills, what if one were to regain understanding of verbal language? In this scenario, a person would retain the hypersensitized nonverbal capacities (at least temporarily) even as they return to the "normal" condition of words making sense. From this position, we might more readily discern the suppressed distress of a partner even when their calm words suggest that they are doing well. Or perhaps we sniff out the deception in a shady salesperson's pricing explanation. We may sense more fully the little interruptions, contradictions, and inner differences of "ordinary" communication, noticing complexity where others see nothing but the obvious content of the words. This greater sensitivity cannot be accomplished by dint of will alone. Few of us would choose aphasia for the purposes of developing it. In a similar way, deformative fictions are often unwelcome in the struggles they create for readers. If we can register the capacities that they may help us expand, though,

---

16. Sacks, "President's Speech."

their costs do not seem so high. In relation to hospitable fictions, journeys with deformative fictions contribute to our ability to attend more fully to the particularity of hospitable fictions. Once we have read deformative fictions, we may see more clearly how we may carry forward their resources into other conditions and texts.

A PATH THROUGH DEBATES ON WORLD LITERATURE

Attending to strategic hospitality offers a way through polarizing debates on contemporary world literature that pit proponents who see it as virtuous and edifying against critics who see it as pandering to and perpetuating neoliberalism.[17] World literature appears innocent and wholesome to many students and ordinary readers. Administrators celebrate it as a source of cross-cultural enlightenment and constructive engagement. They focus on the salubrious effects of world literature: appreciating cultural difference, gaining familiarity with diverse literary traditions, and accessing "windows onto the world," that is, where "world" is all that is foreign and unknown, but familiar enough to be made more familiar through the "window" of empathy and story. This conception is often embedded in general education programs that attempt to enlist literature to introduce "diverse perspectives," encourage "global citizenship," and produce well-rounded undergraduates.

Treating world literature as a panacea for empathy-building and cultural awareness, these efforts embody what Timothy Aubry describes as the "therapeutic paradigm" of reading.[18] Students who come to literature through institutional horizon-broadening efforts often begin from a stance that might be summed up as follows: "What care, enrichment, or advantage will this text offer me?" This question reflects the expectation of some quantifiable benefit, as if they were consumers evaluating a medicinal or therapeutic product in the pharmacy. Such an approach mistakenly allows confirming what we think we already know to pass for learning. Jane Gallop notes that without explicit support to proceed otherwise, we concentrate on the familiar, the elements of the whole that reassure us that what we know is sufficient in relation to the text.[19]

---

17. See Fisk, *Orhan Pamuk*, 165–70, for a trenchant and clear-eyed vivisection of the debates for and against world literature.

18. Aubry, *Reading as Therapy*.

19. Gallop, "Ethics of Reading," 11. See also Ardoin, *Not a Big Deal*: literature can seem to "prove" beliefs that we have already settled on—in part because "our selective attention highlights only the features that *would* prove it correct" (56) and also because it is likely that "competing evidence will just be ignored" (57).

A therapeutic approach also encourages readers to compress a work of literature into the mold of what they expect or would prefer for it to be. Within the therapeutic paradigm, we hew to ourselves while pretending to attend to the world, and congratulate ourselves for it.

Superficial but common promotional materials for the humanities often speak about works of world literature as if they have the power to erase differences of culture, language, history, and privilege, creating a perfectly horizontal, frictionless field for exchanging with a variety of diverse perspectives. This is a convenient fiction. As Doris Sommer points out, "asymmetrical relationships" cannot simply be "flattened out on the smooth surface of print culture."[20] If we treat hospitality or positive reading experiences like goods to which we are entitled, without reflecting on the conditions under which they are offered, we fall into the contradictory role of literary tourists, making texts into "destinations" or "experiences" designed for our enjoyment.[21] Entitlement is a poor starting point for rigorous engagement with the textual or contextual particularities of the work.[22] We may insist that it is not our "fault" if a text makes reading easy (or difficult) for us. But hospitality and literary tourism are not only interrelated phenomena. They are co-constituting and intertwined. Hospitality offers conditions of possibility for literary tourism. Literary tourism produces, and reproduces, the demand for hospitality.

Disregarding these intertwined conditions, and prioritizing our own growth and comfort, risks indifference to the suffering that remains unexpressed in the fictions that reach us. This absence may result from certain portrayals of suffering—deformative ones, for example—that disqualify a book from global circulation. On a more fundamental level, the literature that exists, let alone is translated, excludes most human experiences across the globe. Global capitalism's continual extraction of resources intensifies inequality at every scale. This intensification increases inequalities in culture as well. The consequence is the exclusion of millions whose lives have no room for the luxury or surplus literacy and education required to engage in the creation or consumption of literature. An affirmative vision of world literature is silent on these matters. *Not reading* is far from the worst fate that can befall someone. If our ways of reading shield us from examining the harm that we cause or allow us to feel virtuous simply for opening a book, we participate in turning

---

20. Sommer, *Proceed with Caution*, xiii.

21. See Brouillette, "World Literature and Market Dynamics," 96, for discussion of how world literature has been rhetorically framed as serving "elite consumers' desires to be exposed to exotic or simply unusual experiences or even just to have their own biases confirmed."

22. See Graff, "Inseparability."

reading into a strategy for distancing ourselves from suffering. This may be cruelty rooted in naive reading practices, but it is cruelty nonetheless.

Given the above, it might seem, superficially, that those who oppose the celebration of world literature must be on the side of the marginalized. But that, by itself, is not correct. If solidarity were the overarching goal, there are more effective ways to achieve it than discounting the literary production of popular world writers. For example, we could encourage readers to venture farther from the beaten path by writing articles and circulating public-facing commentaries on the works we want to see others read more often. We could work in literary translation to help texts that do not travel as easily find new audiences. We could build syllabi around literary works that students might never see otherwise and encourage our colleagues to do the same. In other words, constructive means exist to promote a less commercial, more representative encounter with world literature. It is not necessary to scapegoat popular texts. Celebrators of world literature often fail to acknowledge the inequalities that condition the authorship of a given text. Its detractors often fault authors for not responding differently to those conditions.

To its fiercest challengers today, "world literature" reeks of compromise, selling out, aesthetic mediocrity, and an embarrassingly open desire on the part of authors to have their books sold and read.[23] The propensity of some critics to skewer nondominant writers who achieve international commercial success carries an air of affront, or jealousy. I examine one representative instance: "World Lite," an anonymous editorial essay published, tellingly, in the 2013 "Evil" issue of *n+1* magazine. Ostensibly, the *n+1* editors' intervention pertains to popular world *literature*, which they see as watered down into something "lite." Yet the essay barely mentions specific works. Instead, the editors direct indiscriminate scorn at prominent authors. Salman Rushdie, J. M. Coetzee, Kiran Desai, Mohsin Hamid, Chimamanda Ngozi Adichie, Orhan Pamuk, Ma Jian, Haruki Murakami, and other best-selling writers come under attack as representatives of what the editors see as a willingness to stoop to "the tastes of an international middlebrow audience" and an embarrassing eagerness to "transcend their homelands and emerge into a planetary system where their work can acquire a universal relevance."[24] The editors' distress at world literature's entanglement with capitalism seems manufactured, to say the least. In fact, as Sarah Brouillette notes, the likely authors of the essay (Benjamin Kunkel and Chad Harbach) are both successful novelists who themselves

---

23. In Fisk's assessment, for example, Emily Apter's *Against World Literature: On the Politics of Untranslatability* paints world literature as "politically naive, theoretically unenlightened, and crucially caught up in the business of making money." *Orhan Pamuk*, 176.

24. "World Lite."

travel in elite literary circles mostly devoid of oppositional, politically engaged projects. As Poorva Rajaram and Michael Griffith note, the *n+1* editors hold nondominant writers to a much higher standard of political engagement than US-based authors, while simultaneously implying that prioritizing aesthetic concerns is the prerogative of the already privileged.[25]

Global capitalism, neoliberalism, and other pernicious structures determine the compromised and constrained processes by which literary work in general (and not just popular world literature) is produced, circulated, and valorized. These processes encompass the globe. But they affect nondominant writers far more intensely and extensively. Crusades against (too-) popular works of "world lite" cannot produce the more sophisticated, less translatable, more difficult world literary canon that critics like the *n+1* editors claim that they want. Any shift in that direction likely would require far-reaching change to address the inequalities that run in rivulets or gather in enormous reservoirs across the world. These inequalities obstruct basic literacy, access to education, and the prospect of sufficient security for leisure to be possible. The uncomfortable fact remains that "the capacity to represent, portray, characterize, and depict is not easily available to just any member of just any society," as Edward Said puts it bluntly.[26] Those of us with the privilege to read, write, teach, and study literature are also sufficiently privileged to be implicated in the systems that produce these toxic streams. Brouillette observes: "It is not only the case that world literature exists for a small roster of readers, but that *all* literature exists for a small roster of readers."[27] Readers and writers alike "belong to a particular class of people who have tended to be capitalism's beneficiaries," and "the literary marketplace is part of capitalism's cultural infrastructure."[28] Standing "against" world literature diverts attention away from a critical reality. The inequalities of world literature reflect broader, deeper inequalities that are not unique to transcultural or international literary exchange.[29]

This includes levying the highest costs on those already disadvantaged and transferring the resulting gains to the already privileged. To attack or dismiss hospitable fictions is like faulting the performers at a resort for the fact that, to be hired in the first place, they must perform shortened, simplified versions of culturally significant dances. The choice is not between being paid to provide

---

25. Rajaram and Griffith, "Why World Literature."
26. Said, *Culture and Imperialism*, 80.
27. Brouillette, "World Literature and Market Dynamics," 102.
28. Brouillette, "World Literature and Market Dynamics," 102.
29. For broad context, see Harvey, *Brief History of Neoliberalism*; and Piketty, *Capital in the Twenty-First Century*.

a "true" performance or a false one, but between performing in some capacity or not performing at all. The cruelty of world literature's detractors disregards the actual circumstances of the creators and their creations, the constraints that must be navigated to be read, and the losses and exclusions that attend both their writing *and* our reading. "World lite" may offer an unwelcome reminder of the ways that we, too, command hospitable fictions to function within the institutions at whose pleasure we write. These include the stories we tell about the actual good world literature may do for students, the stories that offer a rationale for our teaching and research.[30]

As our encounters with deformative fictions suggest, critics are especially likely to enact cruelty, in reading, when a more inquisitive or critical response would make them vulnerable to uncomfortable implications. Hospitable fictions cut sharply against the grain of what scholars believe (or maintain) that "good" literature should be. They do so in ways that may make us feel implicated in a dirty business. Might it be, then, that some scholars experience hospitality itself as a deformative feature? Some scholarly responses to popular world literature recall the reactions to deformative fictions traced through the case studies in this book. There is the urge to recoil, the sense of offense, and the difficulty in examining the text *as it is* because of the intense desire for it to be different. What more might be possible if we approached hospitable fictions in the same ways that we practice approaching deformative fictions? This experiment, which I regularly undertake with my students, holds promise for heightened curiosity and fuller attention to text, context, and our own responses to each of them.

INVITATIONS TO THE WORK WE *CAN* DO

Of course, proposed strategies for reading deformative fictions or hospitable fictions in Latin American literature, or any literary criticism for that matter, will not suddenly transform what US publishers translate or print, much less mitigate the deeper inequalities that shape access to literacy. Recognizing this fact need not force us into a sense of defeat. Instead, it can free us to focus on what we *can* do. Rhetorical readers can take responsibility for shifting reading practices away from passive literary tourism and toward more active, attentive, and ethical readings. We can invite others into this shift. A responsible approach recognizes hospitable fictions as works worth inquiring about and rejects the assumption that they are "sellout" texts. This underscores Caroline

---

30. See Fisk, *Orhan Pamuk*, 165–88.

Levine's response to the *n+1* editors, Emily Apter's *Against World Literature*, and other detractors of world literature. As Levine reminds us, conscientious readers of world literature do well to ask themselves: "What values and agendas have motivated decisions to translate texts, bringing them to new audiences"? How do "such cultural movements enact or reinforce growing global inequality"?[31] Shifting our practice to foreground these realities, and weave them into our interpretations, means taking responsibility for our own presence, limitations, and thresholds of growth. It means acknowledging that the problems of world literature are problems of Western readers, especially Americans. These problems cannot be solved by criticizing the creators who navigate market demands. Authors who share their work across the globe deserve to have their writings approached as the complex creations they are.

Our encounters with them invite consideration of lived and literary worlds, emerging modes of intertextuality, the itineraries that texts now travel, and how we may reroute our readings to respond to these realities. I see attention to these particularities as an illustration of Spivak's insight that to read "is to make the singular visible."[32] How might rhetorical readers engage the singularity of strategic hospitality, the dimensions of global narratives that diminish discomfort, foreground access, and cultivate connection abroad? For example, hospitable texts (like *Daytripper*) seem to ask for too little reckoning with cultural difference and colonial histories. In the context of world literary systems, we recognize that this is not best understood as authorial deficiency. And rather than passively accepting the empty space or silences presented to us, we could respond with renewed inquiry and attentiveness. With practice, we can teach ourselves to recognize hospitality without feeling entitled to it or mistaking it for a simple welcome. We can cultivate awareness of our host text and its history by attending to undercurrents and sidelines that lie beneath or beside the more palatable and obvious throughlines of a narrative.

The concept of strategic hospitality offers a path for direct, clear-eyed engagement with works of popular world literature—and minoritized literatures more broadly—by addressing two essential elements of the circumstances of their creation. First, we acknowledge the compromised and compromising positions with which the creators contend, and their location within institutions and structures that run contrary to their success and autonomy. In this context, hospitality is a survival strategy. Second, tracking strategic hospitality underscores the persistence of agency and invention through and around these texts. In other words, strategic hospitality is also a narrative resource

---

31. Levine, "For World Literature."
32. Spivak and Damrosch, "Comparative Literature/World Literature," 466.

that articulates authorial agency. We recognize and interpret narrative choices that demonstrate a high level of accommodation of audiences (e.g., a protagonist who is highly relatable to American readers, a de-emphasis on cultural context, or invitations to "universality"). We also may choose to read *past* a text's hospitality and *into* its unique challenges, suppressed or marginal as they may be. Cultivating an ethics of reading that can meet strategic hospitality with curiosity and humility helps us avoid self-congratulatory consumption of world literature as a "good" for personal growth and cultural expansion (that problematic "therapeutic paradigm"). It also supports us in refraining from denigration of or dismissiveness toward world texts written to be legible by global audiences (the reduction of purposeful creative work to "world lite"). In the remainder of this chapter, I trace the presence of strategic hospitality in *Daytripper* and some of the routes we may take toward more attentive and ethically attuned readings of popular world literature. These readings pursue the subtle indications of asymmetrical relationships rather than ignoring them. This effort matters most when it appears not to be required at all.

DAYTRIPPER: ADVENTURES IN STRATEGIC HOSPITALITY

Since 2016, when one of my students first analyzed Moon and Bá's best-selling graphic novel *Daytripper* in a class presentation, I have taught it as the final text in my introduction to world literature courses. It exemplifies many of the qualities of strategic hospitality that set low bars to entry for readers, and consequently draw the ire of world literature's detractors. The novel also creates a powerful occasion for students to redeploy the skill set they develop working with deformative fictions as a resource for reading popular works that circulate globally.

Daytripper's ten chapters focus on a series of moments drawn from the main character's life, or versions of his life. For example, chapter 1 introduces Brás de Oliva Domingos on his thirty-second birthday. He appears there as a brooding obituary writer frustrated with his stymied literary career and struggling to write in the shadow of his father's success. In chapter 2, he is a 21-year-old adventurer on a road trip with his best friend Jorge, a Black Brazilian who frequently points out the racial dimensions of situations that Brás has the privilege to overlook. Chapter 3 finds Brás at age 28, reckoning with the ruins of one failed romantic relationship (linked to an encounter in chapter 2)—and diving into another. Other chapters bring readers into moments from Brás's life at age 41, 11, 33, 38, 47, and 76. Across the chapters, we encounter a range of disruptive events: the birth of Brás's son and the death of his father, a meeting with a secret half sister, a plane crash that catalyzes his literary breakthrough, a quiet childhood day in the country, multiple quests to reconnect with a lost friend, a brutal murder-suicide, deadly car accidents, a fatal tumor, and a heart attack.

This chronology-breaking, leapfrogging movement recalls the strategies of Latin American and Latinx prose novels such as Julio Cortázar's *Rayuela* (*Hopscotch*, 1963) and Ana Castillo's *The Mixquiahuala Letters* (1986).[33] Moon and Bá build on this narrative tradition with a conceit that complicates the interpretation of these slice-of-life episodes in relation to one another. With just two exceptions, the novel's chapters end with Brás's death and a brief obituary-style summary of his life. These obituaries emphasis what sense might be made of his life if assessed externally at the point in the narrative when a given chapter depicts his death. Although *Daytripper*'s jacket copy describes these endings as "a twist he'll never see coming," after a few chapters, readers expect the deaths. Established as a recurring feature, the deaths become an important element in the text, one I will address at greater length as a complication to the rhythm of the chapters as "day trips" for readers. First, I characterize *Daytripper*'s hospitality more fully.

Superficial assessment of the features that render *Daytripper* hospitable to American readers appears to confirm the worst suspicions of world literature's skeptics. The title seems to license short attention spans and partial engagement as readers drop into and out of emotionally charged moments and settings in Brás's life, "daytripping" their way through the chapters with no need to commit to any broader engagement. The novel offers a comfortable textual space where readers can settle into exotic pleasures, from tropical locales to the vibrant visual palette offered by Dave Stewart's lush coloring. There is no need to venture beyond familiar linguistic terrain; conveniently, the locals in *Daytripper* all speak English. Like the stops on a tourist excursion, the novel's chapters direct our attention toward what we can recognize and relate to, or what we will experience as pleasantly different. A tight spotlight on Brás's family, his work, his heterosexual romances, and his immediate social circle keeps the focus on the experiences of white Brazilians. This presentation positions his privileged circumstances as simply given, a welcome framing for readers who may prefer imagining their own advantages as "the way things are" for some people, rather than as manifestations of structural inequality.

Maintaining attention on Brás's life also minimizes the need or opportunity to contextualize those experiences in relation to historical events. For

---

33. For my discussion of the consequences of these strategies for readers, see Pérez, "Navigating Narrative Ambiguity."

example, there is no mention of the repressive military dictatorship that ruled Brazil from 1964 to 1985, despite the overlap between this period and the early years of Brás's life. Local realities remain in the narrative's background, if they are engaged at all. These include inadequate infrastructure, ruthless gentrification, and the persistence of deep, yet often disavowed, racial inequities. Pertinent histories of enslavement, colonialism, and deliberate racial whitening in Brazil remain unaddressed. Only a handful of Afro-Brazilian characters appear in the plot. There is no explicit mention of the substantial Muslim or Japanese communities in São Paulo, despite their being the largest in Brazil. Any notion that "Brás" can stand for "Brasil" itself is contradicted by the gulf between the realities of the Brazilian majority, on the one hand, and Brás's privileged positionality and charmed life, on the other. Light-skinned, wealthy, heterosexual, cisgender, able-bodied, and inattentive to his own privilege or to the limits of his view, Brás is as much like the default literary hero of Western literature as he could be.

Critics of "world lite" find much to object to in these pages. Rather than conclude that a novel like *Daytripper* is irredeemable, I explore how readers may respond meaningfully and ethically to the generosity the work extends. What changes if we remain cautious and curious in the face of apparent hospitality? How might we consider the power dynamics that shape the "welcome" we receive? Where do we find internal resistance to the hospitality that is the text's explicit orientation toward actual audiences? Insights from deformative fictions and intentionally disruptive reading practices help answer these questions and offer alternatives to literary tourism.

HOW TO RESIST LITERARY TOURISM

Progress toward conscious, ethical engagement begins by recognizing that as we may slip into literary tourism, we also can shift out of it. We do so by explicitly disrupting the tendency to prioritize our own comfort, and by deliberately shifting our energies toward more attentive and attuned modes of reading. These actions drive our attention toward the text *as it is* before us, not as would make us most comfortable. In other words, we navigate away from those practices (the presumptions of tourism) that reify circuits of oppression. We consider how hospitality functions, *not* as an add-on, but as "a constitutive feature" of the text in the same way as preemptive translation.[34] These features

---

34. Walkowitz, *Born Translated*, 201.

are central to the narrative particularity that needs to be assessed and interpreted for a responsible reading of popular world literature.

Literary tourism encourages us to expect comfort, but the rigors of deformative fictions dramatize and magnify readers' responsibilities to negotiate texts with attention to their particularity even when they turn away from readers or leave them stranded in difficulties. These ethical entailments are just as present when we engage more accommodating texts, although they may feel less urgent. Because deformative fictions do not allow us to anticipate ease, they also help us recognize how the apparent accommodations within a text create opportunities for closer attention. When we approach hospitable fictions after the rigors of deformation, we may be better prepared to attend to the pockets of narrative resistance or recalcitrance that we find in hospitable fictions. That is, we may seek out, rather than ignore, the information that disrupts our ease or challenges our preconceptions. Attentiveness to what we might otherwise overlook or exclude from our readings opens onto greater engagement with the ethical situation of the text, its authorship, and our response to it. Cultivating mobility and responsiveness in our reading increases the likelihood that we will recognize, analyze, and resist temptations to participate in literary tourism.

An alert and responsive reading strategy contrasts sharply with the cognitive laxness of the literary tourism that hospitable fictions appear to invite. It calls instead for setting aside any sense of entitlement to comfort in favor of curiosity about hospitality as a strategy, a narrative resource for tactical deployment. If we condition our reading of hospitable fictions with the cautions, chastisements, and encumbrances of deformative fictions, we temper the tendency to accept a hospitable fiction's "welcome" at face value as a gift to which we are entitled. We also prevent the folly of criticizing the creations and creators constrained by the demands of a global literary market. Instead, we acknowledge the ethical complexity of nondominant world writers' access to literary markets and consider how peripheral and semi-peripheral writers navigate these constraints in interesting or valuable ways. On the one hand, working with hospitable fictions extends the approaches piloted in the case studies on deformative fictions. On the other, though, it requires some supplementation. Whereas deformative fictions forcefully disrupt expectations, strategic hospitality responds to external circumstances that demand understatement and discretion as a condition of publication. Said's theory of *contrapuntal reading* and Walkowitz's *close reading at a distance* inform approaches that are especially pertinent to hospitable fictions.

Usually focused on the "greats" of Western literature, contrapuntal reading seeks to "draw out, extend, give emphasis and voice to what is silent or marginally present," especially the traces of imperial and colonial legacies most conspicuously ignored by many critics.[35] Said's attention to "what was once forcibly excluded" or sidelined draws attention to historical and political perspectives that the author fails to express.[36] We can modify this approach to inform our reading of strategic hospitality because what is excluded, as much as what is included, may reveal the author's imagining of foreign readers' expectations. An important distinction is called for, though. Whereas Said focuses on dominant writers' disavowal of certain histories and perspectives, in the case of strategic hospitality the salient issue is less erasure than understatement. By definition, strategic hospitality involves muted expression and discretion to avoid impeding the text's international circulation. In other words, with strategic hospitality, the issue is typically not a *lack* of social, cultural, or political perspectives but rather the impact of external constraints on the direct expression of these perspectives.

Walkowitz's *close reading at a distance* highlights the need to address the fundamental inequality that accompanies the efforts of writers whose works often must be born translated to circulate globally. Specifically, when we close read from a distance, we expand our analytical attention, traditionally limited to verbal units (the paragraph, sentence, word), to the visual, paratextual, and historical dimensions of a work, including the terms by which it moves through the world. Applying close reading practices to both text *and* context creates opportunities for challenging the implied centrality and universality of the Western experience, even in those works that depend on specifically Western audiences.[37] A capacity to adjust the range of focus is especially important for reading strategic hospitality in fiction. Authors of such works make critiques that they intend for astute readers to recognize. At other times, any critique may be so thoroughly subordinated to hospitality that greater readerly agency becomes essential if we are to find points of resistance or internal difference within apparent accommodation. In both cases, rhetorical readers need to be active. Even a discernible authorial agenda needs activation and illumination, given the degree of discretion that characterizes strategic hospitality.

To resist literary tourism, rhetorical readers notice the very hospitality that seems to render close critical attention optional, then they reorient themselves accordingly. Analysis benefits from attending more fully to the subtle or sidelined markers of difference and challenge in the text. *Daytripper*, like other works of strategic hospitality, offers invitations to mobilize our attention

---

35. Said, *Culture and Imperialism*, 66.
36. Strauss, *Persecution*, 67.
37. Walkowitz, *Born Translated*, 49–50.

and explore a range of positions, vantage points, and configurations of details that unsettle us from the passivity of literary tourism. Here, I focus on Moon and Bá's novel, but the basic strategies hold promise for ethically responsive engagements with other popular works of world literature, from Latin America and beyond.

FROM DOMINANT READINGS TO MOBILIZED DETAILS

Since resisting literary tourism begins with recognizing it, my students and I start by tracing the dominant reading of *Daytripper*. This is also the most comfortable reading for the literary tourist. It focuses tightly on Brás, considering events and contexts in terms primarily from his perspective, or what they mean for him. In the opening chapter, a gala celebrating his father, an esteemed Brazilian writer, underscores Brás's sense of incomplete achievement and struggle in his father's shadow. Attention lands briefly on what the event means for his friend Jorge, one of the few Afro-Brazilians in attendance, but this functions, because of the focus on Brás, primarily as comic relief. For his part, Brás grapples with race only when it becomes a problem for *him*, as when he is mistaken for a European tourist in his own country. With few exceptions, the chapters focus on Brás's journey toward, or deviation from, the sources of meaning in his life. Identifying with this quest encourages readers to view the rest of Brazil, as well as the other characters, as a backdrop for the story of his soul-searching.

Despite the pull of this dominant reading, the narrative structure of *Daytripper* challenges it. Most chapters (eight of the ten) culminate with Brás's death, creating a dissonant accumulation of aborted trajectories that cannot be wholly reconciled with the other lives presented throughout the novel. In most cases, death itself is the primary deviation. In chapter 3, for example, a delivery truck hits Brás as he races to meet the woman whom he has convinced himself he is destined to marry (and who appears as his wife in several other chapters). Through an exercise of readerly agency, we may find ways of "quarantining" the deaths. We can consider them as an exclamation point after an important event, a repeated reminder to remain attentive to the present moment, or a metaphor for Brás's contemplation of what his life would have "added up to" had he died at a given juncture.

Whatever we make of the deaths, we must still determine how to understand the events that lead up to them. Chapter 6 ends with Brás's death in a car crash on his way to look for his friend Jorge. We may remove the actual death from what we see as the facts of Brás's life within the story, but how far back need we go in our effort to understand? Do we place him on a parallel trajectory to Rio de Janeiro that does not intersect with the sleepy truck driver who causes the crash? Or do we assume that Brás never leaves São Paulo, therefore shifting the events much earlier, when he expresses the need to search for his friend? And how do we relate these events to chapter 7, set five years later, which represents a similar quest and emphasis on loyalty but ends with a gruesome murder-suicide? Other chapters challenge by confronting us with branches that split off more dramatically from the main "trunk" of Brás's life. The events of chapter 8, for example, mostly take place in Brás's absence, after his death from a brain tumor. This means that most of the plot of that chapter remains suspended, its relationship to the rest of the book uncertain.

The dominant reading may encourage us to focus on Brás and his various journeys. Nevertheless, we can choose alternative engagements that expose and question the privilege that this reading takes for granted. One opportunity comes in directing our attention to the implications of the ambiguity that proliferates across these bifurcations. The structure of the narrative undermines efforts to arrange events into a coherent sequence. Although we come into the graphic novel with the expectation of a sturdy protagonist to serve as a screen for our projections, the novel's progression intensifies the disorienting sense that Brás himself is not "one." Parallel universes serve frequently as tropes for comics readers who may imagine *Daytripper* as a series of encounters with multiple "Brás" characters who are not reducible to a single person with a coherent identity or life experience, as in the multiple instantiations of Spider-Man in the Multiverse. Adding to this impression, Brás's appearance varies across, and within, chapters (see figure 5.1). Beyond his changing age, there is the interweaving, sometimes within a single chapter, of the distinctive visual styles of Moon and Bá. Among other differences, Bá inks with pens while Moon uses a brush.[38]

Combined with branching plot lines and temporal leaps, this shifting visual terrain discourages interpretive overconfidence. At the same time, it invites flexibility of perspective, and encourages attentiveness to detail and background. At least initially, we may consider and reconsider even minor visual details in hopes of locating Brás in time and place or establishing linkages between chapters and storylines. For example, tracing the recurrence of kites may tell us about the circumstances in which Brás's carefree delight and sense of freedom support his thriving, and the circumstances that mark him for disaster. But once we begin directing our attention around and behind Brás, these details do more than locate him. We find faint indications of other

---

38. Bá, "If you pay attention."

FIGURE 5.1. Sample images of Brás across *Daytripper*. The differences in Brás's appearance go beyond his age. Clockwise from top left: chapter 3 (78), chapter 4 (83), chapter 4 (98), chapter 6 (138), chapter 9 (209).

realities and other trajectories calling for our engagement. Although it is possible to read *Daytripper* with little regard for history or cultural context, the novel's interpretive possibilities become significantly more complex when we linger over the signs of the world beyond Brás, however lightly figured.

Daytripper provides glimpses of grossly unequal circumstances beneath a rhetorical veneer of equality. Chapter 2, set in the 1980s, follows Brás and his best friend Jorge to Salvador, Bahia. Afro-Brazilians are more numerous than lighter skinned people in the region, so Brás experiences the discomfort of being misapprehended as non-Brazilian. As they explore the historic district of Pelourinho, children and locals hawking their wares encircle Brás. They assume he is from Europe and call him "gringo" (38). In response to Jorge's ribbing, Brás insists, "It's not my fault they all think I'm a foreigner" (39). Jorge's retort, like other bits of dialogue, seems to apply to Brás, but also to many US readers: "As far as they know, you're from another planet, dude.

Planet *White*" (39). Despite the opportunity to reckon with relative privilege, Brás sheds his annoyance, and his engagement with racial issues, as easily as he sheds his clothing before a dip into the ocean. He declares to Jorge, "after I go for a swim, I'm gonna tan until I look just like you" (40). This pretense to innocence regarding racial disparities reflects what Aníbal Quijano describes as "the imposition of 'racial democracy' that masks the true discrimination and colonial domination of blacks."[39] Here and elsewhere, *Daytripper* thematizes Brás's obliviousness to his own privilege, but it does not excuse him.

Readers do not know whether Brás traces his family tree to the historical colonizers of Brazil or if, by contrast, he descends from more recent European immigrants, privileged by national policies focused on *branqueamento* or "racial whitening" of the population.[40] In any case, the fact remains that Brás benefits from the power conferred on white Brazilians. The unexamined dimensions of his life evince how structures rooted in colonial dynamics outlive formal colonialism and continue to privilege those whom the structures were initially instituted to benefit.[41] Among the advantages that accrue to those like Brás is the privilege *not* to notice. In chapter 2, this "not noticing" colors his bid for sympathy with dark irony. The neighborhood where he and Jorge have this conversation is called Pelourinho ("The Pillory," 37). Although neither Jorge nor Brás mentions the history of the area, its iconic colonial architecture is visible in the backgrounds of panels, in particular the one depicting Brás's arrival (see figure 5.2). This panel names Pelourinho explicitly, giving curious readers the starting point needed for learning about the plaza's history. If they do, they learn that it served a pivotal role in the transatlantic project of enslaving African people, both as the first slave market on the South American continent and as the site of public beatings of enslaved people in the pillories that gave the district its name.[42]

Historical events that followed shortly after the time of Brás and Jorge's visit, but that are not addressed in the novel, demonstrate the continuation of practices that divert resources away from Black Brazilians. Pelourinho's 1984 designation as a UNESCO World Heritage Site further deepened the racial and class divides already visible in the novel's background elements. Pelourinho's "revitalization," promoted by a conservative interest group, forced the displacement of four thousand residents of the district, with no provision for relocation. The subsequent redevelopment centered almost exclusively on tourist services and entertainment, with only nine percent of real estate

---

39. Quijano, "Coloniality of Power," 568.
40. Agier, "Racism, Culture, and Black Identity."
41. Quijano, "Coloniality of Power."
42. Straile-Costa, "The Pillory/Pelourinho."

FIGURE 5.2. In chapter 2 of *Daytripper,* Brás arrives at the plaza of the Pelourinho district in Salvador (37). The bustling, sunny scene only partially conceals a history of more sinister activities. Beginning in the colonial period, this was a site for the purchase, sale, and violent punishment of enslaved Africans.

allocated to resident housing.[43] A vibrant, if impoverished, district inhabited by Bahians (as seen in the setting of chapter 2) was transformed into a stage for performing Afro-Brazilian culture as a commodity prepared specifically for tourists.[44]

To be clear, reading *Daytripper* requires none of this context. We can stay on the wide boulevard of a reading focused on the protagonist's experiences, but Moon and Bá tactically signal the multiple side paths away from this dominant reading. This approach differs from Vallejo's rhetorical passing in *La virgen,* with its implication of a conspiratorial audience whose reading includes the satisfaction of imagining targeted readers duped by Vallejo's stratagems. Moon and Bá do not seem to write (and draw) past mainstream readers, nor do they disparage these readers' handling of the text. (They need these readers, after all.) Instead, *Daytripper* invites reformed or reformable literary tourists to reroute, supplement, and contest the dominant reading.

For example, the visual background in chapter 2, and the histories that it subtly surfaces, together encourage attentive readers to confront the problems

---

43. Fernandes and Filgueiras Gomes, "Revisiting the Pelourinho."
44. Straile-Costa, "The Pillory/Pelourinho," 227.

with the uninformed optimism about racial harmony thematized in Brás's remarks. Venturing beyond the dominant reading shifts our interpretation of chapters 2 and 7. Although Brás's deaths are often sudden and extreme (he dies by a gunshot wound in chapter 1, electrocution in chapter 4, and vehicle collisions in chapters 3 and 6), the deaths in chapters 2 and 7 stand out because those directly or indirectly responsible are people Brás knows. In fact, those who "cause" his death are the novel's rare Afro-Brazilian characters. Chapter 2 implicates Brás's love interest Olinda, and chapter 7 makes a murderer of Brás's best friend, Jorge. The contexts for the deaths are complex: a ritual offering to the Candomblé deity Iemanjá in chapter 2 and an apparent psychotic break on Jorge's part in chapter 7.

Detractors of "world lite" might seize on these plot elements as instances of typecasting or recirculation of unhelpful stereotypes of violence. But each also holds open the possibility of death as a signal of transgression or failed engagement, a kind of cosmic correction in response to the unthinking harm of Brás's movements through the world. We may consider these chapters as instances of the sort of narrative resistance or recalcitrance that hospitable fictions often embed in the accommodating main narrative. It is no exposed bed of nails, as it might be in a deformative fiction. But strategic hospitality leaves room for rhetorical readers to feel the sharp edge, if we choose.

Beyond imbuing the protagonist's rosy outlook with less flattering shades, our attention's outward shift to embrace context helps readers separate their perspectives from Brás's. When we do that, it becomes easier to see the privilege that flows through his familial, social, and professional networks. For example, chapter 8 includes a series of panels showing Miguel, Brás's son, in school (184–85). Most of Miguel's classmates are also white despite the much more racially mixed majority in São Paulo; the school sits behind a high fence; and a burly security guard monitors the gated entrance. Although there is no mention of private education, these details suggest that Miguel's school experience likely reinforces rather than challenges white normativity and privilege. The details pattern differently, appearing less inevitable or innocent, when rhetorical readers consider them in relation to racial and class disparities glimpsed elsewhere.

Tracing these subtle markers, students may recognize that the critical lens through which we examine Brás can be turned on ourselves as well. We also note that the opposite of innocence for Brás, and *Daytripper*'s readers, is not guilt. It is awareness. Although we cannot be alert to *everything*, we can resolve to pursue at least some of the invitations that world literature offers us. These include attending to structural factors as they impact the lives that others live, developing a concept of cultural difference as both profound and normal, heightening our sense of responsibility to inquire and inform ourselves, and deepening our recognition that works of world literature do not owe us anything. My students and I learn to ask: What is my part as a reader in this situation? How can I see more clearly from a respectful distance? In what ways can I check my expectations of access? How do I work from the margins? What can I learn about context?

"Born translated," ready to "speak" American individualism, Brás seems constitutionally incapable of these forms of awareness. But *Daytripper* makes room for readers to move in this direction, *if* we are willing to leave the tourist's path of credulity and keep our eyes peeled for differing indications. In his classic analysis of techniques for circumventing state censorship, Leo Strauss describes how a careful writer may place the prevailing emphasis on one idea while carefully placing tinder for other, even diametrically opposed, possibilities within the same text. "Such features," Strauss writes, "do not disturb the slumber of those who cannot see the wood for the trees, but act as awakening stumbling blocks for those who can."[45] An astute and flexible reader activates these features, extending metonymically what may be only intimated in the text itself.[46] When it comes to hospitable fictions, the reasons for authorial reticence and discretion are different, but no less urgent. These works call for an authorial audience willing to direct meticulous attention, as Walkowitz advises, to "those elements that have gone without saying, or without seeing" in most of our encounters with popular world literature.[47] And it is in choosing to activate these elements that rhetorical readers' agency amplifies and enhances authorial agency.[48]

After our first reading of *Daytripper*, my students and I make a second pass through, this time focusing on those elements at the edges of Brás's day trips. Together, we practice activating possibilities. We extend the alternative trajectories they imply and give the weight of our attention to the histories or realities they treat so lightly. Each time they tackle this exercise, my students discover a thicker weave of historical and cultural context in the graphic novel than they initially think is present. Moon and Bá's narrative and stylistic choices make attentive, iterative readings especially rewarding. They encourage attention to the background, margins, and visual elements that might initially appear merely decorative. These details are important in the patterning

---

45. Strauss, *Persecution*, 36.
46. Strauss, *Persecution*, 155–56.
47. Walkowitz, *Born Translated*, 90.
48. There are resonances between this approach and rhetorical passing, but I think of rhetorical passing as being a much more pervasive effect, often with text-wide implications. What Strauss speaks of, and what I see in Moon and Bá's work, is a much more localized strategy.

FIGURE 5.3. *Koinobori* as visual motif in *Daytripper*. The large image on the left is the separator between chapters 8 and 9 (201). The top right image from chapter 9 shows the *koinobori* that hang outside Brás's front door, as seen in other chapters as well (221). The bottom right image shows the *koinobori* on the next page, where they fly (or swim) through the air as part of a dream sequence in chapter 9 (222). Many other panels incorporate *koinobori* into the background or as stylized design elements (see figure 5.4 for a stylized instance).

that we manage across multiple trajectories, possible endpoints, and leaps in time. Background elements, recurring objects, unnamed characters (comic book "extras"), and motifs hint at lives lived largely out of Brás's view and, consequently, out of the reader's view.

As we close read these elements, we ask, whose invisibility or marginal status seems "reasonable" in the frame of the work, and how do we disrupt that positioning? One student tracked the paper cranes and *koinobori* (Japanese carp streamers or windsocks) that appear in at least four chapters (see figure 5.3). In learning their cultural significance, she discovered that the narrative takes place in the Brazilian state with the largest Japanese-descent population.

Another student tracked the repetition of Islamic geometric patterns throughout the novel and learned that São Paulo has the largest Muslim community of any city in Brazil. One student found a trace of indigenous communities in the sign for a hotel called Moronguetá, which means "beautiful conversation" in Tupi-Guarani (165).[49] Other recurring objects include dolls,

---

49. Moronguetá UFPA, "Projeto Moronguetá."

FIGURE 5.4. Divider image before chapter 10 in *Daytripper*. This image also served as the cover art for the tenth issue of the initial limited series version (225).

a Hindu Nataraja statue, and African masks. Figure 5.4 illustrates a more prominent placement of these cultural markers as part of a full-page separator between chapters 9 and 10. These markers make visible, albeit marginally, those communities that are otherwise absent from the story's main narrative.

At times the background details shift the interpretation of Brás's story. Together, the students and I noticed a personal altar to Iemanjá partly visible in the background of Olinda's apartment (see figure 5.5). This suggests her close connection with the deity to whom Brás becomes a sacrifice (or a chance drowning victim). Upon learning that practitioners of the syncretic faith Candomblé often call themselves "children" of the *orixás* they most revere, students reinterpret Olinda's remarks early in the chapter, such as "I have to help my mother" (47). A deity syncretized with the Virgin Mary, Iemanjá is known for being "destructive when angered," a factor that reinforces the "cosmic correction" interpretation of the chapter's conclusion. A fisherman tells Brás that he will take him out to sea to meet "her," but it is not clear whether he means Olinda or Iemanjá (see figure 5.6). The subtle outline that rises like smoke behind the fisherman also appears tethered to him, suggesting an incorporeal

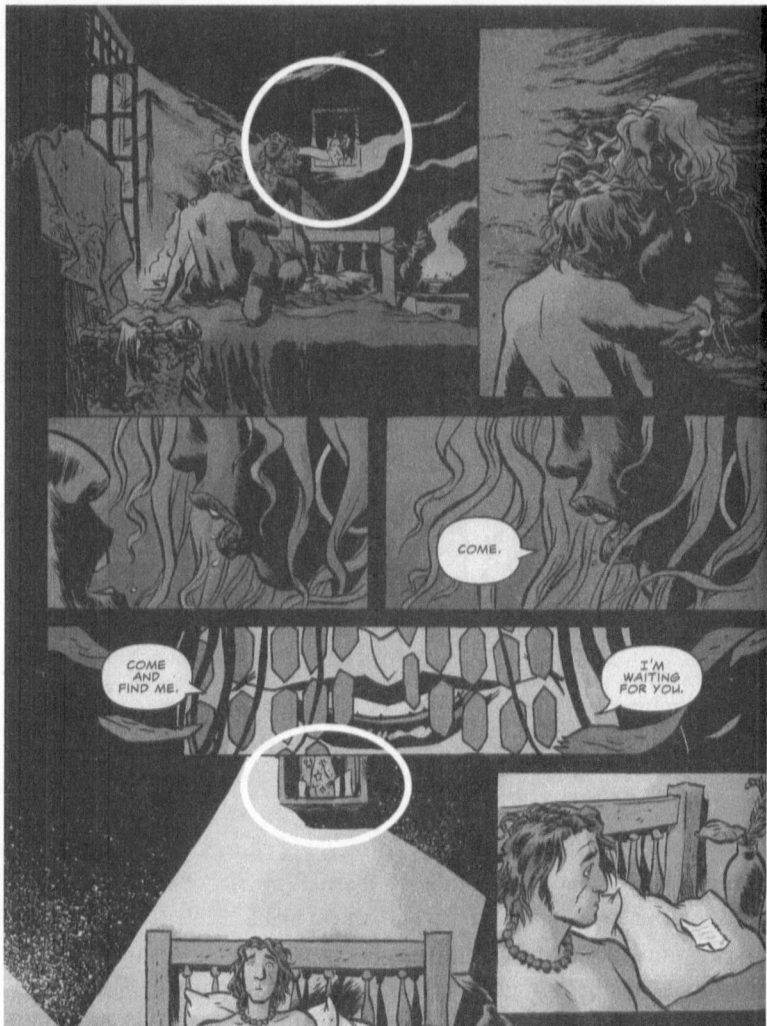

FIGURE 5.5. A small altar to Iemanjá (circled) appears on the wall in two panels in chapter 2 of *Daytripper* (52). The bottom panel, although cropping out the deity's face, shows her characteristic garment covered with stars within the frame of the altar. The top panels depict Brás's sexual encounter with Olinda. The middle divider image between top and bottom is of another woman's face and echoes a dream depicted on the first page of the chapter (35).

presence. Patterned with the other details in the section, this figure seems to imply the aura of a spirit or *orixa* directing the fisherman's action (53). The difference in expression in the bottom left panel—where the shadow seems to smile even as the fisherman frowns—further underscores the possibility of spiritual possession.

FIGURE 5.6. A possessed fisherman guides Brás to "her" in chapter 2 of *Daytripper* (53).

Other focal points that call for attention include recent historical events, such as blackouts, a plane crash in São Paulo, and the inclusion of Portuguese at various junctures. In the two chapters in which Brás dies in collisions, a white vehicle appears with the Portuguese imperative: "Foda" ("Fuck"). In chapter 3, the van that runs Brás over reads, "Foda. Entregas" ("Fuck. Deliveries," 80). In chapter 6, where an overtired truck driver crashes into Brás's car, a motorcycle on the freeway has the sign, "Foda Express" ("Fuck Express," 134). With their heavy-handed foreshadowing, these visual jokes are likely too obvious for a native Portuguese speaker. The authors seem to intend for them to invite, and reward, the attention of English-dominant readers willing to pause and inquire.

These examples may seem underwhelming for readers accustomed to more richly figured narrative worlds, but I have found that tracing them alters how students think about the graphic novel. As we consider the significance of such details, we remind ourselves that *Daytripper* owes us no further service, whether to raise consciousness, inform, or educate. It is not the local hospitality worker's responsibility to clear a path for us out of the brambles of literary tourism. It is ours as rhetorical readers.

CONCLUSION:
READING AS DIVERSION FROM EXPECTATION

Exoticizing foreign locales, focalizing a wealthy white man, delivering Brazil in English, creating a "smooth" travel experience that obviates the need for attention to inequality—these are the marks of hospitality that *Daytripper* extends to an English-reading US public. They are tourist traps we must avoid if we are to engage sincerely with the text. *Daytripper* and other works characterized by strategic hospitality may cultivate, in the margins of a dominant reading, a readership prepared to deconstruct their own position in the literary encounter. By recognizing strategic hospitality, rhetorical readers bring awareness to literary tourism's temptations—and the possibility of pursuing alternative modes of engagement.

Strategic hospitality capitalizes on credulity and presumption, while also weaving in opportunities for unmaking these shortcomings. Effective reading of the texts involves reading *past* the ease it seems to offer and accepting the disappointments of incomplete access, fragmentary glimpses of what lies beyond the narrative's focus, and intimations of culture withheld from view. We should not imagine, however, that we will get around or behind hospitality, as if it were a curtain concealing the "real" text, a genuine artifact the guide might be persuaded to show to those who pass some test.

In *Daytripper,* one expression of authorial agency smooths and straightens readers' paths by offering a vibrant, visually satisfying, and relatable world. Another, more subtle expression of authorial agency introduces interpretive complications through the novel's nonlinear, bifurcating structure. Further opportunities for readers to amplify the text's possibilities come through engagement with the subtle contextual indications of lives very different from Brás's (and most readers'). Remaining sensitive to these choices offers rhetorical readers the opportunity to trace a counterpoint to the main narrative lines through secondary characters and marginal details.

This is not simply a question of deeper contextualization. Awareness of hospitality as a *strategy* demands attention to the stylistic choices that allow literary tourists to receive the narrative as an easy, wide road as well as the opportunities, both intentional and incidental, for other modes of engagement. These modes include deliberately extending our consideration to the edges of the text and beyond; cultivating an attentive, flexible reading practice that makes multiple passes through the text; and returning to details that appear minor and then examining the constellations of possible significance that they intimate. In this way, we create an opportunity to know the text as more than a command performance of hospitality.

What if we read hospitable fictions, not as *diversions* for our pleasure, but as occasions for being *diverted,* that is, for being turned away from the path prepared for our comfort? If we leave the tour, we discover signs in tension with the narratives provided as part of the text's hospitality. These may mark the way to a lookout point, a return to an earlier stage in our trajectory, or a close engagement with something slightly off the trail. When we travel through textual worlds, we may find that there is no world to stand in or explore off the trail. Ours may become an experience marked by incompleteness and unreality. The geographical metaphor only takes us partway. Maintaining an ethical relation to this experience consists, at least to some degree, in allowing the text to be what it is rather than retreating into the sanitized or hospitably defined way through or around. This is a central responsibility of reading hospitable fictions ethically.

Although we may also discern other ways to recognize and engage this responsibility, my students and I find that deformative fictions help us to become readers who *can be interrupted* or, perhaps more importantly for works of strategic hospitality, who *can interrupt our own reading.* Dialing up the deformative qualities of apparently hospitable texts helps us see how our reading can be interrupted, rerouted. That is, we become reacquainted with our agency as readers and its relevance even when, initially, there seemed to be little for us to do. Our goal is to resist familiar arcs of reading that retrace the usual lines of cultural and linguistic power. Each arrival at a work of world literature offers the possibility of retrenching readers' privilege or disengaging from it, even partially. But we must teach ourselves *what else* to do on the shores of these texts instead of following the damaging paradigms of entitlement, appropriation, extraction, and attempted mastery. I hope others will explore and extend these practices. There is a world of hospitable fictions awaiting sincere attention.

CONCLUSION

Readers, Deformative Fictions, and Ordinary Life

We began this journey with Ana Mendieta's *People Looking at Blood, Moffitt*, which offers one vivid dramatization of how deformative fictions work. The blood spilt on the sidewalk in Mendieta's performance interrupts people as they walk their usual morning routes. Beyond the moment of encounter with blood, the larger fiction releases a distressing internal drama for viewers of the performance. This drama does not have a neat resolution. Similarly, the deformative fictions examined in the case studies interrupt the ordinary business of reading as they impose challenges on our literary and ethical imagination.

Texts open some possibilities while closing off others. Readings do, too. Our readings represent an accumulation of choices. We are responsible for how we proceed in the context of the structures, practices, and conventions that we carry with us into any given reading. There are inescapable risks to opening, or closing, the texts we encounter. We abrade their particularity, miss resonances, unconsciously reshape what we read toward what we can accommodate. No amount of effort will prevent these things from happening.

Even as it is important to recognize these shortcomings and necessary failures, we benefit from increasing our awareness of what we do and whom we serve when we read. As rhetorical readers, we may practice pausing, rerouting, and otherwise intervening in our own reading trajectories whenever and however we can. What would be different if we noticed when an expectation of hospitality shadows our reading? When we believe accommodation, satisfaction, and ease is our due? Might we release that expectation and consider the conditions that enable, even prioritize, leisure and comfort? Beyond that, we may also question our reading reflexes, and the stories we tell ourselves about what is, and is not, worth our trouble. Where do we set the limit for the challenges we countenance? Can we erase that line and mark it anew, perhaps farther from our comfort? Close examinations of Ocampo's, Vallejo's, and Bolaño's deformative fictions suggest that we can. But what do we gain when we approach more closely the perspectives that vex or distress us? What do we learn from what we *lose* through these encounters?

Deformative fictions confront rhetorical readers with a fundamentally subtractive experience. They strip away the reassurances of reading, confronting us instead with varied disruptions to our efforts to enter, interpret, and exit narrative worlds. Ocampo's stories block access to character interiority, embarrass us when we hunt for depths, and expose the impulse toward empathy as fundamentally self-serving rather than benevolent. Her defensive project shields characters and texts from our projections and impositions. At the same time, ambiguous and often-opaque scenarios position readers as co-authors of cruelty. We often end up reading cruelty "into" the very stories where empathic access has been blocked. Vallejo's *La virgen* saturates narrative with cruelty, not only in the novel's celebration of death, but even more so in the narrator's evacuation of meaning from the suffering of others, including his teen lovers. Yet another dimension of cruelty in the *telling* emerges in Vallejo's layered assault on targeted readers, an assault conducted for the delight and appreciation of an authorial audience who shares Vallejo's scorn for liberal humanism. *La virgen* hijacks the narrative resources of fiction in an elegant and disturbing bid to maximize the duration of targeted readers' exposure to afflictive diatribe. In *2666*, Bolaño rejects readers' desire to process, interpret, feel past, or otherwise handle cruelty, both literary and factual. This obstruction persists across the novel's many pages, but it finds its most salient expression in the accounts of the murders of women on the US–Mexico border. Bolaño's anti-elegiac project tempts us to seek literary redemption, as if art might repair the experiences it represents, only to refuse that consolation more forcefully. He leaves us with the heavy burden of witnessing without resolution, mourning without release or relief.

Deformative fictions make plain the limits of extracting ethical, moral, or psychological insights from our reading. They suggest that there is much to learn from unlovely voices. In their difficulty, they improve our listening out of necessity. Deformative fictions typically *demand* that we attend to the text closely and scrutinize the preconceptions and schema we bring to it. We learn to contend with, rather than count out, the kind of information or detail that we previously might have ignored. The unlovely voices of deformative fictions also remind us that, too often, we listen only to those voices that speak as we wish.

When I argue for the intentional reading of deformative fictions, I often encounter dear and wise readers who cannot comprehend why anyone would choose to be distressed or frustrated by a text. I do not know that I can convince these readers, but I try. Readers reluctant to approach deformative fictions may benefit from considering the privilege of being able to *choose* whether to walk a difficult road. They might reflect on the contrasting experience of those who suffer in the present or live with the trauma of past harm. What would change if we were to register, alongside our discomfort in reading, the real wounds of intergenerational injustice, structural oppression, systematic disenfranchisement and disposition, and the unfolding aftermath of enslavement and colonialism? It is worth remembering that those who suffer such harms do not have the luxury of choosing, or not choosing, their burdens. In my view, readers with the good fortune to be able to shield themselves from hardship also have a responsibility to develop at least some of the skills to contend with unwanted difficulty. In so doing, we bridge from struggle to wisdom, endurance, insight, strategy, and whatever understanding can come from challenge and distress. We shift the focus to appreciating the *experience* of discomfort, not rushing past it. Reading deformative fictions is an available, albeit incomplete, opportunity to consider the costs of real-life afflictions that we have allowed to become part of our human condition.

I have focused on what deformative fictions mean for narrative ethics in literature. But the ethics of *telling* and the *told*, of *writing* and *reading*, matter beyond the literary domain. Expectations of hospitality and ease feature in our engagement (or lack of engagement) with the varied narrative forms that surround us. Authors make guesses about what hypothetical readers expect from literary fiction. Those who want to gain our attention in fast-paced media spaces, especially online, also ask, *What does it take for this content to be read (or viewed)?* As we navigate the digital and virtual highways, continuous collection of information on our choices hardens into alarmingly detailed, endlessly refined profiles of our specific habits, aversions, and propensities. The intense competition for our attention—to get our eyeballs on content and, especially, the advertisements that accompany it—encourages calculations of what will produce the most clicks.

"Clickability" often corresponds to the appeal that a story or other content holds for a reader, for example, the degree to which it fits into perspectives that they like to have reaffirmed. Challenge drains quietly from our personalized media ecology as each click refines, to our detriment, the future content that we will see. These shifts happen within algorithms we do not see, hiding behind the platforms we use. It does not feel like we have chosen to cede the provocation and opportunity for growth that might be offered by encounters with what we do not want to read.

We may not be able to halt the grinding of algorithms. But we can shape them, and ourselves, by cultivating our sense that it is normal, even beneficial, for some of our reading experiences to unsettle us. We can practice this in all sorts of narrative encounters, ideally including some continued engagement with works of literature that challenge us to navigate the deformation of our expectations. But cultivating responsiveness to deformative fictions also can support greater engagement with the deformative *non*fictions of real life. By this, I mean the experiences that disrupt, distress, and perhaps implicate us: driving through the slums of Calcutta, studying data on disparities in school funding, encountering a display of hundreds of postcards representing the lynchings of Black Americans as if they were picnics, reading letters from refugees in their twenties born in the camps in which they remain imprisoned. Deformative fictions call attention to the ethical significance of the interpersonal capacity to hear and hold distress. They offer the opportunity to expand our tolerance for the many possible stories around and about us. This may be especially important when encountering stories that confront us with our own complicity in harm at varied scales and from various perspectives.

Take one activity from my day: each morning, I take my eight-year-old to school. I can make it part of a story of a hardworking single mom who juggles career and family, packs lunches while listening to her sons' feelings, encourages them to read, and makes time to play board games with them. The story is familiar and familial. What changes, though, if we look at it again, this time from the wounds of the global climate crisis? What if we place my actions in the context of other actions? I am among hundreds of residents in my neighborhood who drive their kids one mile to school. Consider my drive multiplied across all the neighborhoods and suburbs of my city, then across Ohio and the entire United States. Look at the story from the perspective of the world's peoples, including those who walk miles daily to access clean water. Assess this "innocent" action from the perspectives of climate refugees forced to leave their homes because of unbearable rises in temperatures. Such confrontations and reframings are the stuff of deformative fiction. Where other stories might protect tranquility even as harm proceeds, deformative tactics demand attention to what we would rather not see, feel, or understand. Parents like me may rattle off justifications. We face tight morning schedules for school and work; one child plays the cello; another must carry their equipment for evening baseball games; midwestern winter mornings are dark; icy sidewalks can be treacherous. Coal plants, we have heard, are far more serious polluters. These reasons wilt under the gaze of those upon whom the consequences of my choice are inflicted. *Rightly so.* My choice is not malicious, but neither is it innocent.

Sincere engagement in narrative encounters with the world does not end often with reassurance or confirmation of our innocence. We tend to avoid stories that make us feel bad even when we *should* feel bad. The rigors and suspended satisfactions of deformative fictions provide training for the everyday stories that tell of our complicity. We can muster the stamina to face them, not avoid or resist them, and then to seek ways of belonging to alternative narratives. Seeing another parent bicycle his child to school makes me grateful, but it does not negate my driving. The days I carpool with a nearby family help, but they do not free me from responsibility. Even if I were to put my car up on blocks, that would not be *enough,* at least not if we imagine "enough" to mean releasing ourselves from feelings, and facts, of responsibility. Reading stories and cultivating a willingness to see ourselves in an unflattering light is one important action. It is not the only one we should take, but it is an ethically significant one.

By "we," I refer especially to US-based readers, like myself, who often benefit from the relative and unearned privileges conferred by legacies of colonialism, slavery, and other extractive practices. Intersections of identity complicate privilege, to be sure. Some Americans bear more scars than others, depending on their vulnerability to structural racism, police brutality, and the dark fruits of past thefts. These thefts include the seizure of indigenous lands and culture, people in transatlantic trafficking, labor from those enslaved or underpaid, and resources from colonized spaces. We may observe that these problems, and the limitations of any given reader's reading practices, have sources that long precede their own choices, or those of anyone now living. That does not lessen our responsibility to engage with the disasters we inherit. In *Caste: The Origins of Our Discontents,* Isabel Wilkerson offers a powerful metaphor for this situation:

> We in the developed world are like homeowners who inherited a house on a piece of land that is beautiful on the outside, but whose soil is unstable loam and rock, heaving and contracting over generations, cracks patched but the deeper ruptures waved away for decades, centuries even. Many people may rightly say, "I had nothing to do with how this all started. I have nothing to do with the sins of the past. My ancestors never attacked indigenous people, never owned slaves." And, yes. Not one of us was here when this house was built. Our immediate ancestors may have had nothing to do with it, but here

we are, the current occupants of a property with stress cracks and bowed walls and fissures built into the foundation. We are the heirs to whatever is right or wrong with it. We did not erect the uneven pillars or joists, but they are ours to deal with now.[1]

Wilkerson's analogy underscores a fundamental insight of deformative fictions. There are problems that we may face, claim, and respond to, even when nothing that we can do by ourselves will achieve adequate repair. Whatever the inadequacy of our efforts, we would do well to keep training our narrative and ethical imagination on this difficult story. It is not enough, to be sure. But it is still worth discovering what becomes possible when we sustain attention to unflattering reflections and unpleasant experiences.

Contending with deformative fictions expands our capacity to turn toward narratives and situations that we would rather turn away from. We may become readers of literature, and the world, who remain with a difficult story and our difficult feelings about it. We may practice living with ourselves as people learning to do *something* even when that action, by itself, is not enough. We may cultivate mobility in reading. We may work at holding, simultaneously, the facts of our sincere wishes for the well-being of others, often those close to us, and the facts of our capacity for harm, whether directly or through the passive perpetuation of privilege and disadvantage.

Does this book inspire you to steer toward deformative fictions and notice the varied relational structures of fictional cruelty? Has it presented you with new ways to think about either your wish to approach or to pull away from uncomfortable narratives? Will you think differently, even a little, when you pick up a book that seems written with readers *just like you* in mind? I am satisfied with any answers of yes. I seek to contribute to ongoing efforts to articulate more fully the interconnectedness of reading and living. By "interconnectedness," I mean the sense that reading is an experience of living *and* the sense that reading practices can shape our living.[2] To emphasize the interrelationships between reading and living is not to say that they are the same thing, nor that what we do or imagine in reading predicts what we will do in real life. Our goal is to encourage greater negotiation between the two. Rhetorical readers can cultivate the capacity for responses that treat reading as a central activity in life, not a departure from it. Like the hardships we would not choose in our lives, deformative fictions teach us something. I hope this book makes you curious to continue to discover what it is.

---

1. Wilkerson, *Caste*, 16.
2. Phelan, *Somebody Telling Somebody Else*, 259.

AFTERWORD

Current Attacks on Difficulty in Literature

Deformative Fictions makes a case for the value of engaging with especially difficult narratives. While writing this book, however, I also witnessed the harm that comes from a collective refusal to tolerate challenge or difficulty in literature, as seen in unprecedented right-wing book-banning campaigns across the country.[1] These campaigns have focused on books in high school libraries, including my third novel, *Out of Darkness*, a work of historical fiction that takes the catastrophic 1937 school explosion in New London, Texas, as the backdrop for an interracial love story. The novel was published in 2015 to critical acclaim and was on high school library shelves for more than half a decade without a single challenge. But beginning in 2021 with removals in central Texas, *Out of Darkness* quickly became one of the most targeted works in the epidemic of book banning.[2] My efforts to respond publicly to this alarming trend draw most obviously on my insights as a novelist and an educator (first as a high school teacher, now as a university professor), but I have

---

1. For an excellent overview of the issues and current data, see two recent reports by PEN America: Friedman and Johnson, "Banned in the USA: Rising School Books Bans"; and Friedman and Johnson, "Banned in the USA: Growing Movement to Censor Books."

2. *Out of Darkness* has been challenged or banned in more than seventy-five school districts across eighteen states (September 2021 through September 2023) and removed unofficially in many more. Its inclusion in library and school spaces has also been upheld in dozens of district reviews, with strong support for its value from educators, community members, and young people. PEN America, EveryLibrary.org, and the American Library Association provide the most current data on bans and challenges.

also found myself drawing significantly on what I have learned from teaching and writing about deformative fictions. Here, I consider how the ideas in this book relate to book banning and the attacks on inquiry and imagination that accompany it.

Book banners' outrage in response to the array of literature in high school libraries has little to do with the books and much more to do with their aversion to reading and unabashed ignorance of how literature explores and imagines human experiences. It bears emphasizing that (to my knowledge) none of the hundreds of books targeted by right-wing groups meets the definition of deformative fiction. Most are typical of young adult literature. Some books, like mine, *are* especially intense thematically and narratively challenging. But this challenge is consistent with the works of literature frequently held up by the book banners as appropriate, namely, the Bible, Shakespeare's plays, and other classics. Certainly, not all readers are ready for them, or interested in the kinds of experiences they offer. That is just as it should be; the library offers diverse choices to diverse readers. Books that one person finds too difficult may be exactly what another reader needs.

Bans and removals hinge on the notion that if *someone* finds a book difficult—often for ideological reasons—it must be a bad book, and students need to be protected from it. Unlike the relatively modest and sporadic efforts to ban books in decades past, right-wing groups have adopted a new approach of bulk banning, often coordinating their efforts with Republicans in public office.[3] Groups like Moms for Liberty distribute lists of books to target and encourage their members to challenge dozens—or hundreds—of books at a time.[4] The timing of the bans makes clear that they are not an expression of sincere parental concern; most of the targeted books have been on library shelves for many years without incident or challenge. Only now, when it is politically opportune for the far right, have they been made an issue. Book banning in schools is part of a coordinated national effort to suppress discourse on important issues and narrow the range of life experiences students imagine through their reading.

The books most often challenged serve as symbols of the identities and human experiences right-wing groups and politicians seek to denigrate or

---

3. For example, Texas state representative Matthew Krause sent letters to school districts that included a list of 850 book titles and challenged their inclusion—as well as the inclusion of any other books addressing gender, human sexuality, race, and other "controversial" topics. Although Krause has no authority over local school districts' library collections, free speech organizations documented widespread removals of many of the books on the list from libraries. Lopez, "Texas House Committee."

4. The *Washington Post* found that the majority of book challenges come from a small number of people who challenge ten or more books each. Natanson, "Objection to Sexual, LGBTQ Content."

dismiss. They frequently characterize targeted books as "pornography" or "indoctrination" to tap into the sensitivities and anxieties of certain segments of the public.[5] Sometimes this is because books portray something shameful (and true) about the past, such as genocide, land theft, and enslavement, or because they draw attention to ongoing harms such as structural racism and police brutality. In other cases, groups object to the books' representations of specific identities, with a special aversion to nonbinary gender identity and expression, interracial relationships, and nonheteronormative sexual orientation or family structure. Although their official challenges focus on claims that the books are too sexual, violent, traumatic, liberal, or mature for readers, these concerns seem to crop up primarily when they intersect with identities or topics that right-wing groups object to. It is no accident that the targeted books are overwhelmingly by or about people with queer, Black, Latinx, or other nondominant identities.

As adults mobilized by right-wing groups denounce award-winning literature as "filth," others have stepped up to defend the books under attack. Young readers of all backgrounds want access to diverse and challenging literature, and they and their allies express persistent, well-informed support for banned books that underscores their literary merits and value to readers. They rightly argue that, for those who read and appreciate them, challenged books like *Out of Darkness* do more than confront difficult realities. They also show repair and transformation. These books are redemptive in ways that inspire hope and persistence and community support. They are healing, important, and validating for many readers, even as they are threatening and difficult for others. This is the way of literature.

I deeply appreciate this essential advocacy, but the fragility of a "redeeming qualities" defense makes me uncomfortable. It too easily may be reversed to suggest that books without obvious "merit" (in the narrowed eyes of the censors) should be removed. This is especially concerning since today's book banners reject books without reading them, on the basis that difficulty and presumed inhospitality renders a book worthless. Banners have little concept of how individual scenes function in the context of a whole work, nor of the value of literary imagination more broadly. Despite rhetoric about "protecting" young people, the bans are the work of frightened adults, often white, who unabashedly seek to protect their own privilege. They insist that school spaces prioritize their comfort, their worldviews, their cultural centrality,

---

5. Efforts at censorship that first focused on school libraries have spread to public libraries. See Waller and Reynolds, "Push to Ban Books." Bookstores and authors have been targeted as well, as in a (now dismissed) lawsuit in Virginia that alleged, among other things, that books that address queer experiences are inherently pornographic. Holpuch, "Virginia Judge Dismisses Case."

regardless of what the increasingly diverse students in public schools want or need. Book banners aim to strip libraries of all but those works that they deem hospitable.

Book banners represent an alarming extreme along a spectrum of engagement (or nonengagement) with literature. They stand far beyond the point of readers who themselves prefer not to read books that challenge and discomfit, beyond nonreaders who are apathetic to literature. Book banners are *anti*-readers who wish to prevent others from engaging with ethically and narratively complex books. I am not naive enough to imagine that those who seek to ban my fiction will bother to read my novels completely, much less this book. But I remain hopeful that, for all its ugliness, this moment underscores the importance of efforts to build capacity for reading, and defending, difficult works.

I also have found myself reflecting on what bans, and the chilled environment they create, mean for writers' process, especially our capacity to exercise creative choice. We work with a range of possibilities any time we approach a given scene or work on a book. Censorship, both explicit (book bans) and implicit (librarians' reluctance to purchase books that might be deemed controversial) threatens to narrow that range, constraining imagination to the inoffensive and anodyne. Our libraries need all kinds of writing, to be sure—light, breezy reads; engrossing graphic narratives; page-turners; hefty historical novels; fantasy novels to spin new worlds out of words. But even the most seemingly wholesome narrative depends on the existence of a wider spectrum to be read against. It is one thing for a writer to *choose* to write a chaste kiss because of what they want to show about a character. It is quite another to have no other option, if one wishes for the book to reach readers. Writers may choose to engage in strategic hospitality, but I hope they do not abandon difficult topics as a bid—likely futile—to avoid backlash. It will take resolve and persistence to keep writing to the fullest breadth of our imaginations.

The need to defend books, and the need to defend the rights of the young people who want to read them, lends a rare urgency to conversations about why we read and how—the conversation that *Deformative Fictions* contributes to in its modest way. Even readers who don't (right now) want to read difficult or deformative books may nevertheless recognize their value to someone else. Perhaps the most important insight from *Deformative Fictions*, in terms of responding to censorship, is the conviction that we become more sensitive readers by approaching books whose value we do not recognize immediately. I leave readers with this, then: *that* we choose to read difficult books in the first place, and how we read them, matters to our understanding of ourselves and the world beyond us.

BIBLIOGRAPHY

Agier, Michel. "Racism, Culture and Black Identity in Brazil." *Bulletin of Latin American Research* 14, no. 3 (1995): 245–64. http://www.jstor.org/stable/3339326.

Alberca, Manuel. "¿Existe la autoficción hispanoamericana?" *Cuadernos del CILHA* 7, no. 7–8 (2005–6): 115–34.

Aldarondo, Hiram. *El humor en la cuentística de Silvina Ocampo*. Madrid: Editorial Pliegos, 2004.

Almodóvar, Pedro, dir. *Kika*. Warner Española S.A., 1993. 1 hr., 54 min.

Alonso, Amado. "Aparición de una novelista." Preface to *La última niebla*, by María Luisa Bombal, 7–34. 2nd ed. Santiago: Editorial Nascimento, 1941.

Amícola, José. "Silvina Ocampo y la *malseánce*." In *La ronda y el antifaz: Lecturas críticas sobre Silvina Ocampo*, 129–38. Compiled by Nora Domínguez and Adriana Mancini. Buenos Aires: Editorial de la Facultad de Filosofía y Letras, Universidad de Buenos Aires, 2009.

Apter, Emily. *Against World Literature: On the Politics of Untranslatability*. New York: Verso, 2013.

Arcimboldo, Giuseppe. *Summer*. 1573. Oil on canvas. Web Gallery of Art. http://commons.wikimedia.org/.

Ardoin, Paul. *Not a Big Deal: Narrating to Unsettle*. Frontiers of Narrative. Lincoln: University of Nebraska Press, 2021. https://doi.org/10.2307/j.ctv1s5nzwv.

Arguedas, José María. *El zorro de arriba y el zorro de abajo*. Paris: ALLCA XXe (Université Paris X, Centre de recherches latino-américaines), 1990. First published in 1971 by Losada (Buenos Aires).

Artaud, Antonin. *The Theater and Its Double*. Translated by Mary Caroline Richards. New York: Grove Press, 1958. First published in 1938 by Gallimard (Paris).

Aubry, Timothy. *Reading as Therapy: What Contemporary Fiction Does for Middle-Class Americans*. Iowa City: University of Iowa Press, 2011. https://doi.org/10.2307/j.ctt20mvcgt.

Avelar, Idelbar. "The Ethics of Interpretation and the International Division of Intellectual Labor." *SubStance* (Johns Hopkins University Press) 29, no. 1 (January 2000): 80–103. https://doi.org/10.1353/sub.2000.0001.

———. *The Letter of Violence: Essays on Narrative, Ethics, and Politics*. New York: Palgrave Macmillan, 2004.

Bá, Gabriel. Reply to "Fábio Moon and Gabriel Bá AMA [Ask Me Anything]." "If you pay attention to inking techniques, you may notice I ink with pens and Fábio uses a brush." Reddit Comics Forum (*Reddit*), October 26, 2015. https://www.reddit.com/r/comicbooks/comments/3qazku/comment/cwdmh3k/?utm_source=share&utm_medium=web2x&context=3.

Bá, Gabriel, and Fábio Moon. "Bá and Moon Go 'Daytripping.'" Interview by Steve Sunu. Comic Book Resources. November 18, 2009. https://www.cbr.com/ba-and-moon-go-daytripping/.

Bakhtin, Mikhail. *Problems of Dostoevsky's Poetics*. Edited and translated by Caryl Emerson. Theory and History of Literature. Minneapolis: University of Minnesota Press, 1984. https://doi.org/10.5749/j.ctt22727z1.

Balderston, Daniel. "Los cuentos crueles de Silvina Ocampo y Juan Rodolfo Wilcock." *Revista Iberoamericana* 49, no. 125 (1983): 743–52.

Baraz, Daniel. *Medieval Cruelty: Changing Perceptions, Late Antiquity to the Early Modern Period*. Ithaca, NY: Cornell University Press, 2003. http://www.jstor.org/stable/10.7591/j.ctvm2036f.

Baron-Cohen, Simon. *The Science of Evil: On Empathy and the Origins of Cruelty*. Philadelphia: Basic Books, 2012.

Bernstein, Michael André. *Foregone Conclusions: Against Apocalyptic History*. Berkeley: University of California Press, 1994.

Bersani, Leo. *The Culture of Redemption*. Cambridge, MA: Harvard University Press, 1990.

Biron, Rebecca E. *Murder and Masculinity*. Nashville: Vanderbilt University Press, 2000. https://doi.org/10.2307/j.ctv176kv4g.

Blocker, Jane. *Where Is Ana Mendieta?: Identity, Performativity, and Exile*. Durham, NC: Duke University Press, 1999.

Bolaño, Roberto. *2666*. Barcelona: Anagrama, 2004.

———. *2666*. Translated by Natasha Wimmer. New York: Farrar, Straus and Giroux, 2008.

———. *Estrella distante*. Barcelona: Anagrama, 1996.

———. *La literatura nazi en América*. Barcelona: Seix Barral, 1996.

———. *Los detectives salvajes*. Barcelona: Anagrama, 1998.

———. *Nocturno de Chile*. Barcelona: Anagrama, 2000.

Bolaño, Roberto, and Mónica Maristain. "The Last Interview." In *Roberto Bolano: The Last Interview & Other Conversations,* edited by Mónica Maristain, translated by Sybil Perez, 93–123. The Last Interview Series. Brooklyn: Melville House, 2009.

Bombal, María Luisa. *La última niebla*. 2nd ed. Santiago: Editorial Nascimento, 1941. First published in 1935 by Colombo (Buenos Aires).

Booth, Wayne C. "Resurrection of the Implied Author: Why Bother?" In *A Companion to Narrative Theory*, edited by James Phelan and Peter J. Rabinowitz, 75–88. Hoboken, NJ: Blackwell, 2005.

———. *The Rhetoric of Fiction*. 2nd ed. Chicago: University of Chicago Press, 1983.

Borges, Jorge Luis. "Preface." In *Leopoldina's Dream*, by Silvina Ocampo, vii–viii. Translated by David Balderston. Ontario: Penguin Canada, 1988.

Borges, Jorge Luis, and Adolfo Bioy Casares. *Seis problemas para Don Isidro Parodi*. Madrid: Alianza Editorial, 1998. First published 1942 by Sur (Buenos Aires).

Breithaupt, Fritz Alwin. "Empathic Sadism: How Readers Get Implicated." In *The Oxford Handbook of Cognitive Literary Studies*, edited by Lisa Zunshine, 440–60. Oxford: Oxford University Press, 2015. https://doi.org/10.1093/oxfordhb/9780199978069.013.0022.

———. *The Dark Sides of Empathy*. Translated by Andrew B. B. Hamilton. Ithaca, NY: Cornell University Press, 2019.

Brooks, David G. "Ambiguity, the Literary, and Close Reading." *CLCWeb: Comparative Literature and Culture* 12, no. 4 (2010): 1–8. https://doi.org/10.7771/1481-4374.1677.

Brouillette, Sarah. "World Literature and Market Dynamics." In *Institutions of World Literature: Writing, Translation, Markets*, edited by Stefan Helgesson and Pieter Vermeulen, 93–106. Abingdon: Routledge, 2016.

Browning, Richard L. *Childhood and the Nation in Latin American Literature: Allende, Reinaldo Arenas, Bosch, Bryce Echenique, Cortázar, Manuel Galván, Federico Gamboa, S. Ocampo, Peri Rossi, Salarrué*. New York: Peter Lang, 2001.

Brütsch, Matthias. "Irony, Retroactivity, and Ambiguity: Three Kinds of 'Unreliable Narration' in Literature and Film." In *Unreliable Narration and Trustworthiness: Intermedial and Interdisciplinary Perspectives*, edited by Vera Nünning, 221–44. Berlin: de Gruyter, 2015.

Burke, Kenneth. "Psychology and Form." In *Counter-Statement*, 29–44. Berkeley: University of California Press, 1986. First published July 1925 by *The Dial* 79, 34–46.

Butler, Octavia E. *Kindred*. Garden City, NY: Doubleday, 1979.

Candia Cáceres, Alexis. "Todos los males el mal: La 'estética de la aniquilación' en la narrativa de Roberto Bolaño." *Revista Chilena de Literatura* 76 (April 2010): 43–70. http://dx.doi.org/10.4067/S0718-22952010000100003.

Casanova, Pascale. *The World Republic of Letters*. Translated by M. B. DeBevoise. Cambridge, MA: Harvard University Press, 2005.

Castellanos, Rosario. *Mujer que sabe latín*. Mexico City: Fondo de Cultura Económica, 2003.

Castillo, Ana. *The Mixquiahuala Letters*. Binghamton, NY: Bilingual Press/Editorial Bilingüe, 1986.

Céline, Louis-Ferdinand. *Voyage au bout de la nuit*. Paris: Gallimard, 1952. First published 1932 by Éditions Denoël (Paris).

Chambers, Ross. "Attending to AIDS: Elegy's Rendez-Vous with Testimonial." In *The Oxford Handbook of the Elegy*, edited by Karen Weisman, 382–96. Oxford: Oxford University Press, 2010. https://doi.org/10.1093/oxfordhb/9780199228133.013.0022.

Close, Glen S. *Contemporary Hispanic Crime Fiction: A Transatlantic Discourse on Urban Violence*. New York: Palgrave MacMillan, 2008.

Cortázar, Julio. *Rayuela*. Buenos Aires: Sudamericana, 1963.

Deckard, Sharae. "Peripheral Realism, Millennial Capitalism, and Roberto Bolaño's 2666." *Modern Language Quarterly* 73, no. 3 (September 2012): 351–72. https://doi.org/10.1215/00267929-1631433.

Derrida, Jacques. *The Beast and the Sovereign*. Translated by Geoffrey Bennington. Seminars of Jacques Derrida. Chicago: University of Chicago Press, 2009.

Díaz, Valentín. "Como el agua en el agua: Formas del no-saber y la influencia en Silvina Ocampo." In *La ronda y el antifaz: Lecturas críticas sobre Silvina Ocampo*, 91–105. Compiled by Nora Domínguez and Adriana Mancini. Buenos Aires: Editorial de la Facultad de Filosofía y Letras, Universidad de Buenos Aires, 2009.

Dieste, Rafael. *Testamento geométrico*. A Coruña: Ediciones del Castro, 1975.

Dostoevsky, Fyodor. *Notes from Underground*. Translated by Richard Pevear and Larissa Volokhonsky. New York: Vintage Classics, 1993. First published 1864 by *Epoch*.

Duchamp, Marcel. "Interview with Marcel Duchamp: 'I Propose to Strain the Laws of Physics.'" By Francis Roberts. *Art News* 67, no. 8 (December 1968): 46–47, 62–64.

———. *Le Readymade Malheureux*. 1919. Ready-made [original lost]. Anonymous photograph of the original, now held by the Philadelphia Museum of Art, 1920.

Dunbar-Ortiz, Roxanne. *An Indigenous Peoples' History of the United States*. Boston: Beacon Press, 2014.

Eagleton, Terry. *Criticism and Ideology: A Study in Marxist Literary Theory*. London: Verso, 1976.

Espinoza-Vera, Marcia. "Unsubordinated Women: Modernist Fantasies of Liberation in Silvina Ocampo's Short Stories." *Hecate: An Interdisciplinary Journal* 35, no. 1/2 (2009): 219–27.

Farred, Grant. "The Impossible Closing: Death, Neoliberalism, and the Postcolonial in Bolaño's 2666." *Modern Fiction Studies* 56, no. 4 (2010): 689–708.

Fernandes, Ana, and Marco A. A. de Filgueiras Gomes. "Revisiting the Pelourinho: Preservation, Cultural Heritage, and Place Marketing in Salvador, Bahia." In *Contemporary Urbanism in Brazil: Beyond Brasilia,* edited by Vicente del Rio and William Siembieda, 144–63. Gainesville: University Press of Florida, 2008. https://doi.org/10.5744/florida/9780813032818.003.0007.

Fishburn, Evelyn, ed. *Short Fiction by Spanish-American Women*. Hispanic Texts. Manchester: Manchester University Press, 1998.

Fisk, Gloria. *Orhan Pamuk and the Good of World Literature*. New York: Columbia University Press, 2018. https://doi.org/10.7312/fisk18236.

Flaubert, Gustave. *Madame Bovary*. Edited by Jacques Neefs. Paris: Livre de Poche, 1999. First published 1857 by Michel Lévy Frères (Paris).

Franco, Jean. *Cruel Modernity*. Durham, NC: Duke University Press, 2013.

———. "Questions for Bolaño." *Journal of Latin American Cultural Studies* 18, no. 2–3 (2009): 207–17. https://doi.org/10.1080/13569320903361903.

———. *The Decline and Fall of the Lettered City: Latin America in the Cold War*. Cambridge, MA: Harvard University Press, 2002.

Frantzen, Mikkel Krause. "The Forensic Fiction of Roberto Bolaño's 2666." *Critique: Studies in Contemporary Fiction* 58, no. 4 (August 8, 2017): 437–48. https://doi.org/10.1080/00111619.2016.1246412.

Franzen, Jonathan. "Conversation with Jorge Volpi." Opening of the Literary Salon (Address) presented at the Feria Internacional del Libro de Guadalajara, Auditorio Juan Rulfo, Expo Guadalajara. Guadalajara, Mexico, November 25, 2012.

Friedman, Jonathan, and Nadine Farid Johnson. "Banned in the USA: Growing Movement to Censor Books in Schools." PEN America. September 19, 2022. https://pen.org/report/banned-usa-growing-movement-to-censor-books-in-schools/.

———. "Banned in the USA: Rising School Book Bans Threaten Free Expression and Students' First Amendment Rights." PEN America. April 2022. https://pen.org/banned-in-the-usa/.

Gallop, Jane. "The Ethics of Reading: Close Encounters." *Journal of Curriculum Theorizing* 16, no. 3 (Fall 2000): 7–17.

Gamerro, Carlos. *Ficciones barrocas: Una lectura de Borges, Bioy Casares, Silvina Ocampo, Cortázar, Onetti y Felisberto Hernández*. Buenos Aires: Eterna Cadencia, 2011.

Garrido, Francisco Villena. *Las máscaras del muerto: Autoficción y topografías narrativas en la obra de Fernando Vallejo*. Bogotá: Editorial Pontificia Universidad Javeriana, 2009.

———. "'La sinceridad puede ser demoledora': Conversaciones con Fernando Vallejo." *Ciberletras* 13 (2005). https://www.lehman.cuny.edu/ciberletras/v13/villenagarrido.htm.

Gekoski, Rick. "Reading Is Overrated." *The Guardian*, February 17, 2011. https://www.theguardian.com/books/booksblog/2011/feb/17/reading-overrated-rick-gekoski.

González, Aníbal. *Killer Books: Writing, Violence, and Ethics in Modern Spanish American Narrative*. Austin: University of Texas Press, 2001. https://doi.org/10.7560/728394.

González Espitia, Juan Carlos. *On the Dark Side of the Archives: Nation and Literature in Late Nineteenth-Century Hispanic America*. Ithaca: Cornell University Press, 2002.

González Rodríguez, Sergio. "La vida inconclusa." In *Huesos en el desierto*, 257–73. Barcelona: Anagrama, 2002.

Graff, Harvey J. *Searching for Literacy: The Social and Intellectual Understanding of Literacy Studies*. London: Palgrave Macmillan, 2022. https://doi.org/10.1007/978-3-030-96981-3.

———. "The Inseparability of 'Historical Myths' and 'Permanent Crises' in the Humanities." *Journal of Liberal Arts and Humanities* 3, no. 9 (September 15, 2022): 16–26.

Graff Zivin, Erin. *Anarchaeologies: Reading as Misreading*. New York: Fordham University Press, 2020. https://doi.org/10.2307/j.ctvsf1qzf.

———, ed. *The Ethics of Latin American Literary Criticism: Reading Otherwise*. New Concepts in Latino American Cultures. New York: Palgrave Macmillan, 2007.

Harvey, David. *A Brief History of Neoliberalism*. Oxford: Oxford University Press, 2007.

Hall, Kari René. *Beyond the Killing Fields*. New York: Aperture, 1992.

Hall, Stuart. "The Work of Representation." In *Representation: Cultural Representations and Signifying Practices*, edited by Stuart Hall. Culture, Media and Identities. London: SAGE Publications (The Open University), 1997.

Hallie, Philip Paul. *The Paradox of Cruelty*. Middletown, CT: Wesleyan University Press, 1969.

Halpern, Faye. "Charles Chesnutt, Rhetorical Passing, and the Flesh-and-Blood Author: A Case for Considering Authorial Intention." *Narrative* 30, no. 1 (January 2022): 47–66. https://doi.org/10.1353/nar.2022.0002.

Harris, Daniel. "Cuteness." *Salmagundi*, no. 96 (1992): 177–86. http://www.jstor.org/stable/40548402.

Harshav, Benjamin. "Fictionality and Fields of Reference." In *Explorations in Poetics*, 1–31. Palo Alto, CA: Stanford University Press, 2007.

Hassan, Wail S. *Immigrant Narratives: Orientalism and Cultural Translation in Arab American and Arab British Literature*. Oxford: Oxford University Press, 2011. https://doi.org/10.1093/acprof:oso/9780199792061.001.0001.

Hemingway, Ernest. "Big Two-Hearted River." In *In Our Time*, 131–56. New York: Scribner, 1996. First published 1925 by Scribner's Sons.

———. *Death in the Afternoon*. New York: Scribner's, 1932.

Herlinghaus, Hermann. *Narcoepics: A Global Aesthetics of Sobriety*. New York: Bloomsbury, 2013.

———. *Violence without Guilt: Ethical Narratives from the Global South*. New York: Palgrave, 2009.

Holpuch, Amanda. "Virginia Judge Dismisses Case That Sought to Limit Book Sales." *New York Times*, August 31, 2022. https://www.nytimes.com/2022/08/31/us/virginia-obscenity-book-ban.html.

Horne, Luz, and Daniel Noemi Voionmaa. "Notes toward an Aesthetics of Marginality in Contemporary Latin American Literature." *LASA Forum* 40, no. 1 (2009): 36–41.

Hume, Kathryn. *Aggressive Fictions: Reading the Contemporary American Novel*. Ithaca, NY: Cornell University Press, 2012.

Insua, Juan, ed. *Archivo Bolaño = Bolaño Archive: 1977–2003*. Barcelona: Centre de Cultura Contemporània de Barcelona. Exhibition catalog published in conjunction with an exhibition of the same title, organized by and presented at Centre de Cultura Contemporània de Barcelona, March 5–June 30, 2013.

James, Conrad. "Ana Mendieta: Art, Artist, and Literary Afterlives." *Revista Canadiense de Estudios Hispánicos* 41, no. 3 (Spring 2017): 569–95.

Joset, Jacques. *La muerte y la gramática: Los derroteros de Fernando Vallejo*. Bogotá: Taurus, 2010.

Justice, Daniel Heath. *Why Indigenous Literatures Matter*. Waterloo: Wilfrid Laurier University Press, 2018.

Kanafani, Ghassan. *Men in the Sun and Other Palestinian Stories*. Translated by Hilary Kilpatrick. Boulder, CO: Lynne Rienner Publishers, 1999.

Kaplan, Betina. *Género y violencia en la narrativa del Cono Sur (1954–2003)*. NED-New edition. Martlesham, UK: Boydell & Brewer, 2007. http://www.jstor.org/stable/10.7722/j.ctt9qdnb9.

Kekes, John. "Cruelty and Liberalism." *Ethics* (The University of Chicago Press) 106, no. 4 (1996): 834–44. https://www.jstor.org/stable/2382037.

Kilapán, Lonko. *O'Higgins es araucano: 17 pruebas tomadas de la historia secreta de la Araucanía*. Santiago (Chile): Editorial Universitaria, 1978.

Kirsch, Adam. "Slouching towards Santa Teresa: Roberto Bolaño's Utterly Strange Masterpiece." Review of *2666*, by Roberto Bolaño. *Slate*, November 3, 2008. https://slate.com/culture/2008/11/roberto-bolano-s-2666.html.

Klingenberg, Patricia. *Fantasies of the Feminine: The Short Stories of Silvina Ocampo*. Lewisburg, PA: Bucknell University Press, 1999.

———. "The Mad Double in the Stories of Silvina Ocampo." *Latin American Literary Review* 16, no. 32 (1988): 29–40.

Kraniauskas, John. "Porno-Revolution: *El fiord* and the Eva-Peronist State." *Angelaki Journal of Theoretical Humanities* 6, no. 1 (April 2001): 145–53. https://doi.org/10.1080/713650371.

Lamborghini, Osvaldo. *El fiord*. Buenos Aires: Chinatown, 1969.

Lancelotti, Mario A. Review of *Las invitadas*, by Silvina Ocampo. *Sur* 278 (1962): 74–76.

"Land-Grab Universities: A High Country News Investigation." *High Country News*, n.d. https://www.landgrabu.org/.

Landy, Joshua. *How to Do Things with Fictions*. New York: Oxford University Press, 2012. https://doi.org/10.1093/acprof:oso/9780195188561.001.0001.

Lee, Robert. "Morrill Act of 1862 Indigenous Land Parcels Database." *High Country News*, March 2020. https://github.com/HCNData/landgrabu-data.

Leonard, Kathy S. *Cruel Fictions, Cruel Realities: Short Stories by Latin American Women Writers*. Pittsburgh: Latin American Literary Review Press, 1997.

Levine, Caroline. "For World Literature." *Public Books*. January 6, 2014. https://www.publicbooks.org/for-world-literature/.

Levinas, Emmanuel. *Totality and Infinity: An Essay on Exteriority*. Translated by Alphonso Lingis. Pittsburgh: Duquesne University Press, 1969. First published 1961 by Martinus Nijhoff (The Hague).

Levinson, Brett. "Case Closed: Madness and Dissociation in 2666." *Journal of Latin American Cultural Studies* 18, no. 2–3 (2009): 177–91. https://doi.org/10.1080/13569320903361879.

Lopez, Brian. "Texas House Committee to Investigate School Districts' Books on Race and Sexuality." *Texas Tribune*, October 26, 2021. https://www.texastribune.org/2021/10/26/texas-school-books-race-sexuality/.

Lutz, Edwin. *Animated Cartoons: How They Are Made, Their Origin and Development*. New York: Scribner's Sons, 1920.

Machado de Assis, Joaquim Maria. *Dom Casmurro*. Edited by *Maximiano de Carvalho e Silva*. São Paulo: Edições Melhoramentos, 1966. First published 1899 by Livraria Garnier (Rio de Janeiro).

Mackintosh, Fiona J. *Childhood in the Works of Silvina Ocampo and Alejandra Pizarnik*. Woodbridge, UK: Tamesis, 2003.

Maier, Gonzalo. "'Dogs Don't Vote': Diatribe and Animality in *Peroratas*, by Fernando Vallejo." *Journal of Latin American Cultural Studies* 29, no. 3 (2020): 349–61. https://doi.org/10.1080/13569325.2020.1832449.

Manzoni, Celina, ed. *Violencia y silencio: Literatura latinoamericana contemporánea*. Buenos Aires: Corregidor, 2005.

Martel, James R. "Nietzsche's Cruel Messiah." *Qui Parle* 20, no. 2 (2012): 199–223. https://doi.org/10.5250/quiparle.20.2.0199.

Martínez Cabrera, Erika. "Silvina Ocampo, fantástica criminal." In *Miradas oblicuas en la narrativa latinoamericana contemporánea: Límites de lo real, fronteras de lo fantástico*, edited by Jesús Montoya Juárez and Ángel Esteban, 129–39. Madrid: Iberoamericana, 2009.

Mathew, Shaj. "Ciudad Juárez in Roberto Bolaño's 2666: Mexico's Violent Cradle of Modernity." *Critique: Studies in Contemporary Fiction* 57, no. 4 (August 7, 2016): 402–16. https://doi.org/10.1080/00111619.2015.1091287.

Medina, Alberto. "Arts of Homelessness: Roberto Bolaño or the Commodification of Exile." *Novel* 42, no. 3 (November 1, 2009): 546–54. https://doi.org/10.1215/00295132-2009-054.

Meehan, Thomas C. "Los niños perversos en los cuentos de Silvina Ocampo." In *Essays on Argentine Narrators*, 31–44. Valencia: Albatros Hispanófila, 1982.

Mendieta, Ana. *Untitled (People Looking at Blood, Moffitt)*. 1973. Super-8 color, silent film. Running time 3:12 minutes. Documentation of performance in Iowa City, IA, 1973.

———. *Untitled (Rape Scene)*. 1973. Photograph, color on paper. Documentation of performance in artist's apartment in Iowa City, IA. Support: 254 × 203 mm; frame: 399 × 309 × 32 mm. Tate. https://www.tate.org.uk/art/artworks/mendieta-untitled-rape-scene-t13355.

Molloy, Sylvia. "Silvina Ocampo, la exageración como lenguaje." *Sur* 320 (October 1969): 15–24.

———. "Simplicidad inquietante en los relatos de Silvina Ocampo." *Lexis* 2, no. 2 (December 1978): 241–51.

Moon, Fábio, and Gabriel Bá. *Daytripper*. New York: Vertigo, 2011.

Moretti, Franco. "Conjectures on World Literature." *New Left Review* 1 (February 2000): 54–68.

Moronguêtá UFPA. "Projeto Moronguetá." Memorial do Livro. November 14, 2013. https://moronguetaufpa.blogspot.com/2013/11/projeto-morongueta.html.

Murillo, Javier H. Introduction to *El río del tiempo*, by Fernando Vallejo. Bogotá: Alfaguara, 1999.

Nabokov, Vladimir. *Lolita*. Paris: Olympia Press, 1955.

Natanson, Hannah. "Objection to Sexual, LGBTQ Content Propels Spike in Book Challenges: An Analysis of Book Challenges from across the Nation Shows the Majority Were Filed by Just 11 People." *Washington Post,* May 23, 2023. https://www.washingtonpost.com/education/2023/05/23/lgbtq-book-ban-challengers/.

Nelson, Maggie. *The Art of Cruelty: A Reckoning.* New York: Norton, 2011.

Nemrava, Daniel, ed. *Disturbios en la tierra sin mal: Violencia, política y ficción en América Latina.* Buenos Aires: Ejercitar la Memoria Editores, 2013.

Newton, Adam Zachary. *Narrative Ethics.* Cambridge, MA: Harvard University Press, 1995.

———. *To Make the Hands Impure: Art, Ethical Adventure, the Difficult and the Holy.* New York: Fordham University Press, 2015. https://doi.org/10.2307/j.ctt1287fz7.

Ngai, Sianne. *Ugly Feelings.* Cambridge, MA: Harvard University Press, 2007.

Nietzsche, Friedrich. *Beyond Good and Evil: Prelude to a Philosophy of the Future.* Translated and edited by Walter Kaufmann. New York: Vintage Books, 1966.

Ocampo, Silvina. *Silvina Ocampo: Cuentos completos.* 2 vols. Buenos Aires: Emecé, 1999.

———. *Forgotten Journey.* Translated by Suzanne Jill Levine and Katie Lateef-Jan. San Francisco: City Lights Publishers, 2019.

———. *La furia y otros cuentos.* Buenos Aires: Alianza Tres, 1993. First published 1959 by Sur (Buenos Aires). Page references are to the 1993 edition.

———. *La promesa.* Lumen, 2011.

———. *Leopoldina's Dream.* Stories selected and translated by Daniel Balderston. Ontario: Penguin Canada, 1988.

———. *Lo amargo por dulce.* Buenos Aires: Emecé Editores, 1962.

———. *Los nombres.* Buenos Aires: Emecé Editores, 1953.

———. *Silvina Ocampo.* Translated by Jason Weiss. NYRB Poets. New York: New York Review of Books, 2015.

———. *The Promise.* Translated by Suzanne Jill Levine and Jessica Powell. San Francisco: City Lights Publishers, 2019.

———. *Thus Were Their Faces.* Translated and selected by Daniel Balderston. NYRB Classics. New York: New York Review of Books, 2015.

———. *Viaje olvidado.* Buenos Aires: Sur, 1937.

Ocampo, Victoria. Review of *Viaje olvidado,* by Silvina Ocampo. *Sur* 35 (1937): 118–21.

Oliveros Cordoba, Milagros. "Fernando Vallejo: Attacking the World's Evils." *Bogotá Post,* May 2, 2016. https://thebogotapost.com/Fernando-Vallejo-attacking-worlds-evils/14918/.

Ovejero, José. *La ética de la crueldad.* Barcelona: Anagrama, 2012.

Paz, Octavio. "Arcos." In *Libertad bajo palabra: Obra poética (1935-1957),* 62. Mexico City: Fondo de Cultura Económica, 1960.

Pelaez, Sol. "Counting Violence: Roberto Bolaño and 2666." *Chasqui* 43, no. 2 (November 1, 2014): 30–47.

Pérez, Ashley Hope. "Against *Écriture Féminine*: Flaubert's Narrative Aggression in *Madame Bovary.*" *French Forum* 38, no. 3 (2013): 31–47.

———. "Navigating Narrative Ambiguity in Ana Castillo's *The Mixquiahuala Letters.*" In *Teaching the Narrative of Mexicana and Chicana Writers,* edited by Elizabeth Martínez, 158–65. Options for Teaching Series. New York: MLA, 2021.

———. *Out of Darkness.* Minneapolis: Carolrhoda Lab, 2015.

———. "Reading Cruelty in Silvina Ocampo's Short Fiction: Theme, Style, and Narrative Resistance." In *New Readings of Silvina Ocampo: Beyond Fantasy,* edited by Patricia N. Klingenberg and Fernanda Zullo-Ruiz, 75–108. Suffolk: Boydell & Brewer, 2016. http://www.jstor.org/stable/10.7722/j.ctt1c3gxks.10.

———. "Translating María Luisa Bombal's *La última niebla*." *Translation Review* 75, no. 1 (2008): 21–26. https://doi.org/10.1080/07374836.2008.10523969.

Phelan, James. "Estranging Unreliability, Bonding Unreliability, and the Ethics of *Lolita*." *Narrative* 15, no. 2 (May 2007): 222–38. http://www.jstor.org/stable/30219252.

———. *Experiencing Fiction: Judgments, Progressions, and the Rhetorical Theory of Narrative*. Theory and Interpretation of Narrative. Columbus: The Ohio State University Press, 2007. http://hdl.handle.net/1811/29256.

———. *Living to Tell about It: A Rhetoric and Ethics of Character Narration*. Ithaca, NY: Cornell University Press, 2005.

———. *Somebody Telling Somebody Else: A Rhetorical Poetics of Narrative*. Theory and Interpretation of Narrative. Columbus: The Ohio State University Press, 2017.

Piglia, Ricardo. "Tesis sobre el cuento." In *Formas breves*, 92–100. Buenos Aires: Temas Grupo Editorial SRL, 1999.

Piketty, Thomas. *Capital in the Twenty-First Century*. Translated by Arthur Goldhammer. Cambridge, MA: Belknap Press, 2017.

Pollack, Sarah. "After Bolaño: Rethinking the Politics of Latin American Literature in Translation." *PMLA* 128, no. 3 (2013): 660–67. http://www.jstor.org/stable/23489303.

Pound, Ezra. *The Cantos*. New York: Farrar & Rinehart Inc., 1925.

Quijano, Aníbal. "Coloniality of Power and Eurocentrism in Latin America." *Nepantla: Views from South* 1, no. 3 (2000): 533–80. https://muse.jhu.edu/article/23906.

Rabinowitz, Peter J. *Before Reading: Narrative Conventions and the Politics of Interpretation*. Ithaca, NY: Cornell University Press, 1987.

———. "'Betraying the Sender': The Rhetoric and Ethics of Fragile Texts." *Narrative* (The Ohio State University Press) 2, no. 3 (October 1994): 201–13.

Rajaram, Poorva, and Michael Griffith. "Why World Literature Looks Different from Brooklyn." Tehelka.com. August 16, 2013. http://blog.tehelka.com/why-world-literature-looks-different-from-brooklyn/ (site discontinued). Web Archive: http://web.archive.org/web/20131207103507/http://blog.tehelka.com/why-world-literature-looks-different-from-brooklyn/. Quoted in "'The Rest Is Indeed Horseshit,' Pt. 6: *On World Lit #BEEF*" (anonymous editorial). *n+1*, August 23, 2013. https://www.nplusonemag.com/online-only/horseshit/the-rest-is-indeed-horseshit-pt-6/.

Rama, Ángel. *La ciudad letrada*. Hanover, NH: Ediciones del Norte, 1984.

Reese, Debbie. American Indians in Children's Literature. https://americanindiansinchildrensliterature.blogspot.com/.

Rekdal, Paisley. *Appropriate: A Provocation*. New York: W. W. Norton & Company, 2021.

Ruiz, P. "*Lolita* of the Andes." Review of *La virgen de los sicarios* by Fernando Vallejo. Amazon.com. August 18, 2009. https://www.amazon.com/gp/customer-reviews/R3Q0K7M1XI96HD?ASIN=1852426470.

Ruskin, John. "Of the Pathetic Fallacy." In *The Works of John Ruskin*, edited by Edward Tyas Cook and Alexander Wedderburn, 201–20. Cambridge, MA: Cambridge University Press, 2010.

Sacks, Oliver. "The President's Speech." In *The Man Who Mistook His Wife for a Hat and Other Clinical Tales*, 80–84. New York: Harper & Row, 1985.

Sacks, Peter. *The English Elegy: Studies in the Genre from Spenser to Yeats.* Baltimore: Johns Hopkins University Press, 1987.

Said, Edward. *Culture and Imperialism.* New York: Knopf, 1993.

Sánchez Prado, Ignacio M. *Strategic Occidentalism: On Mexican Fiction, the Neoliberal Book Market, and the Question of World Literature.* Evanston, IL: Northwestern University Press, 2018. https://muse.jhu.edu/book/60236.

Schroeder, Barbet, dir. *La virgen de los sicarios.* Paramount Classics, 2000. 1 hr., 38 min.

Selnes, Gisle. "The Feminine (Ob)Scene of Cruelty: On the Fantastic, Its Genealogy and Margins." *Orbis Litterarum* 63, no. 6 (December 2008): 510–28.

Shen, Dan. "Dual Narrative Progression as Dual Authorial Communication: Extending the Rhetorical Model." *Style* 52, no. 1–2 (2018): 61–66.

———. *Style and Rhetoric of Short Narrative Fiction: Covert Progressions behind Overt Plots.* New York: Routledge, 2013. https://doi.org/10.4324/9780203093122.

———. "Unreliability." In *The Living Handbook of Narratology,* edited by Peter Hühn et al., Hamburg University. Accessed April 3, 2023. http://www.lhn.uni-hamburg.de/article/unreliability.

Silva, José Asunción. *De sobremesa.* Buenos Aires: Losada, 1992. First published 1925 (Bogotá).

Sommer, Doris. *Proceed with Caution, When Engaged by Minority Writing in the Americas.* Cambridge, MA: Harvard University Press, 1999.

———. "Resistant Texts and Incompetent Readers." *Poetics Today* 15, no. 4 (1994): 523–51. https://doi.org/10.2307/1773099.

Sontag, Susan. *Against Interpretation.* New York: Farrar, Straus and Giroux, 1966.

Spargo, R. Clifton. "The Contemporary Anti-Elegy." In *The Oxford Handbook of the Elegy,* edited by Karen Weisman, 413–30. Oxford: Oxford University Press, 2010. https://doi.org/10.1093/oxfordhb/9780199228133.013.0024.

Spivak, Gayatri. "Criticism, Feminism and the Institution." By Elizabeth Gross. *Thesis Eleven* 10–11, no. 1 (1985): 175–87. https://doi.org/10.1177/072551368501000113.

Spivak, Gayatri Chakravorty, and David Damrosch. "Comparative Literature/World Literature: A Discussion with Gayatri Chakravorty Spivak and David Damrosch." *Comparative Literature Studies* 48, no. 4 (December 1, 2011): 455–85. https://doi.org/10.5325/complitstudies.48.4.0455.

Steig, Michael. *Stories of Reading: Subjectivity and Literary Understanding.* Baltimore: The Johns Hopkins University Press, 1988.

Steintrager, James. *Cruel Delight: Enlightenment Culture and the Inhuman.* Bloomington: Indiana University Press, 2004.

Straile-Costa, Paula D. "The Pillory/Pelourinho in Open Air Museums in the US and Brazil: A Site of Racism and Racial Reconciliation." In *Erasing Public Memory: Race, Aesthetics, and Cultural Amnesia in the Americas,* edited by Joe Young and Jana Braziel, 209–42. Voices of the African Diaspora. Macon, GA: Mercer University Press, 2007.

Strauss, Leo. *Persecution and the Art of Writing.* Glencoe, IL: The Free Press, 1952.

Styron, William. *The Confessions of Nat Turner.* New York: Random House, 1967.

Taylor, Kathleen Eleanor. *Cruelty: Human Evil and the Human Brain.* Oxford: Oxford University Press, 2009.

Terada, Rei. *Feeling in Theory.* Cambridge, MA: Harvard University Press, 2001. http://www.jstor.org/stable/j.ctv1smjnpf.

Three Percent (a resource for international literature at the University of Rochester). "About." Accessed May 10, 2023. http://www.rochester.edu/College/translation/threepercent/about/.

Tomassini, Graciela. *El espejo de Cornelia: La obra cuentística de Silvina Ocampo.* Buenos Aires: Plus Ultra, 1995.

Twain, Mark. *The Adventures of Huckleberry Finn.* London: Chatto & Windus, 1884.

Ulla, Noemí. *Encuentros con Silvina Ocampo.* 2nd ed. Buenos Aires: Leviatán, 2004.

Vaage, Margrethe Bruun. "On the Repulsive Rapist and the Difference between Morality in Fiction and Real Life." In *The Oxford Handbook of Cognitive Literary Studies,* edited by Lisa Zunshine, 421–39. Oxford: Oxford University Press, 2015. https://doi.org/10.1093/oxfor dhb/9780199978069.013.0021.

Valdés, Marcela. "Alone among the Ghosts: Roberto Bolaño's *2666.*" *The Nation,* December 8, 2008. https://www.thenation.com/article/archive/alone-among-ghosts-roberto-bolanos-2666/.

Vallejo, Fernando. *La virgen de los sicarios.* Bogotá: Alfaguara, 2008. First published 1994.

———. *Our Lady of the Assassins.* Translated by Paul Hammond. London: Serpent's Tail, 2001.

———. *Peroratas.* Madrid: Alfaguara, 2013.

Venuti, Lawrence. *The Translator's Invisibility: A History of Translation.* New York: Routledge, 2017.

Walker, Carlos. "El tono del horror: *2666* de Roberto Bolaño." *Taller de letras* 46 (2010): 99–112.

Walkowitz, Rebecca. *Born Translated: The Contemporary Novel in an Age of World Literature.* Literature Now. New York: Columbia University Press, 2015. https://doi.org/10.7312/walk16594.

Waller, Allyson, and Kevin Reynolds. "The Push to Ban Books in Texas Schools Spreads to Public Libraries." *Texas Tribune,* December 20, 2021. https://www.texastribune.org/2021/12/20/texas-library-books/.

Washington Valdez, Diana. *The Killing Fields: Harvest of Women: The Truth about Mexico's Bloody Border Legacy.* Los Angeles: Peace at the Border, 2006.

Wilkerson, Isabel. *Caste: The Origins of Our Discontents.* New York: Random House, 2020.

"World Lite: What Is Global Literature?" (anonymous editorial). *n+1* 17 (Fall 2013). https://www.nplusonemag.com/issue-17/the-intellectual-situation/world-lite/.

Wright, Melissa W. *Disposable Women and Other Myths of Global Capitalism.* New York: Routledge, 2006.

Zapata, Mónica. "Rire: Entre le plaisir et l'horreur: Les Récits courts de Silvina Ocampo." *Études littéraires* 28, no. 1 (1995): 9–19.

Zola, Émile. *Nana.* Les Rougon-Macquart. Paris: G. Charpentier, 1880.

Zunshine, Lisa. *Why We Read Fiction: Theory of Mind and the Novel.* Theory and Interpretation of Narrative. Columbus: The Ohio State University Press, 2006.

INDEX

Adventures of Huckleberry Finn (Twain), 14, 52
affect: flattening or obscuring of character's, 39, 45, 53–55, 143; flattening or obscuring of narrator's, 141–45
aggrieved antihero, examples of, 86–87
Aldarondo, Hiram, 57n27
Almodóvar, Pedro, 25
Alonso, Amado, 55–56
ambiguity, 31–33, 101, 151; in Moon and Bá, 200; in Ocampo, 39, 45–46, 49, 53, 66, 69, 72–73, 155. *See also* indetermination
anti-elegy, 127, 129, 176
appearance, trope of, 139–40, 139n17, 151, 154–55, 172
Arcimboldo, Giuseppe, 149–50, 149 fig. 4.1
"Arcos" (Paz), 74–75
Ardoin, Paul, 181, 181n2, 188n19
Arguedas, José María, 87
Artaud, Antonin (Antoine Marie Joseph Paul Artaud), 68, 68n34
Aubry, Timothy, 188
audience: authorial, 23–24, 26, 95n19, 145, 182n5, 205; conspiratorial, 87, 95n19, 100–101, 103–4 (*see also* readers: conspiratorial); naïve, 98; narratorial, 26, 69; targeted, 83n2, 87, 95n19, 99–100, 103–4. See also *La virgen de los sicarios* (Vallejo): audiences in
author: as cruel, 22, 29–30, 34, 41, 70, 144; flesh-and-blood, 8, 70, 87, 95, 97. *See also* implied author
authorial and narratorial intention, 97–98, 101
authorial agency, 193–94, 205, 210
authorial audience, 23–24, 26
author-reader contract, 12, 33
autoficción, 105
Avelar, Idelbar, 35–36, 169
awareness: of narrative strategies, 77, 193, 210; of preexisting beliefs and expectations, 14, 36, 39–40, 82, 204–5, 212–13

Bá, Gabriel, 179, 185, 194–95, 200, 203, 205; reviews of work by, 186
Bakhtin, Mikhail, 91, 93
Balderston, Daniel, 40, 75n37
Bernstein, Michael, 175

"Big, Two-Hearted River" (Hemingway), 44
Bioy Casares, Adolfo, 55
blood, 1–5, 15, 212, 131
Bolaño, Roberto: biography and legacy of, 131; cruelty in fiction by, 127–28, 130–31, 143–44, 154–55, 167–68; other works by, 156, 156n43, 167n59; strategies of, 18, 128–32, 140, 150–51, 155, 157–58, 163, 213. *See also* indetermination; *2666* (Bolaño)
Bombal, María Luisa, 55–56
book bans, 218–21, 218nn1–2
Booth, Wayne C., 97
Borges, Jorge Luis, 39, 41n6, 44–45, 55, 57n27
"born translated," 183, 185, 198, 205
Breithaupt, Fritz, 13
Brouillette, Sarah, 189n21, 190–91
Browning, Richard, 59n29
Buenos Aires, 39, 41, 41n5, 46, 55
Burke, Kenneth, 27
Butler, Octavia, 7

Cantos (Pound), 7
Caste (Wilkerson), 216–17
Castellanos, Rosario, 76
Castillo, Ana, 29, 195
causality, 39, 43, 45, 47, 49, 52
Céline, Louis-Ferdinand (Louis Ferdinand Auguste Destouches), 86
censorship, 205, 211–12
Chambers, Ross, 146
character interiority, 25, 29; in Bolaño, 142, 168; in Bombal, 56; in Ocampo, 26, 45–46, 53–54, 58, 60
Chekhov, Anton, 43
Chesnutt, Charles, 95–96, 98
Chopin, Kate, 96
Ciudad Juárez, 128, 135n12, 156, 162; Santa Teresa vs., 156–57, 156n40, 157n44
"clickability," 214
cognitive theories of reading, 101, 101nn30–31, 181n2
Colombia, 111. *See also* Medellín
complaint, 90–91
compound composition, 130, 150

Confessions of Nat Turner (Styron), 14
contact, 24
context, 31, 90, 98, 100, 183, 194, 198, 204
"Cordelia effect, the," 60, 60n33
Cortázar, Julio, 195
cruelty: definition of, 5, 68, 68n34; semantics of, 28n14, 31, 31n17, 168. *See also* author: as cruel; fictional cruelty; narrator: as cruel; readers: as cruel
cuento, 43
cultured intellectual, the, 107. *See also letrado*

Damrosch, David, 193n32
Daytripper (Moon and Bá), 179, 185–86, 194–96, 199–210
De sobremesa (Silva), 87
defamiliarization, 4, 12, 52–53
defense, 38–39, 52, 57, 79–82
deformative fictions: anti-elegiac, 127, 129, 147, 176; assaultive, 83, 90, 125; characterizing, 3–6, 11–14, 25–27, 33, 45, 47; "formative fictions" vs., 6–7, 10–11, 33; as instructive, 15–17, 20–21, 36–37, 81–82, 126, 162–63, 178–80, 187–88, 197, 213–17; over time, 14–15. *See also* Bolaño, Roberto: strategies of; Ocampo, Silvina: strategies of; Vallejo, Fernando: strategies of
Derrida, Jacques, 24
detective fiction, 27, 33, 44, 137, 137n15, 140–41, 141n16, 147. *See also* mystery
diatribe, 90–93, 101–3, 128
Díaz, Valentín, 75n37
Dieste, Rafael, 171
difference, 21, 24, 35, 204–5
"disappeared, the," 165–66
disco mágico. *See* thaumatrope
discomfort, avoidance of, 21–23, 26, 145–46, 150, 218–21; through interpretation and consideration of theme, 163–66, 166n58
dislocation, exposure and, 171, 174–75
Dom Casmurro (Machado de Assis), 87
Dostoevsky, Fyodor, 26, 86, 93
Duchamp, Marcel, 171–74

Eagleton, Terry, 23n6
El fiord (Lamborghini), 34

"El vestido de terciopelo" (Ocampo), 46–55, 61, 65–66, 76; possible explanations of a death in, 48–51, 51n20

El zorro de arriba y el zorro de abajo (Arguedas), 87

elegy, 127, 129, 146–47

empathy, 13, 17, 45, 55, 58, 116–17

encounter: everyday, 1–3, 21, 187–88, 212, 215–17; reading, 4–11, 14, 15–16, 22–23, 26, 28, 36, 81, 83, 130, 163, 176, 184n10, 210, 214–17; with world literature, 190, 192–94, 205

Espinoza-Vera, Marcia, 42n8

ethics: Levinasian, 22, 117 (*see also* Levinas, Emmanuel); of *reading*, 8–9, 16, 36, 46, 67, 70, 125, 162, 180, 194; of *telling*, 8, 12, 52, 55, 70, 162; of the *told*, 8, 17, 45, 52, 70; of *writing*, 8, 10, 46, 55, 131–32, 180

evaluating, 109

exposure, dislocation and, 171, 174–75

Farred, Grant, 135n12

femicides: context of, 128–29, 158–59, 165–66; characterizing narration of, 141–47, 159–61, 161n52; patterns of, in *Crímenes*, 136–40, 147–50, 154–56, 165n56, 166, 166n57. *See also* indetermination; *maquiladoras*

Fernando (narrator): characterizing narration of, 84–88, 92, 104–8, 123; claims to innocence, 110–12, 121–22; devaluation of victims, 114; diatribe, 100–103; Fernando Vallejo vs., 98; inflated efficacy, 112–13; as unreliable, 97–98, 100–101, 108–10, 115–19. *See also* imperfect tense; *La virgen de los sicarios*; *letrado*; narrator: as cruel; *se inocente*

fiction and nonfiction, 4, 4n4, 92–93, 157

fictional cruelty, 5–6, 28n15, 36; assets of, 31–33; in Bolaño's fiction, 127–28, 130–31, 143–44, 154–55, 167–68; characterizing, 27–31; apart from deformative fictions, 33; explanations for, in Ocampo, 23, 51–52; expressions of, 28–31, 33–34; as reflecting reality, 34–35, 35n24; in Ocampo, 38–39, 51, 54, 57n27, 61, 69–70, 73–74, 81; in Vallejo, 83, 125–26, 130–31. *See also* author: as cruel; cruelty

fictionality, 4n4, 25–26, 67, 91–93, 105–6, 115–16, 156–58

"First World," 132, 132n10, 136, 147, 167, 169, 171, 216–17

Fishburn, Evelyn, 60n30

Fisk, Gloria, 190n23

flatness, 39, 45–46, 54, 59–60, 75, 80

Flaubert, Gustave, 34, 34n20

flesh-and-blood author, 8, 70, 87, 95, 97. *See also* author; implied author

"forensic aesthetic," 161

Forgotten Journey (Ocampo), 41, 56–57

form, 27

formative fictions, 6

Franco, Jean, 35, 156n40, 168

Frantzen, Mikkel Krause, 161

Gallop, Jane, 188

Gekoski, Rick, 20

genre, 4, 14, 44, 48–49; readers' expectations of, 25, 27, 33, 105, 137, 137n15, 147; relief from cruelty through, 29, 30, 33, 51, 51n20, 58. *See also* detective fiction; diatribe; elegy; mystery

González Rodríguez, Sergio, 158–60

"Goophered Grapevine, The" (Chesnutt), 95

Hall, Kari René, 32 fig. 1.1

Hallie, Philip Paul, 31n17

Halpern, Faye, 93, 95–96, 115

Hammond, Paul, 83n1, 86n4, 103, 111, 111n38

Harris, Daniel, 60

Harshav, Benjamin, 4n4

Hemingway, Ernest, 44–45, 44n16

Herlinghaus, Hermann, 161n53

historia, 43

Horne, Luz, 84

hospitable fictions, 10, 178–86, 191–93, 195–97, 205, 211. *See also* formative fictions; strategic hospitality

Hume, Kathryn, 91

iceberg theory, Hemingway's, 44, 44n16, 45

imperfect tense, 121–22

implied author, 8–9, 52–53, 69–70, 93–97, 115n40; continuity and discontinuity between, and narrator, 87, 93n13, 114, 144;

flesh-and-blood vs., 70; in Ocampo, 46, 71, 74, 145; in Vallejo, 100, 115, 115n40, 122. *See also* author; flesh-and-blood author

indetermination, 140, 143, 151, 153–56. *See also* ambiguity; overdetermination

"Informe del Cielo y del Infierno" (Ocampo), 77–79, 153

interiority. *See* character interiority

interpreting, 108, 113–14

Joset, Jacques, 103n32

Journey to the End of the Night (Céline), 86

Kafka, Franz, 44
Kanafani, Ghassan, 7
Kekes, John, 31n17
Kika (Almodóvar), 25
Kilapán, Lonko, 157
Kindred (Butler), 7
Kirsch, Adam, 151
Klingenberg, Patricia, 51n22, 59n29, 77n39
Krause, Matthew, 219n3

"La Belle Zoraïde" (Chopin), 96
"La boda" (Ocampo), 58
"La casa de azúcar" (Ocampo), 54
"La casa de los relojes" (Ocampo), 61–71; implied author in, 69–71; possible readings of, 67–69; unreliable narration in, 61–67
La ciudad letrada (Rama), 107
"La furia" (Ocampo), 71–75; cruelty as instructive in, 72–73; possible locations of cruelty in, 74–75
La furia y otros cuentos (Ocampo), 17, 41, 76
"La oración" (Ocampo), 58
La parte de Amalfitano, 2666 (Bolaño), 134, 136, 151, 153, 171–72, 173–74
La parte de Archimboldi, 2666 (Bolaño), 135–36, 154n39, 164
La parte de Fate, 2666 (Bolaño), 134, 136–37
La parte de los crímenes, 2666 (Bolaño), 128, 130, 132–37, 132n11, 141, 141n19, 150–51; indetermination in, 154–56. *See also* femicides; *maquiladoras*

La parte de los críticos (Bolaño), 133–34, 136, 162, 167–71
La última niebla (Bombal), 55
"La vida inconclusa," *Huesos en el desierto* (González Rodríguez), 158–60
La virgen de los sicarios (Vallejo), 13, 17–18, 26, 83–86; audiences in, 26, 83n2, 87–88, 95n19, 98–104, 116, 119–26; diatribe in, 90–93; expressions of unreliability in, 110–15; Fernando's positionality in, 104–8; rhetorical passing in, 85, 88, 89, 94–97, 101–4. *See also* Fernando (narrator); Vallejo, Fernando; unreliability: in Vallejo

Lamborghini, Osvaldo, 34
Lancelotti, Mario A., 41n6
Landy, Joshua, 6, 36n28
Larson, Nella, 94–95
Latin American literary studies, 13, 131; of Ocampo, 39, 41–42, 42n8; thematic concerns in, 6, 24, 27–28, 34–36, 34n21, 35nn24–25, 84, 182
Le Readymade malheureux (Duchamp), 171–73, 172n64
letrado, 107, 123
Lettered City, The (Rama), 107
Levinas, Emmanuel, 22–23, 24n7, 117
Levine, Caroline, 192–93
Levite's concubine (Judges 19), 30
literary redemption, 176
literary tourism, 107, 186, 189, 196–97, 203
literature: as affliction and antidote, 175–77; as instructive, 13, 188–89, 194; interpretations of, 9–10, 220; Latin American, 34–35, 34n21, 35n25, 39; race in, 14, 95–96, 116, 185, 194–96, 199, 201–2, 204; as "slow," 7. *See also* Latin American literary studies; world literature
Lolita (Nabokov), 87, 97–99
los desaparecidos, 165–66
Los detectives salvajes (Bolaño), 156, 156n43

Machado de Assis (Joaquim Maria Machado de Assis), 87
machismo, 148n32
Mackintosh, Fiona, 41n6, 59n29
Madame Bovary (Flaubert), 34, 34n20

"magic disc." *See* thaumatrope
Maier, Gonzalo, 90n8, 108
Man Who Mistook His Wife for a Hat, The (Sacks), 187
maquiladoras, 135n12, 147–50, 148n32
marianismo, 148n32
Martínez Cabrera, Erika, 51, 75n37
Mathew, Shaj, 162
Medellín, 84, 104–5
Meehan, Thomas, 59n29
Men in the Sun (Kanafani), 7
Mendieta, Ana: *People Looking at Blood, Moffitt*, 1–5, 2 fig. 0.1, 15, 212; *Rape Scene*, 3; themes in performances by, 3
"Mimoso" (Ocampo), 58
"mind-reading," 101, 101nn30–31. *See also* cognitive theories of reading
misreading, 23. *See also* discomfort, avoidance of
Mixquiahuala Letters, The (Castillo), 29, 195
Moffitt Building Piece (Mendieta), 1–5, 2 fig. 0.1, 15
Molloy, Sylvia, 51
Moms for Liberty, 219
Moon, Fábio, 179, 185, 194–95, 200, 203, 205; reviews of work by, 186
mourning, 129, 146, 164
mystery, 25, 30, 33, 137. *See also* detective fiction

Nabokov, Vladimir, 87, 97, 99
Nana (Zola), 29
narrative, 9–10, 43, 91–92, 125–26; impropriety, 25, 61; moral judgments of, 25–26
narrative ethics, 8, 12, 123, 132. *See also* ethics
narrative opacity, 39, 45, 49–50
narrator, 108; child, 46, 52, 61, 66; continuity and discontinuity between, and implied author, 87, 114, 144; as cruel, 29–30, 34, 112, 117, 120, 131, 144, 162, 164; unreliable, 50, 52–53, 61, 87, 93, 93n13, 98, 100–101, 108–23 (*see also* unreliability; Fernando [narrator])
narratorial audience, 26, 69
narratorial intention. *See* authorial and narratorial intention

Nelson, Maggie, 2
Newton, Adam Zachary, 8
Nietzsche, Friedrich, 68, 68n34, 72, 103
noir fiction, 137, 140, 141. *See also* novela negra
Notes from the Underground (Dostoevsky), 86, 93
nonfiction. *See* fiction and nonfiction
novela negra, 137, 141. *See also* noir fiction

Ocampo, Silvina, 17, 23, 44–46; accessibility of, 40–41; biography of, 39; Borges on, 41n6; cruelty in fiction by, 38, 41–42, 51, 57n27, 66–68, 77; reviews of work by, 56–58; strategies of, 17, 26, 38–40, 42, 213. *See also* affect: flattening or obscuring of character's; ambiguity: in Ocampo; character interiority: in Ocampo; fictional cruelty: explanations for, in Ocampo; fictional cruelty: in Ocampo; implied author: in Ocampo; Ocampo, Silvina, works of
Ocampo, Silvina, works of: "El cuaderno," 58–60; "El goce y la penitencia," 76; "El vestido de terciopelo," 46–51; "Informe del Cielo y del Infierno," 77–79, 153; "La boda," 58; "La casa de azúcar," 54; "La casa de los relojes," 61–71; "La furia," 58, 71–75; *La furia y otros cuentos*, 41, 76–77; "La oración," 58; *La promesa*, 41; "La propiedad," 54; *Las invitadas*, 41n6; *Leopoldina's Dream*, 40; "Mimoso," 58; *Viaje olvidado*, 41, 56–57; "Voz en el teléfono," 80
Ocampo, Victoria, 56–57
On Earth We're Briefly Gorgeous (Vuong), 98
other, the, 24, 117
Our Lady of the Assassins (Vallejo). *See La virgen de los sicarios*
Out of Darkness (Pérez), 218, 218n2
Ovejero, José, 28n15, 144
overdetermination, 150, 154. *See also* indetermination

parataxis, 161, 161n53
Passing (Larsen), 94–95
Paz, Octavio, 74
pedagogy of reading, 16, 29n15, 39–40, 181–82, 184–85, 188; in *Daytripper*, 194, 199–201, 204–9, 211. *See also* deformative fictions:

as instructive; literature: as instructive; reading: close, at a distance

Pelaez, Sol, 161n52

Pelourinho, 201–2, 203 fig. 5.2

People Looking at Blood, Moffitt (Mendieta), 1–5, 15, 212

Pérez, Ashley Hope: other works by, 34n20, 38n1, 56n25, 195n33; *Out of Darkness*, 218, 218n2

Phelan, Jim, 10, 12, 52, 95n19, 97, 115n40

Piglia, Ricardo: "Tesis sobre el cuento," 42–46

Poe, Edgar Allan, 44–45

Pope, Paul, 186

Pound, Ezra, 7

Promise, The (Ocampo), 41

pseudo-reference, 157–58

Quijano, Aníbal, 202

Rabinowitz, Peter J., 25, 94–95, 95n19, 96, 100n29

Rachilde (Marguerite Vallette-Eymery), 14

Rama, Ángel, 107

rape: in fiction, 143, 146, 155, 160, 176; representations of, vs. murder, 25–26. *See also* Mendieta, Ana: *Rape Scene*

Rayuela (Cortázar), 195

readers, 9, 11; anti-, 221; conspiratorial, 18, 87–88, 88n5, 101, 103, 106, 116, 119–21 (*see also* audience: conspiratorial); as cruel, 30–31, 76, 145, 162, 190, 192; norms expected by, 6, 27, 39, 43, 45, 47, 80, 205, 212–13; rhetorical, 10–11, 24, 89, 101, 109, 115, 122, 142, 153, 163, 179–80, 192–93, 198, 212–13; targeted, 18, 83–85, 87–88, 94, 100–103, 106, 114–16, 120–22. *See also* audience; awareness: of preexisting beliefs and expectations; book bans; *La virgen de los sicarios* (Vallejo): audiences in; US readers

reading, 8–14, 20, 36, 179, 184, 212; close, at a distance, 197–98, 200–209; contamination through, 69, 75–76, 79–80, 88, 110, 124, 146, 150, 162, 167, 171, 176 (*see also* readers: as cruel); contrapuntal, 197–98; discharging responsibility through, 13, 18, 129, 147, 166, 177, 189–90 (*see also* discomfort, avoidance of); formation through, 6–7, 13, 20; interconnectedness of, and living, 217. *See also* ethics: of *reading*

readymade, 174–75

relato, 43

reporting, 108, 113

reviews, 41, 41n6, 44, 55–57, 88n5, 97, 186

rhetorical passing, 18, 85, 87–88, 94–97, 100–101, 116, 205n48

right-wing groups, 219

Room (Donaghue), 52

Ruskin, John, 79

Sacks, Oliver, 187

Sacks, Peter, 129

Sade, Marquis de (Donatien Alphonse François), 14

Said, Edward, 191, 197–98

Sánchez Prado, Ignacio M., 184n9

Santa Teresa, 128, 132n10, 133–34, 135n12, 136, 147–49, 147n31, 156n43; Ciudad Juárez vs., 156–57, 157n44

Savage Detectives, The (Bolaño), 156, 156n43

Schroeder, Barbet, 84

se inocente, 111

Selnes, Gisle, 41n6

Shen, Dan, 96

sicarios, subculture of, 84–86, 109, 113, 122

silence, 144–45

Silva, José Asunción, 87

solidarity, 23, 51, 58, 60, 183, 190

Sommer, Doris, 60n33, 184n10, 189

Sontag, Susan, 143

Spargo, Clifton, 129

Spivak, Gayatri, 183, 193

Stewart, Dave, 195

story: translations into Spanish of, 43

strategic essentialism, 183–85

strategic hospitality, 18, 179–83, 193–98, 210–11. See also *Daytripper* (Moon and Bá)

strategic Occidentalism, 184n9

Strauss, Leo, 205

Styron, William, 14

Summer (Arcimboldo), 149 fig. 4.1, 150

Sur, 55–57

taboos: activation of, 25
teaching considerations, 81, 98, 181–82, 184–85, 190, 192
Terada, Rei, 142
thaumatrope, 151–53, 152 fig. 4.2, 171, 175
theory of omission. *See* iceberg theory
"Third World," 132n10, 135n12, 167, 169. *See also* "First World"
Thompson, Craig, 186
To Kill a Mockingbird (Lee), 52
translation: limited, of non-English works, 40–41, 90, 99, 182, 189–90; characterizing a, 86n4, 111n38. *See also* "born translated"
Twain, Mark (Samuel Langhorne Clemens), 14, 52
2666 (Bolaño), 18, 26–27, 127–33, 147, 150–51, 175–77; summary and parts of, 133–36, 137n15. *See also* Bolaño, Roberto; femicides; *maquiladoras*; pseudo-reference; Santa Teresa; thaumatrope; *and specific part titles*

Unhappy Readymade (Duchamp), 171–73, 172n64
unreliability, 52, 93; in Ocampo, 50, 52–53, 61, 63, 66–67; in Vallejo, 93n13, 98, 100–101, 108–23. *See also* narrator: unreliable
US readers, 216; of English, 180, 182, 193, 195, 201, 209

Vaage, Margrethe Bruun, 25–26

Vallejo, Fernando, 13, 17–18, 83–84, 90, 98–99, 103–8; cruelty in fiction by, 88–89, 108, 115, 120, 125–26; on Hammond's translation, 86n4; reviews of work by, 88n5, 97; strategies of, 17–18, 85, 89, 104, 123–24, 213
Venuti, Lawrence, 182
Viaje olvidado (Ocampo), 41, 56–57
violence: in Latin American literature, 28, 34, 34n21; semantics of, 28n14
Voionmaa, Daniel Noemi, 84
Voyage au bout de la nuit (Céline), 86
"Voz en el teléfono" (Ocampo), 80
Vuong, Ocean, 98

Walkowitz, Rebecca, 183, 196–98, 205
Wilkerson, Isabel, 216–17
women writers, expectations and norms of Latin American, 25, 39, 41, 42n8, 54, 56
"World Lite" (anonymous essay), 190, 192
"world lite" (concept), critics of, 190, 196, 204
world literature, 35, 35n25, 131, 178n1, 180–86, 188–90, 189n21, 190n23, 191–92. *See also* literature
Wright, Melissa, 148

Zapata, Mónica, 75n37
Zola, Émile, 29
Zunshine, Lisa, 101, 101n30

THEORY AND INTERPRETATION OF NARRATIVE

James Phelan, Katra Byram, and Faye Halpern, Series Editors
Robyn Warhol and Peter Rabinowitz, Founding Editors Emeriti

Because the series editors believe that the most significant work in narrative studies today contributes both to our knowledge of specific narratives and to our understanding of narrative in general, studies in the series typically offer interpretations of individual narratives and address significant theoretical issues underlying those interpretations. The series does not privilege one critical perspective but is open to work from any strong theoretical position.

Deformative Fictions: Cruelty and Narrative Ethics in Twentieth-Century Latin American Literature by Ashley Hope Pérez

Post-Postmodernist Fiction and the Rise of Digital Epitexts by Virginia Pignagnoli

Becoming Pynchon: Genetic Narratology and V. by Luc Herman and John M. Krafft

The Story of Fictional Truth: Realism from the Death to the Rise of the Novel by Paul Dawson

Fictionality and Literature: Core Concepts Revisited edited by Lasse R. Gammelgaard, Stefan Iversen, Louise Brix Jacobsen, James Phelan, Richard Walsh, Henrik Zetterberg-Nielsen, and Simona Zetterberg-Nielsen

A New Anatomy of Storyworlds: What Is, What If, As If by Marie-Laure Ryan

Narrative in the Anthropocene by Erin James

Experiencing Visual Storyworlds: Focalization in Comics by Silke Horstkotte and Nancy Pedri

With Bodies: Narrative Theory and Embodied Cognition by Marco Caracciolo and Karin Kukkonen

Digital Fiction and the Unnatural: Transmedial Narrative Theory, Method, and Analysis by Astrid Ensslin and Alice Bell

Narrative Bonds: Multiple Narrators in the Victorian Novel by Alexandra Valint

Contemporary French and Francophone Narratology edited by John Pier

We-Narratives: Collective Storytelling in Contemporary Fiction by Natalya Bekhta

Debating Rhetorical Narratology: On the Synthetic, Mimetic, and Thematic Aspects of Narrative by Matthew Clark and James Phelan

Environment and Narrative: New Directions in Econarratology edited by Erin James and Eric Morel

Unnatural Narratology: Extensions, Revisions, and Challenges edited by Jan Alber and Brian Richardson

A Poetics of Plot for the Twenty-First Century: Theorizing Unruly Narratives by Brian Richardson

Playing at Narratology: Digital Media as Narrative Theory by Daniel Punday

Making Conversation in Modernist Fiction by Elizabeth Alsop

Narratology and Ideology: Negotiating Context, Form, and Theory in Postcolonial Narratives edited by Divya Dwivedi, Henrik Skov Nielsen, and Richard Walsh

Novelization: From Film to Novel by Jan Baetens

Reading Conrad by J. Hillis Miller, Edited by John G. Peters and Jakob Lothe

Narrative, Race, and Ethnicity in the United States edited by James J. Donahue, Jennifer Ann Ho, and Shaun Morgan

Somebody Telling Somebody Else: A Rhetorical Poetics of Narrative by James Phelan

Media of Serial Narrative edited by Frank Kelleter

Suture and Narrative: Deep Intersubjectivity in Fiction and Film by George Butte

The Writer in the Well: On Misreading and Rewriting Literature by Gary Weissman

Narrating Space / Spatializing Narrative: Where Narrative Theory and Geography Meet by Marie-Laure Ryan, Kenneth Foote, and Maoz Azaryahu

Narrative Sequence in Contemporary Narratology edited by Raphaël Baroni and Françoise Revaz

The Submerged Plot and the Mother's Pleasure from Jane Austen to Arundhati Roy by Kelly A. Marsh

Narrative Theory Unbound: Queer and Feminist Interventions edited by Robyn Warhol and Susan S. Lanser

Unnatural Narrative: Theory, History, and Practice by Brian Richardson

Ethics and the Dynamic Observer Narrator: Reckoning with Past and Present in German Literature by Katra A. Byram

Narrative Paths: African Travel in Modern Fiction and Nonfiction by Kai Mikkonen

The Reader as Peeping Tom: Nonreciprocal Gazing in Narrative Fiction and Film by Jeremy Hawthorn

Thomas Hardy's Brains: Psychology, Neurology, and Hardy's Imagination by Suzanne Keen

The Return of the Omniscient Narrator: Authorship and Authority in Twenty-First Century Fiction by Paul Dawson

Feminist Narrative Ethics: Tacit Persuasion in Modernist Form by Katherine Saunders Nash

Real Mysteries: Narrative and the Unknowable by H. Porter Abbott

A Poetics of Unnatural Narrative edited by Jan Alber, Henrik Skov Nielsen, and Brian Richardson

Narrative Discourse: Authors and Narrators in Literature, Film, and Art by Patrick Colm Hogan

An Aesthetics of Narrative Performance: Transnational Theater, Literature, and Film in Contemporary Germany by Claudia Breger

Literary Identification from Charlotte Brontë to Tsitsi Dangarembga by Laura Green

Narrative Theory: Core Concepts and Critical Debates by David Herman, James Phelan and Peter J. Rabinowitz, Brian Richardson, and Robyn Warhol

After Testimony: The Ethics and Aesthetics of Holocaust Narrative for the Future edited by Jakob Lothe, Susan Rubin Suleiman, and James Phelan

The Vitality of Allegory: Figural Narrative in Modern and Contemporary Fiction by Gary Johnson

Narrative Middles: Navigating the Nineteenth-Century British Novel edited by Caroline Levine and Mario Ortiz-Robles

Fact, Fiction, and Form: Selected Essays by Ralph W. Rader edited by James Phelan and David H. Richter

The Real, the True, and the Told: Postmodern Historical Narrative and the Ethics of Representation by Eric L. Berlatsky

Franz Kafka: Narration, Rhetoric, and Reading edited by Jakob Lothe, Beatrice Sandberg, and Ronald Speirs

Social Minds in the Novel by Alan Palmer

Narrative Structures and the Language of the Self by Matthew Clark

Imagining Minds: The Neuro-Aesthetics of Austen, Eliot, and Hardy by Kay Young

Postclassical Narratology: Approaches and Analyses edited by Jan Alber and Monika Fludernik

Techniques for Living: Fiction and Theory in the Work of Christine Brooke-Rose by Karen R. Lawrence

Towards the Ethics of Form in Fiction: Narratives of Cultural Remission by Leona Toker

Tabloid, Inc.: Crimes, Newspapers, Narratives by V. Penelope Pelizzon and Nancy M. West

Narrative Means, Lyric Ends: Temporality in the Nineteenth-Century British Long Poem by Monique R. Morgan

Understanding Nationalism: On Narrative, Cognitive Science, and Identity by Patrick Colm Hogan

Joseph Conrad: Voice, Sequence, History, Genre edited by Jakob Lothe, Jeremy Hawthorn, James Phelan

The Rhetoric of Fictionality: Narrative Theory and the Idea of Fiction by Richard Walsh

Experiencing Fiction: Judgments, Progressions, and the Rhetorical Theory of Narrative by James Phelan

Unnatural Voices: Extreme Narration in Modern and Contemporary Fiction by Brian Richardson

Narrative Causalities by Emma Kafalenos

Why We Read Fiction: Theory of Mind and the Novel by Lisa Zunshine

I Know That You Know That I Know: Narrating Subjects from Moll Flanders *to* Marnie by George Butte

Bloodscripts: Writing the Violent Subject by Elana Gomel

Surprised by Shame: Dostoevsky's Liars and Narrative Exposure by Deborah A. Martinsen

Having a Good Cry: Effeminate Feelings and Pop-Culture Forms by Robyn R. Warhol

Politics, Persuasion, and Pragmatism: A Rhetoric of Feminist Utopian Fiction by Ellen Peel

Telling Tales: Gender and Narrative Form in Victorian Literature and Culture by Elizabeth Langland

Narrative Dynamics: Essays on Time, Plot, Closure, and Frames edited by Brian Richardson

Breaking the Frame: Metalepsis and the Construction of the Subject by Debra Malina

Invisible Author: Last Essays by Christine Brooke-Rose

Ordinary Pleasures: Couples, Conversation, and Comedy by Kay Young

Narratologies: New Perspectives on Narrative Analysis edited by David Herman

Before Reading: Narrative Conventions and the Politics of Interpretation by Peter J. Rabinowitz

Matters of Fact: Reading Nonfiction over the Edge by Daniel W. Lehman

The Progress of Romance: Literary Historiography and the Gothic Novel by David H. Richter

A Glance Beyond Doubt: Narration, Representation, Subjectivity by Shlomith Rimmon-Kenan

Narrative as Rhetoric: Technique, Audiences, Ethics, Ideology by James Phelan

Misreading Jane Eyre: *A Postformalist Paradigm* by Jerome Beaty

Psychological Politics of the American Dream: The Commodification of Subjectivity in Twentieth-Century American Literature by Lois Tyson

Understanding Narrative edited by James Phelan and Peter J. Rabinowitz

Framing Anna Karenina: Tolstoy, the Woman Question, and the Victorian Novel by Amy Mandelker

Gendered Interventions: Narrative Discourse in the Victorian Novel by Robyn R. Warhol

Reading People, Reading Plots: Character, Progression, and the Interpretation of Narrative by James Phelan

www.ingramcontent.com/pod-product-compliance
Lightning Source LLC
Chambersburg PA
CBHW020646230426
43665CB00008B/330